D0049204

Customer-Centered Products

Customer-
Centered
Products

Creating Successful
Products through
Smart Requirements Management

Ivy F. Hooks & Kristin A. Farry

*Karl —
Keep talking — one day
we'll get them to do it right
Ivy*

AMACOM
American Management Association

New York • Atlanta • Boston • Chicago • Kansas City • San Francisco • Washington, D. C.
Brussels • Mexico City • Tokyo • Toronto

This publication is designed to provide accurate and authori-
tative information in regard to the subject matter covered. It
is sold with the understanding that the publisher is not engaged in rendering legal, accounting, or other professional
service. If legal advice or other expert assistance is required, the services of a competent professional person
should be sought.

Library of Congress Cataloging-in-Publication Data

Hooks, Ivy
    Customer-centered products: creating successful products through smart
    requirements management/ Ivy F. Hooks & Krisitn A. Farry.
        p.   cm.
    Includes biographical references and index.
    ISBN 0-8144-0568-1
    1. New products.   2. Production management   3. Production planning.
    I. Farry, Kristin A.   II. Title
    TS170.H66 2000
    658.5'75—dc21   00-026631
                                                                          CIP

Printing number

10   9   8   7   6   5   4   3   2   1

Contents

List of Figures

List of Tables

Chapter 16

Chapter 17

Foreword

"What do I need?" It's such a simple question, one that we pose often in daily life. I know my first lessons in answering this question came from my mother, when she asked, "What do you need to take to school tomorrow, Kathryn?" Each time we evaluate options for a new car, plan the appliances and personal electronics for a new home or pack for a business trip, we're defining requirements. Sometimes we rely solely on past experience and other times we do more deliberate research. Given how simple and commonplace this question is, one would think that defining requirements—answering the simple "What do I need?" question—would be second nature to us all. Why then are the headlines, and our own professional lives, full of cases in which there was clearly a failure to answer the question well enough to deliver what was needed at the time and cost expected?

This book reveals the key factors behind such disappointments and offers clear and sound guidance on how to avoid them. Those of you looking for sophisticated analytical techniques or elaborate methodologies may be disappointed. The authors present a clear and convincing case that the underlying causes are actually quite simple: inadequate experience or knowledge, unclear reasoning, unrecognized biases, hidden assumptions, and sloppy and inaccurate communications. Their central message is aimed at executives and managers responsible for the products and systems that depend on sound requirement definition, and it is this: Your team doesn't need a slick new tool, they need you! They need you to recognize the paramount importance of doing the front-end preparatory work well and give them the resources for this. They need you to insist that the organization set up processes that uncover and remedy the shortcomings mentioned above. They need you to enforce the sound use of these processes by all levels and players in the undertaking.

I can attest to the effectiveness of the processes and techniques offered here. Ivy Hooks began teaching me about such things informally as soon as I moved to Houston to join the astronaut corps in 1978. She took pity on a penniless, freshly-minted Ph.D., housing me in a spare bedroom until I found an apartment near the space center; my lessons began at her dinner table.

Almost ten years later, I took one of her courses in requirement definition at NASA. Ivy's case studies hit very close to home for everyone in the class. We absorbed eagerly the techniques and guidance she offered, hoping to avoid future disasters. I found countless opportunities to apply those lessons during the rest of my NASA tenure and my tour as chief scientist of the National Oceanic and Atmospheric Administration. When she asked me to write this foreword, I'm sure Ivy imagined I would cite instances from those years to illustrate the benefit of reading this book. When I saw the full manuscript, though, I realized my most powerful example of how to succeed by applying these techniques comes from my recent experience in nonprofit education and construction.

In 1996, I was recruited to become CEO of one of the country's oldest and most innovative hands-on science centers and also to lead the design and construction of its $125 million new building. Most of the project work was outsourced to an extremely lean array of contractors and consultants. Only about five members of the museum staff were closely involved with the project, none of whom had ever tackled a project of this scope. As owner and eventual operator of this new facility, we had to specify the new business systems for the building, ranging from telephones to ticketing, point-of-sale to restaurant operations. By culture, the institution was predisposed to learning-by-doing and experimentation, with a premium on individual creativity. Our team, although very talented and smart, included no real expertise in the equipment, technologies, or operations involved in many of these systems. All of the systems would have to serve virtually every division in the organization from guest services to finance, education to marketing. We had neither the staff nor the funds to implement elaborate, sophisticated systems or pay for changes and rework.

What did we do? All the things this book tells you to do: As CEO, I made it very clear that we would not release any requests for proposals until we had a crisp definition of our needs that had been developed through a clear and consistent process. It's amazing what happens when the boss makes clear that both the output and the quality of the process have to pass scrutiny before you can proceed! We engaged outside experts to deepen our domain knowledge where needed. We developed operating scenarios with input from all key stakeholders. We prioritized requirements, established vendor interview templates, and defined prioritized evaluation criteria. We asked ourselves over and over again whether we had asked the right questions and distilled the system requirements correctly from all the input received. We used no elaborate software or analytical tools, just plain English, business mathematics, and word processing. We met or beat the budget and schedule target on every system and opened the new building on time, at full strength.

Ivy Hooks and Kristin Farry have written a wonderful book that will help anyone trying to answer the question, "What do we need?" Whether you're a product developer or customer, a current leader or aspiring manager, dealing with a large budget or a small one, in a high-tech or low-tech endeavor, you'll find clear insight, great advice, and adaptable techniques that will improve your performance.

—Kathryn D. Sullivan, Ph.D.
President & CEO, Center of Science & Industry (COSI), Ohio
NASA Astronaut (ret)
Captain, USNR

Preface

A Book on Requirements
Especially for Managers

Good requirements—defining the job that needs to be done or the characteristics of the product we want to buy, develop, build, modify, or have developed, built, or modified—are essential to improved productivity. It doesn't matter how good a manager you are, what you manage, or where you are in the management chain. If you have poor requirements, you will end up being either over budget, behind schedule, with an unsatisfactory product, or all three.

Ten years ago, I began teaching classes on how to write and manage requirements. The classes were arranged after witnessing incredible failures of programs because of bad requirements. The failures were not all total losses. Some were simply burned-up resources and burned-out people. I found that writing good requirements was a lost art. At the time, I naively believed if I showed people how to write better requirements, rapid improvements would follow. Although I have witnessed some incredible success stories, improvements have not matched my expectations.

My students tell me *lack of management commitment is a major impediment to good requirements*. People in many different types of organizations—government to commercial, large to small, complex development to simple upgrade, single product to integrated systems—tell me that managers want to see *results*. Rooms of programmers writing code, fancy computer screens, metal being cut and shaped: Managers don't think anything is happening without these products. Managers, according to those below them, don't understand what it takes to analyze the problem and to write good requirements.

The demands on a manager's time make attending lengthy

classes difficult. A book offers time flexibility, but until now, books about requirement engineering have always targeted the line engineer or analyst rather than the manager. A busy manager doesn't have time to wade through 350 pages of detail on requirement writing, nor does he need that much detail, because he is supervising the job, not doing it. A manager needs a process and the knowledge to both implement it and recognize when the process is yielding good results. A manager also needs to understand the problems he will face in implementing the process. Thus, we have written a book about requirements especially for the managers.

You can build and acquire better products faster and cheaper with good requirements. We believe that reading this book and applying what you learn to your world will help you get those good requirements.

—Ivy Hooks
March 17, 2000

Acknowledgments

We would like to extend our thanks and eternal gratitude to the people who have helped us make this book reality.

Managers Larry Fellows, Kevin Jackson, Sue Liles, Philip Shaffer, Marvin Shugerman, and Ralph Young reviewed the manuscript and made many suggestions to improve and enrich its content. Jeffrey Farry provided valuable ideas on requirements in often-neglected life-cycle phases.

Alexis Latner spent many hours assisting us in finding references and polishing the manuscript. Susanne Henslee kept us sane with help in formatting, configuration control, securing permissions, and chasing thousands of details in its preparation.

Nicholas Smith of Altair Literary Agency mentored us from an idea of a book all the way through its sale and writing.

Alan Binder, Harry Botsford, Bob Collings, Ron Ebbets, Larry Fellows, Brian Lawrence, John Leinhard, Jaclyn Mayorga, William Rice, Barney Roberts, Robert Spinrad, and Buddy Webb contributed time in interviews or "lessons learned" quotes, or both, without compensation.

Tim Kreiter once again took handwaving and unclear requirements and constructed great cartoons.

Kathy Sullivan managed to both read the manuscript and write a foreword, in spite of a busy schedule.

Any errors, of course, are ours.

—Ivy Hooks and Kristin Farry

Introduction

Managers and Requirements

Imagine producing, delivering, or buying a product for 50 percent of what your competition spends. What could your company do with such a large competitive advantage? What would be the impact on your career?

You could achieve that 50 percent cost reduction by changing your approach to defining the requirements for what you are producing or procuring. Smart requirement management offers the potential of eliminating rework, which consumes half of a typical project's resources!

Everyone in management has some requirement responsibilities. If you are in the government, you may be the manager responsible for acquiring a new airplane. You specify the top-level requirements. If you are a manager at an airplane manufacturer, you are responsible for managing the development and delivery of the airplane. You interpret the customer requirements and develop a design and the requirements for the parts and pieces of the airplane, including avionics requirements. If you are a manager at an avionics firm, you are responsible for supplying and possibly developing new avionics for the airplane. You interpret the aircraft manufacturer's requirements for avionics, develop a design, and define requirements for the parts that your system needs. If you are a manager at an avionics parts supplier, you are responsible for providing parts that meet the requirements specified by the avionics vendor.

The scenario varies only slightly if you are a large commercial aircraft manufacturer. Instead of a customer writing the top-level requirements, you have to solicit the requirements and determine the needs of all of your potential customers. Similar scenarios occur for developing a new automobile, new kitchen appliances, new computers, and other consumer products. The customer base is larger and broader, and the top-level requirements are usually determined by marketing.

If you are a systems integrator, your marketing people and your developers define requirements for a suite of products that can be integrated. You develop potential solutions using many existing products, developed by you or others. Marketing consults with customers for unique requirements to tailor the product to the customer. Your initial requirements are critical to developing a sellable product. If you miss, you will never sell the integrated system or you won't be able to deliver at the time and to the schedule demanded by the customer.

If you are a retail company, a bank, or an insurance company, you do not manufacture or integrate products, but you still have requirements. In this day and age, everyone is computer driven. You have requirements for systems to manage every aspect of your business. Even if you are not yet ready for e-commerce, you have computers to track inventory, shipping, payroll, employee training, and a multitude of customer information data. You may build your software in-house, contract out to have software developed, or buy off-the-shelf software. It doesn't matter. If you don't know the requirements before you develop or buy, you are going to waste time and money.

Information technology (computers, software, and associated support) spending in the United States alone, accounted for three trillion dollars over the last decade. Charles Wang, CEO of Computer Associates, estimates that one trillion of this money was wasted,[1] because in the end what is bought or built is not what is really needed. The disconnect—between what is needed and what is delivered—is poor, missing, ambiguous, or just flat wrong requirements.

The *Wall Street Journal* carried a series of articles about companies who bought new computer systems and suffered many embarrassing setbacks. Hershey Foods Corporation couldn't deliver Halloween candy and Whirlpool Corporation couldn't supply distributors and retailers with appliances when they went online with new distributions systems. Other companies, such as Waste

Management, Inc., and Allied Waste Industries, Inc., have simply given up after spending over $100 million on new management systems.[2]

Similar problems are plaguing many government entities. Why? Because the requirements were not understood before selecting a "solution." Companies bought software based on what the software sales force told them. They did not really understand what they needed, but believed that someone was going to save them. Talk about buying the proverbial pig in a poke!

The same problem will happen to other companies facing needs to upgrade existing systems unless management makes some changes. There is no magic in replacing systems. The new technology can be great, but you alone can determine what product you need and plan for the deployment to avoid major disruptions. Understanding requirements will set the stage for success—*your* requirements, not those of the vendor. One vendor has been known to sell systems to high-level managers for a price of at least $100 million. The vendor then goes to "interview" the corporate personnel about what they need. Only when the changes have risen to an additional $50 million does the CFO or CIO become aware of what is happening. A common response is to cry, "stop, no more changes!" The system implemented is not what the staff needs, partial changes are in place, and operations are a nightmare. The vendor then has to be employed to fix things. The vendor's fees are very expensive, but overall cost to the business is even larger.

And, if you thought Y2K was bad and expensive, wait until you see what we are about to experience in e-commerce! If you are a customer who has bought an airline ticket when you only thought you were checking flights, had your child disappointed by a toy not shipped at Christmas, or spent hours tracking down something on the Internet only to loop back in a circle or simply fall off the electronic cliff, you already know some of the problems of e-commerce. Those of you who think you can just hire someone to get you into e-commerce are in for some surprises—and not good surprises. If you don't do the thinking and the planning, who is going to? Who in the e-commerce building business understands your business? No one. Oh, you're going to build it in-house? Well, you know your business, but do you know how to define what it will be in the e-commerce world?

E-commerce takes more thinking, more planning, and clearer requirements than ever before, because it is new and you haven't done it before, and because if done wrong it can put you out of business fast. Without a change in your requirement process you face major problems. Managers must make the change—it cannot bubble up from below. This is a management call.

You probably don't know what to change or you would have already done so. This book is to help you understand what needs to be done and to help define your role. As a young manager told me recently, it doesn't work if management just sends everyone to classes and then stands back with crossed arms and says, "Okay, let's see what you can do." Managers have to manage what happens. Managers have to understand what is going on, what is working, what is failing, what needs pushing and shoving. Managers have to understand what and when to measure, and what and when to applaud and when to get tough. Otherwise, nothing is going to change.

This book will help you identify and make the needed changes. If your company has need of products or integrated systems; if your company creates products, develops software, integrates systems, or if your company is responsible for testing any of the above, *and* you want better, faster, cheaper results, then you need this book. If you are anywhere in the management chain—in marketing, in development, in quality or test—you need this book. If you are an engineer, a programmer, an analyst, or a test engineer—you need to read this book and take a copy to your manager.

This book will give you an understanding of how you can achieve faster, better, and cheaper results—all three—from implementing or improving a requirement process in Chapter 1. We give you insight into cultural barriers to improvements in Chapter 2 and how to surmount them in Chapter 17. We present a practical requirement management process in Chapter 3 that can be easily integrated into your existing processes and discuss how to implement it in chapters 4 to 12. The book then covers follow-through to ensure that your requirements are implemented in Chapters 13 to 16. You can read the whole book or you can skip to the chapters that address particular problems that plague your organization (see Table 3-1). At every step, we tell you what a manager's role is in requirement management. We give you checklists ("sanity checks") to make sure you are doing what needs to be done to *do it right the first time*.

—Ivy Hooks

Chapter 1
Requirements
Structure for Success

The so-called "Y2K bug" wasn't a "bug" at all. It was a requirement problem. No one told the developers that their systems had to operate past the year 1999.

—Kristin Farry

"Better, cheaper, faster!"

You have no doubt heard this refrain coming down your management chain. It has become a product development mantra for staying competitive in the new millennium. The exact order in which you have heard the words may depend on your industry, but they translate into the same headaches for everyone. If you are a product development manager, you must develop and deliver higher quality products in less time and for less money than you have in the past. If you are in charge of procuring products for use in your company, you must procure a quality product faster and cheaper than ever before. Otherwise, you will not stay in business.

Many of you have been struggling with using the words *faster*, *better*, and *cheaper* in the same sentence. Conventional wisdom says that you must sacrifice "better" to get "faster" or "cheaper," not to mention "faster" and "cheaper." You grew up with ads saying that "quality takes time" and "you get what you pay for." You may have recently been on a project in which someone above arbitrarily cut your budget or reduced your schedule or both, and yet did not lower (or even increased) their expectations on product quality. If so, you know that you can't get there by simply driving your people faster. You nod glumly when your colleagues mutter, "Best we can get is two out of three" or "We're doing well to get only one!"

If you are a development manager, you are already streamlining manufacturing and testing processes, reducing material waste, increasing process yields, and automating the most labor-intensive or operator error-prone steps. These steps reduce time and cost and improve quality, but they usually do not lead to breakthrough savings or revolutionary quality improvements. The savings are limited by the product design. What drives design? Product requirements: the needs the product must meet to be a success. Increasing your investment before product design or purchase—ensuring that you have a complete, correct set of product requirements in the eyes of all stakeholders—is the real key to better, cheaper, and faster product development or procurement.

Consider one of your recent product development or procurement efforts. What requirements did the effort start with? Were these requirements clear? How many times did they change? Did crises occur during developmental testing? Did you discover that you had missed or misunderstood a requirement in acceptance testing? Did operational deployment go smoothly? You may be shrugging the problems off, thinking, "No worse than usual!" Or saying, "That's just the nature of product development or procurement."

But wait! If you are a typical American manager, your culture may blind you to alternatives. "Never time enough to do it right, but always time enough to do it over" is not just a joke. It is ingrained in American culture. Reconsider for a moment: Does development rework resulting from misunderstanding the users' needs add to the final product's quality? Do the delays caused by that rework or unanticipated manufacturing or testing requirements add anything to the product's performance in the field? Do product features that your users don't need add to their satisfaction? No. Do they add to development time and cost? Do they add to procurement and installation costs? Yes. Raymond Dion of Raytheon found that approximately 40 percent of the total budget the chapters that address particular problems that plague your organization (see Table 3-1). At every step, we tell you what a manager's role is in requirement management. We give you checklists ("sanity checks") to make sure you are doing what needs to be done to *do it right the first time*.

—Ivy Hooks

for software projects that he studied was rework.[1] Barry Boehm, developer of the most widely used software cost estimation model, estimates that the cost of rework approaches 50 percent on large software projects![2]

The biggest mistakes in any large system design are usually made on the first day.[3]
—Dr. Robert Spinrad
Vice President
Xerox Corporation, Rochester, New York

Bell Labs and IBM studies have determined that 80 percent of all product defects are inserted in the requirement definition stage of product development,[4] the stage when you should define a product's needs and uses. In the 1970s and early 1980s, experts were reporting that 45 to 56 percent[5] of all software product defects are inserted during requirement definition. Are we getting worse at defining requirements? No. We are getting better at everything else! We have made considerable progress in measuring performance and fixing problems in all other phases of product development. The next major advance in product quality has to be in requirement definition.

The good news is: "Better, cheaper, and faster" is possible. Eliminating rework and gold-plating (unnecessary features) rooted in poor requirement definition can make product development or procurement faster and cheaper without sacrificing better. At the same time, improving fit between the product and the customers' needs also makes it better. You can frame the structure of success—good requirements—early in a project. Start with good requirements, and win on quality, cost, and schedule.

Now, the bad news: You have to change your approach to product development or procurement to realize "better, cheaper, and faster." Repeating the mantra is not enough. Nor is it enough to tell your requirement definition team to "write better requirements." You, as manager, must identify the areas needing improvement and empower your people to change. Only a manager can eliminate many of the causes of bad requirements. The seeds of schedule and cost overruns as well as operational failures are planted early in projects, typically with pressure, often from management, to procure or begin developing a product before defining its needs and use.

Customers frequently do not understand their own needs before engaging a developer. When customers do understand their needs, they may not communicate these needs clearly. Sometimes customers describe a possible solution to their needs rather than the needs themselves. Developers make assumptions about the customers' needs and do not check their assumptions with the customer before charging into development. Customer expectations drift while the development or procurement is underway.

Sometimes the original requirements are too ambitious for the budget and schedule. The requirement risk assessment before development start is inadequate. Partway through development, it becomes clear that the original requirements cannot be met. The descoping and redefining process involves scrapping much of the development work done to date, or procuring an entirely different product.

Even worse is the situation when the product enters acceptance testing before the miscommunications become apparent. The customer finds that the product does not meet their needs and reject it, perhaps citing a huge list of "bugs." These are bugs only in the context of the customer's needs. They are mismatches with the customer's expectations, not technical flaws in the product. Still, the development team must redesign and rebuild the product to meet the customer's now all-too-clear needs. Much of the work that went into the first product, the product that did not meet the customer's needs, is wasted.

> In a [1995] survey of the nation's top utilities . . . Tennessee Gas (Tenneco) ranked last behind 10 of the other most-mentioned pipelines serving the Northeast [U.S.], based on several criteria, including quality of service and price.
> Tenn-Speed has been a big part of the problem.
> The first of its kind, the system was designed to give customers a single spot in which to make quick pipeline transactions by computer, rather than by telephone and fax, as was customary.

> While some customers say Tenn-Speed was a good concept, Tenneco Energy was in such a hurry to beat its competitors, it pushed the system into service before it was ready.
>
> "The customers provided feedback, and we [utility executives] provided feedback and Tenneco . . . was hell-bent on getting this thing out . . . without listening to the customers," said an executive in the gas supply purchasing department at a major Northeast utility, who asked not to be identified. . . .
>
> The result was a massive failure in which Tenn-Speed rejected between 75 and 85 percent of the orders in late 1993, customers said.
>
> "We had a month from hell," recalls Withers from KCS, adding his company lost business because of it.
>
> [Tenneco Energy chairman and CEO] Chesebro' acknowledges Tenn-Speed required more computer power and sophistication than customers had in 1993, and the company didn't take enough time to test and debug the system.
>
> —Hillary Durgin
> Houston Chronicle, March 12, 1996

Many people have difficulty separating problems with meeting requirements—the real bugs—from requirement problems. Figure 1-1 shows types of nonclerical requirement errors (77 percent of the total requirement errors) for an aircraft technology program[6] (incorrect facts or assumptions, omissions, inconsistencies, ambiguities, and misplacements) and their frequency of occurrence. Inconsistent requirements are often discovered during design because they present design difficulties, but errors such as ambiguities may become apparent only in testing, when the test engineer or customer interprets an unclear requirement differently than the design engineer. Some ambiguities, as well as omitted requirements and bad assumptions, may not be discovered until postinstallation use or even disposal. Out in the field, these requirement errors often look like design errors. Frequent breakage of a particular part may be a design error (the part is too weak for its designed role), but the breakage may also happen because people are using the product differently from what the designer expected and their unanticipated use is overstressing the part. The mismatch between the designers' expectations and the actual use is a requirement problem.

Figure 1-1. Types of Requirement Errors

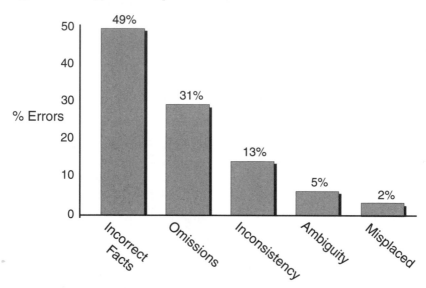

You wouldn't test something that you hadn't yet built, would you? You also know that building a product before designing it is a prescription for rework and waste. Similarly, designing or purchasing a product before defining its requirements is asking for trouble.

In 1994, Federal Aviation Administrator Hinson pulled the plug on the FAA's Advanced Automation System (AAS), the project intended to modernize air traffic control. Hinson canceled the project after the entire initial budget of $2.5 billion was spent without a working product. Auditors estimated that completing the project would require $7.6 billion.[7]

The FAA's AAS implementation began with disagreement between regional centers whose local air traffic control practices differed from one another. The centers could not agree on a uniform way of doing business to be "automated." Instead of resolving this dispute internally and at the beginning of the project, the FAA gave the AAS contractor requirements so vague that they would not preclude any center's operations preferences. The contractor could not build and test a system that would meet these vague requirements. "The failure to do [AAS] came from the inability of the FAA to control its wants and determine its needs," said Neil Planzer, director of the Air Traffic System Requirements Service of the FAA.[8] ". . . FAA researchers did not focus adequately on what end users, such as controllers, need or how the technology would be deployed or maintained," Gerald Dillingham of the United States General Accounting Office testified in 1995 Congressional hearings.[9]

The air traffic control community has learned from this experience. The FAA has since managed a more modest project (Display System Replacement or DRS) well. The DRS project incorporated some of the aborted AAS software; it passed its acceptance testing ahead of schedule.[10] An August 1999 tour of the new control room in Houston's Air Route Traffic Control Center only weeks after its commissioning found air traffic controllers already at ease with new traffic and weather displays and traffic management software showing thousands of flights in progress. The FAA personnel were justifiably proud of their progress.

The lessons of AAS apparently spread beyond U.S. shores. Developers of a large information display system for European air traffic control spent 13 percent of their total budget on requirements definition[11]—nearly twice the 7 percent that the COCOMO[12] cost estimation model suggested. The overall effort compared favorably with other projects of the same size and kind. The product had significantly fewer faults after delivery than other similar products, and few of these faults were specifications or requirements problems.[13]

—Kristin Farry

Bad requirements result in cost overruns, schedule slips, frustrated and overworked employees, unhappy customers, lost profitability, and limited careers. All else being equal, high-quality requirements contribute to high-quality products completed on schedule and within budget. Quality products begin long before manufacturing and testing. They begin before design. Never will you have more leverage—dollar for dollar—on your product's quality than you have in the requirement definition phase (Figure 1-2). The cost of fixing a requirement error goes up astronomically as you progress through design toward operations.[14]

Figure 1-3 shows this cost growth for software development projects. We haven't found equivalent statistics for hardware projects, but our experience suggests that the requirement error cost growth is higher in hardware-intensive projects, because you must factor in manufacturing tooling, test equipment, and other plant costs. Because a requirement error has longer to accumulate cost than design or later errors, Dean Leffingwell (Vice President of Rational Software) estimates that requirement errors account for 70 to 85 percent of software project rework costs.[15] Recalling that rework consumes 40 to 50 percent of software project budgets, this estimate means that requirement errors take a 28 to 42.5 percent bite out of your total software development resources!

The ultimate cost of requirement errors is even larger, but it is impossible to completely quantify it. Requirements drive more than product quality. They drive personnel skill levels for both product development and operation. They determine how the product will be used. Requirements for ease of operation, for

Figure 1-2. Raising Product Quality

Figure 1-3. Cost of Requirement Errors[18]

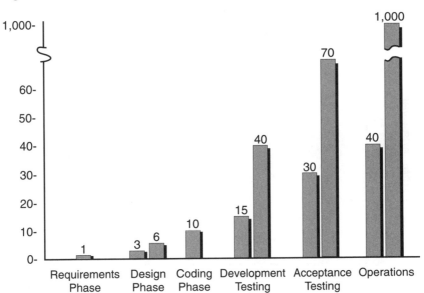

example, lead to products that require less training before use and less time to accomplish tasks. Omitting operability requirements will result in a product that is inexpensive to purchase but costly to use. Worse, operators may make more mistakes in the product's use.

If you increase your investment in requirement definition, what return can you expect? Studies conducted by NASA in 1991 and 1992 revealed average cost and schedule overruns of approximately 65 percent on 29 programs. Figure 1-4 compares cost overrun on pre-1990 NASA projects to the investment in requirement definition, including feasibility and trade studies.[16] The greater the requirement definition investment (as a percentage of the total investment), the lower the cost overrun (also shown as a percentage of the total cost). Those projects that invested 10 percent or more of their total resources before freezing requirements had 0 to 50 percent overruns. Cost overruns of 100 to 200 percent were common for projects that spent 5 percent or less on requirement definition.

In the early 1990s, "better, cheaper, faster" products officially became NASA's goal. In 1996, Strategic Resources, Inc.,

Figure 1-4. Cost Growth

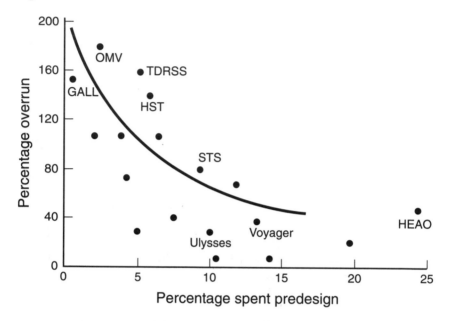

analyzed "fast track" projects inside and outside of NASA.[17] This study concluded that thorough planning and teamwork were two of the three primary project management policies necessary for fast-track project success. Strategic Resource's recommendations included:

- "Require and allow time for the actual project manager and team to plan at the front end . . . with the understanding of the importance of controlling project and programmatic requirements throughout the life cycle."
- "Use . . . bilateral agreements . . . to ensure common requirement understanding and to control requirement creep."
- "Use metrics for each project that will measure progress and value."

Recent, successful NASA projects (the 1997 Pathfinder mission to Mars and the 1998 Lunar Prospector mission to the Moon, for example) had a large early investment. They didn't overrun their budgets. The projects were well-grounded in reality by the time full-size spacecraft development began. The investment began even before formal requirement definition, sometimes under generic "technology development" programs rather than the mission-specific programs, which makes it hard to trace this investment to a specific mission. In the case of the Lunar Prospector, NASA did not make this early investment. The program grew out of an all-volunteer effort started in 1989 by Dr. Alan Binder. Several engineer-years went into defining the requirements, the mission, and the spacecraft before NASA adopted the project and began tracking its budget in early 1995.[19] Thus, these successful projects were more front-end loaded than official budgets show.

Public projects are often larger and affect more people than private sector projects; this fact, and the obligation of our government to be open with the public, results in most project failure headlines being about government projects. These headlines can give the impression that government administrators are not managing projects as well as their private sector counterparts. Not so! Just as many incomplete, overbudgeted, and ill-conceived products exist in the private sector as in the public sector![20] In private businesses, the label "proprietary information" can hide a multitude of sins. Consequently, we can't publish much quantitative data on how investment in the early stages of a product's development affects quality from the private sector, but private sector data that we have seen show the same trend as the NASA data.

There is quite a collection of documented evidence that requirements defects are the most expensive to fix once they propagate into designs and products. In my experience with project retrospectives, I've found that around 80 percent of serious defects are attributed to poor requirements.

If dealing with requirements takes the most time and produces the worst problems, then why don't we concentrate more on doing it better? There's more gold in this quality mine than in any other.[21]

—Brian Lawrence
Cutter Information Corporation,
Arlington, Massachusetts

Public or private, for-profit or not-for-profit, service or man-ufacturing, it doesn't matter what your industry or product. Good requirements are crucial to a project's success. Managers from all areas must take responsibility for ensuring quality require-ments. If you are managing an effort to define requirements for a procurement, requirements are your first product. If you are directing the procurement, the requirements guide the purchase. If you are managing the development of the product being pro-cured, the requirements guide the development effort. If your product is a service, defining the requirements to be met is just as important in the consumer's perception of quality as when your product is a widget. It will be tempting for those whose prod-uct is not specifically a set of requirements to say, "Hey, I don't write them! I just have to meet them!" When all is said and done, however, the customer or user will not separate the blame for failure to meet their expectations into such neat packages. The finest design, workmanship, and materials will still be labeled poor quality if it fails to do the job for the customer. Everyone in the chain from product concept to realization must concern themselves with the quality of the requirements. Managers must set the pace for their people in this effort.

Around 400 BC, Plato said, "The beginning is the most im-portant part of the work." This is not arcane philosophy or rocket science. No doubt you've sworn "Never again!" after a project, only to find yourself buried in rework on the next project, in spite of your best efforts to prevent it. We have been there too. We have learned that it's not enough to just say, "manage your require-ments."

So, we start this book with a look at how our culture and education work against your intentions to produce good require-ments (Chapter 2). Next, we explain doing it right the first time, showing you a practical process for requirement definition (Chapter 3) if you do not already have one. You have enough to do just getting a quality product out the door. You don't need to waste resources defining processes from scratch! We expand each step in this process, including the "what" and "how" of good requirements, in Chapters 4 through 12. If you already have a requirement definition process, but aren't completely happy with its output, you can incorporate one or more of our steps into your current process and reduce specific types of requirement errors. In Chapters 13 through 16, we cover techniques and tools to manage the requirements after you define them. In each chapter, we include "sanity checks" to help you evaluate your particular situation and progress.

We end the book with suggestions on overcoming cultural and corporate inertia to make all this happen in your organization (Chapter 17). Throughout this book, we give examples and share stories—lessons learned the hard way—from our own and others' experiences.

All of the early [Boeing] 747s and 757s came back for one or two sets of significant modification," Barry Gosnold, British Airways' executive vice president for engineering and contracts told *Aviation Week* in April 1994.

"There was a famous quote in the [airline] industry about that time [1989] that said: 'The 747-400 is a beautiful airplane. I can't wait until Boeing finishes building it.' That was the way we all felt at the time. Boeing could have done a better job on that airplane and they have certainly turned around [with the 777]," added Gordon McKinzie, manager of New Technology Engineering for United Airlines.[22]

Before the 777 program, Boeing spent about 15 percent of the total effort on a new model airplane in requirement definition and early engineering stages. As the design matured, they built a complete airplane to find and correct problems. On the 767, 13,341 changes were made on the doors alone![23] At the beginning of the 777 effort, Boeing announced a new approach to developing airplanes, which included elimination of "physical mockups" (whole airplanes built to check design and then scrapped), increased use on computer modeling, a new test philosophy, and more effort in requirement definition. In August 1990, *Aviation Week* reported that "[t]he present [777] schedule . . . provides an extra year beyond the classic 48 months usually allotted for this process. This will allow more time to make sure that requirements are correct for that costly changes down the line—one of the major problems in the 747-400 delays—can be avoided."[24]

Gordon McKinzie was pleasantly surprised at the trouble Boeing took to consult potential customers on the 777. "Al-

most a year ahead of our decision date, they were pulling airlines into Seattle and getting our opinion. . . . [Boeing] made
a point inside the meetings of repeating back to us what we
had told them and then they followed up after each meeting
with a little document that says: 'Here's what we thought we
heard. . . .' It was great."[25] Four of the major airlines established offices at Boeing to participate in the program.[26]

Inside Boeing, this new philosophy was known as "No
more chain saws." Ron Ostrowski, director of engineering, explained it this way: "Traditionally, we found that as we got
more customers involved . . . we would have to come in and
change our design after we had put it in place. Maybe we'd
even got hardware being built. Or maybe the airplane is sitting
out there and it doesn't meet the customer's expectations in
some specific way. The chainsaw approach was that you
crank that chain saw up and go into the plane and rip up structure, rip up systems, in a broad sense of the word, because
you had to replace it with something that was closer to those
expectations. It's very expensive. It disrupts the engineering
process. And it's very difficult for manufacturing."[27]

The chainsaws fell silent at Boeing, and the 777 trip cost
per seat and overall trip costs are lower than other aircraft in
its class.[28]

—Kristin Farry

Chapter 2
Why Johnny Can't Write Requirements
Cultural, Educational, and Management Influences of Requirement Definition

How do so many projects end up with bad requirements time after time? Why do the same product development experiences and nightmares seem to happen over and over?

You are an intelligent and capable leader. They put you in charge of defining requirements, developing a product, or both. Your team has a lot of talent. You may have read textbooks and taken classes on project management or systems engineering that discuss the importance of requirements. You probably started the last project planning effort using the textbook method, only to find that the ideas just did not catch on with your team right away. Before you could figure out why, your boss called to schedule a progress briefing. Telling your boss "we're still trying to figure out what to do" seemed career-limiting, and then you were too caught up in the melee of trying to get something out the door to think about, let alone implement, a new process.

Now, reflecting on the stress and workload during the final days leading to product delivery, you may be wondering why it turned out that way—essentially, the same set of lessons learned all over again. This situation is especially frustrating if you tried to do something different up front. The gap between that textbook theory and the workplace reality seems bigger than ever.

In that "gap" between textbook and reality are cultural forces, both mainstream and workplace, and shortfalls in individual workers' educations, all of which conspire against producing good requirements. These forces (especially the mainstream cultural ones) may be invisible to you. As a more-than-typically successful American, you have bigger-than-average servings of the traits that our culture values. Believe it or not, these "success" traits can make it difficult to follow the processes required to develop products on schedule and within budget.

To keep from running around in circles in product development—to prevent major rework across multiple phases of the development process—you must gain a perspective on your culture and education and that of your team. This chapter gives you an overview of these in the context of requirement definition and product development. Understanding the pressures and problems that you and your people face will help you implement long-lasting process improvements.

American Culture

In their book, *The Stuff Americans Are Made Of*, Joshua Hammond and James Morrison identify "seven cultural forces that define Americans"[1]:

1. Insistence on choice
2. Pursuit of impossible dreams
3. Obsession with big and more
4. Impatience with time
5. Acceptance of mistakes
6. Urge to improvise
7. Fixation on "what's new"

Unharnessed, these forces trample good intentions to do it right the first time. All are at work in product development. Neither customers nor developers want any limits on their choices.

We all think big and view those trying to scope us down as "unimaginative" or lacking that "can do" attitude that made America great. After all, "nothing ventured, nothing gained!" And we are certain that the newest technology is going to solve all of our problems.

Three of these cultural forces—impatience with time, acceptance of mistakes, and the urge to improvise—cause the biggest product development headaches. Hammond and Morrison's cultural factors aren't the only ones that create product development problems. We would add a bias toward making assumptions instead of asking questions to the list. Let's elaborate on each.

Impatience with Time

Not only do we want it all, we want it all now. Customers want it yesterday. Product developers got into the development business because they love creating things. They want to start creating this product now. In their view, all of this "requirements garbage" gets in the way of starting the design that is forming in their heads before the end of the project kick-off meeting (Figure 2-1). In fact, most of your team stopped listening to you halfway through the introduction of the customer's needs. They're already mentally designing the product to their own requirements. If their experience with requirement definition has always been long, tedious meetings over vague and voluminous documents that were seldom revisited during the design process, who can blame them?

Charging into design results in a product built to many incorrect assumptions. These assumptions remain unidentified until very late and are costly to fix. Time saved in requirement definition gets wasted in rework as the test team asks for modifications to the almost-finished product to make it testable. Even more is wasted in rework requested by the customer during acceptance testing.

Acceptance of Mistakes

Hammond and Morrison call America "the land of comeback opportunities . . . [where] you get three strikes and as many foul

Figure 2-1. Rush to Err

balls as you want. In fact, you often get more than three 'strikes' in business, politics, and personal pursuits."[2] In the United States, we tend to forget the trials and tribulations of the process and focus only on the end result, saying "Because it worked out okay, there's nothing to learn." In fact, we admire comebacks more than people who never failed in the first place. We are more loyal to a supplier who quickly fixes a mistake he makes than we are to a supplier who never makes a mistake.

Most people in product development assume that mistakes are inevitable. Some mistakes are; however, we often confuse some preventable ones (like those caused by poor preparation and inadequate understanding of the customer's requirements) with the inevitable ones.

Urge to Improvise

We tamed most of a continent with what we could carry on our backs, in saddlebags, or on (what luxury!) a wagon. We brought a crippled spacecraft (Apollo 13) back from its disaster-stricken voyage to the moon with duct tape and ingenuity. Our heroes are the improvisors. Combine our easy acceptance of mistakes with our love the challenge of solving a problem on the spot and whatever we have and you have a recipe to maximize rework.

A fireman was arrested for starting fires in the Los Angeles basin a few years ago. He wanted to create situations in which he could be the firefighter who saved lives and homes. His actions cost one man his life and many others their homes. That was lunacy, of course. Few people intentionally start fires just to display firefighting heroics; however, a culture that rewards firefighters and ignores fire preventers will have few people willing to invest much effort in fire prevention.

We have worked with project managers and engineers who believed that solving the unanticipated problems under the gun was "the fun part of the project." These people resisted requirement definition because they believed it reduced the need to improvise and, hence, their fun, not to mention their chance to shine. Consider, however, the fiery consequences when they can't solve the problem they've created! Good requirement definition is fire prevention.

Bias Toward Making Assumptions

Often, people do not ask a critical question because they think they are supposed to know the answer already. This reluctance to reveal ignorance starts during their formal education or perhaps earlier. In her book, *Beamtimes and Lifetimes: The World of High Energy Physicists*, anthropologist Dr. Sharon Traweek writes:

> A European postdoc[toral researcher] at SLAC [Stanford Linear Accelerator Center] observed to me that many American postdocs simply don't ask questions— they seem to feel that they might come across as uninformed or even stupid if they did. Another, a non-American and one of the few women in the community . . . found all this hesitation silly and asked many questions; she says that others privately thanked her for

doing so. Yet another postdoc suggested that it was difficult to trust anything one heard because everyone was trying to impress the others by sounding off; he thought it best to learn on one's own.[3]

Men feel greater pressure to keep silent than women do. In requirement definition classes, we have noticed that technical professionals have more inhibitions against asking questions than nontechnical professionals, thus compounding the problem.

The silence of your team is not always due to posturing. On team projects, people tend to assume that someone else knows when things are going wrong. The Wirthlin Group of the American Quality Foundation found that 68 percent of all employees don't speak up when they do become aware that something is wrong and needs fixing.[4]

Samples from Other Cultures

It would take volumes to do justice to the diversity of the world's cultures; however, it's worth mentioning a few differences to highlight how culture affects requirement definition and product development.

The stereotype image of Germans as planners is rooted in fact. Germans invest heavily in exploring needs and defining requirements before beginning development. They develop a detailed plan and then execute it. They find the American reliance on improvisation maddening!

Resource scarcity shaped Russian technical culture. Russian engineers have never had enough resources to do the "cut-and-try" product development so prevalent in America. This lack of resources, combined with an extremely low tolerance for mistakes, forces them to analyze ideas carefully before starting to build anything. Their analysis skills are excellent, and they can build amazingly effective products out of very little. Designs that appear crude to American engineers are in fact clever ways of addressing Russian operational requirements. For instance, Russians used air pressure to actuate brakes on certain airplanes instead of hydraulic oil-based systems. Air pressure systems do not have the performance of oil-based systems, but those air pressure systems work in artic cold and tolerate dirty conditions at unpaved airfields better than oil-based systems. Aerospace engineering lore includes a comparison between the Russian and American space pioneers: American engineers supposedly spent a million dollars redesigning the ink pen so that it would write in zero-gravity conditions, whereas their Russian counterparts issued pencils to the cosmonauts. We don't know if this writing instrument story is literally true, but it contrasts the two cultures well with respect to requirement engineering.

Although Russians are very good at analysis of requirements, they have had little practice in interacting with customers (other than their government and military) to explore their needs. The Japanese, on the other hand, interact well with customers. In Japan, the tendency is to begin with a set of requirements and then iterate frequently between the requirements and implementation. Japanese product development is a process of continuous refinement. The Japanese have also developed sophisticated methods for analyzing customer priorities.[5]

It's also worth noting that optimism is not a universal cultural trait. We have noticed that Americans are much more optimistic than any other people about what can be accomplished with a set of resources. This optimism is both a blessing and a curse in requirement definition and product development. In fact, the same could be said of any of the cultural traits that we have discussed. A culture's biggest strength can be its biggest weakness! As a manager, you must cultivate balance.

Corporate Requirement Management Myths

Not only do you have American culture sabotaging your efforts to get a project off to the right start with good requirements, you might face problems in your immediate work environment. Inside a typical company, we see five "Management Myths" about requirement definition. These are:

1. Everyone knows what this project is about.
2. Everyone knows how to write requirements.

3. We already have a requirement management process in place.
4. Everyone understands our requirement management process.
5. Nothing can be done about bad requirements.

Let's expand on each of these myths a little.

Everyone Knows What This Project Is About

No one can write good requirements without a clear understanding of the scope of the product, its mission, and its operation. A requirement author also needs to know the goals, objectives, and constraints of the project. A manager involved in early discussions with the customer in which the idea for a product is born has this knowledge. He may fail to communicate it to others joining the project later. The manager overestimates his requirement developers' project understanding.

Communication up the management chain may be just as bad: Managers create problems when they try to manage a project to an outdated vision of the product. The product design evolves as the developers learn more about customers' needs, but a development manager left uninformed of these evolving requirements may veto necessary changes.

We have also seen some projects in which well-meaning managers brought in a person whose job consisted entirely of "the documentation." Isolated from the customer and the mainstream project activity, this "documentation person" struggled in vain to produce a coherent and meaningful requirement document with few inputs from the development team members, who were "too busy building a product to be bothered with that paper chase."

Everyone Knows How to Write Requirements

You just write what the project is about. Right? Stating customer needs clearly is not that simple! The major cause of bad requirements is simple: People do not know how to write requirements!

To compound this problem, managers may lack the knowledge to educate their people in writing requirements. One senior manager that we know reviewed a report critiquing a set of requirements for one of his projects. The report listed each requirement, explained what was wrong with it, and then gave a correct rewrite. The manager was amazed. "I would have thought that the current requirements were okay as written," he said.

We Already Have a Requirement Management Process in Place

This "process in place" often consists of inviting wish lists from a large group of people. Next, a junior engineer (more about him later) gets stuck with consolidating these fuzzy lists into a requirement document. His document is then circulated for review by more senior (and presumably more experienced) people.

Many managers rationalize assigning the requirement writing to a junior person because they believe that the "review process" will catch the problems. This reasoning is false: Reviews cannot make a bad requirement document good. They can cost a great deal, however. Reviews can make a bad document worse, especially when reviewers do not recognize a good requirement when they see one. Failure to communicate the same vision of the product to all reviewers also does not help the process converge on a coherent set of requirements.

Everyone Understands Our Requirement Definition and Management Process

It seems so obvious: Just write this document, get it reviewed and signed, and forget about it until testing. But do you understand your company's requirement process? Have you discussed the process with your team? If not, you can be sure that your team's understanding is not even as good as yours. It's likely that Johnny Low-on-the-Totem-Pole, bombarded with inputs from hither and yon, has no idea which inputs are important and correct. As a junior employee, he also has no way to find out.

When I joined the Space Shuttle Mission Control team, one of the "initiation rites" for new flight controller trainees was a writing assignment. It was a ten-page paper, usually on some piece of the Space Shuttle, summarizing material from various voluminous Shuttle handbooks. My manager, however, noticed my software development experience and stuck me with "The Shuttle Flight Software Change Control Process." This was the process for getting new requirements implemented in the Space Shuttle's on-board software. People often added unprintable adjectives when the topic came up in meetings.

I couldn't find a single piece of paper documenting this process, even though the Shuttle had been flying for seven years. After a dozen referrals, I found the guys who handled all these requirement change requests. It took quite a few hours to pick their brains and diagram the process. It was so complicated, I sent the resulting paper back to those change request guys for an accuracy check. A week went by with no word from them, and I got worried enough to call them. They assured me that it was accurate. In fact, they had sent it to the print shop for me, but 500 copies would take a while.

"Five hundred! I need only ten copies!" I pointed out.

"*You* need ten copies. *We* need the other four hundred and ninety. This is the first time anyone has gotten this all written down, so we are giving this paper to everyone who even thinks that they have a better idea on Shuttle flight software. It'll save a lot of time and grief."

—Kristin Farry

Nothing Can Be Done About Bad Requirements

If you remain blinded by the above four corporate myths as well as the broader cultural forces discussed earlier, this mindset is natural. "But wait!" those of you getting requirements from outside the company are saying. "The customer gave us this garbage that they call requirements, so we are stuck with it. We can't do anything about it." Not true! You can, and must, help your customer define good requirements early. Otherwise, your product will look bad to them—it won't solve their problem. You can be sure that they won't mention their poorly defined requirements when they complain about your product to your might-have-been future customers. You can help your customer give you good requirements in the beginning.

> In each of my requirement courses, I ask the class, "How many of you have had to write requirements?" and then, "How many of you have had to review or verify someone else's requirements?" Most respond to one or both questions. Then I ask, "How many of you have been happy about either process?" Rarely does anyone raise their hand on this final question.
>
> —Ivy Hooks

The Individual

Take a trip back to where you started in this business of acquiring or developing products. Individuals like Susie Engineer or Johnny Programmer end up doing most of the work of writing requirements. They are good, resourceful, educated people. What about their education, temperament, or experience renders them unable to write good requirements?

We've found four reasons that an individual fails requirement writing. The writer doesn't know what to do, doesn't understand why, would rather be doing something else, or sees no reward.

Johnny Doesn't Know What to Do

Often, he has no training for the job, cannot write, does not have all of the necessary information, and does not know what the need is.

He has no training for the job

He didn't learn "requirement writing" in college. A typical engineering or computer science curriculum focuses on building a product to meet requirements, not on defining requirements.

Schools reward individual work, not teamwork. They foster competition between students. Their product is a future professor, not an industry executive or a project manager. Requirement definition is a cooperative team effort. It involves synthesizing often vague inputs into a clear, concise needs statement. This effort bears little resemblance to a typical homework assignment.

Schools think that Johnny will get "on the job training" in defining requirements, but his industry mentors never got any formal training in it either. They can't teach him what they don't know. They may be teaching him the wrong way!

So, stuck and floundering, Johnny finds an existing requirement document and models his requirements on that example. If he gets an electronic version, so much the better. Then he thinks that he just has to change a few sentences here and there to get his own set of requirements. The example document is often flawed. Worse, it may itself have been based on a flawed example. After a few generations of this, any resemblance the results might have to valid requirements is purely coincidental.

He cannot write

Poor writers make poor requirement writers. It's possible to get a technical degree from many schools without taking a single course on writing. Although even a generic writing course is better than nothing, the only mention of requirements in a generic writing course is in the context of the minimum amount of work required to pass. Thus, few technical people have any specific training in writing requirements.

On the other hand, a background in creative writing can get Johnny in trouble when writing requirements. The purpose of requirements is to explicitly define a product, not to stimulate imagination or generate interest.

He doesn't have the necessary information

Johnny doesn't understand the scope of the project or the eventual use of the product. Even if he's writing lower level requirements from high-level requirements, he probably does not understand why those high-level requirements exist. He doesn't know what trade studies or analysis took place to arrive at those requirements.

He doesn't know what the need is

A requirement is a precise statement of a need. Not understanding what is needed guarantees bad requirements. As Yogi Berra said, "If you don't know where you are going, you might end up somewhere else." Johnny may not have any domain knowledge for the product—the understanding of the environment in which the product will be used. The more junior Johnny is, the greater the likelihood that Johnny will not even know how to get the necessary domain knowledge.

Why doesn't Johnny research the domain and needs? Johnny is under pressure to "do something, anything, now!" Someone establishes a date for the product to be in the stores or the system to be installed. They back up from that date to allow for distribution or operator training, and, without any knowledge of how much might be needed, they choose a conservatively large time. Then, they back up much further to cover the development and testing. Next, they put time in the schedule for the procurement process, which is always lengthy on competitively bid contracts. These dates keep leaping backward until they reach the date when the requirements are needed, and it is NOW! Johnny has to deliver requirements before he has a chance to research the needs.

Johnny Doesn't Understand Why He Should Do It

He doesn't understand the impact of the requirements and thinks that "it's just documentation."

He doesn't understand the impact of the requirements

He doesn't know how they drive cost and schedules, which is not surprising, because estimating the cost and schedule for a project is often done by someone else. Sometimes someone dictates these without referring to the requirements anyway!

He thinks that "it's just documentation"

He suspects that he's just filling a square. Johnny may get this idea from his manager when that manager doesn't assign the most knowledgeable people to requirement definition or doesn't support Johnny in requests for help from these people. Working a few projects in which the requirement document was ignored until testing started, then changed to match what was built, will also convince him that it's unimportant. Johnny's attitude nearly always reflects that of his supervisors.

Johnny Would Rather Be Doing Something Else

He would rather do design. He doesn't have enough time, and he believes that the review process will catch his errors.

He would rather do design

Design work is much more fun than writing requirements. Johnny went to school to do design. Nobody ever told him that writing requirements was part of the job.

He doesn't have enough time

There's always a tight deadline. Management wants to see some action *now,* which means jumping into design or procurement as soon as possible. Or, someone is screaming for his time to fix the problems of the last product, leaving Johnny little peace to address this new one that isn't even close to reality yet.

He believes that the review process will catch his errors

The reviewers may not have enough time to do the job right either. The right people may not be reviewing the requirements, and small "reviewer-type" changes to a definition that is way off the mark won't make it a bull's-eye. You can't "review" a bad requirement into a good requirement!

Johnny Sees No Reward

No matter what requirements he writes, reviewers who could not or would not take the time to participate in writing will batter Johnny. Because many reviewers don't know how to write a good requirement, they may batter his good requirements along with his bad ones. When something he missed rears its ugly head part way through the project (and there will always be something, even if he has the time and training to do a good job), he gets the blame for all of the project's problems. People focus on a 1 percent error and forget the 99 percent done right. Johnny gets tired of being a scapegoat.

At the end of the project, the awards go to the bailout artists and firefighters. No one thinks about the problems that they didn't have because he filled those holes in the requirements early. No one measures requirement quality; so, no one can tell who is writing good requirements. Johnny may suffer in ratings with respect to his peers, because he was writing requirements while they were doing more heroic deeds.

After one round of abuse and no recognition, Johnny refuses additional requirement-writing assignments. Thus, he never becomes an expert on requirements.

What Is the Solution?

Teaching Johnny to write requirements is helpful, but it is not enough. A single individual in an organization's bowels cannot solve the requirement problem by learning to write requirements.

Given inadequate time and emphasis, inadequate domain knowledge, poor communications, undefined processes, and lack of reward, even an individual with consummate requirement-writing skill will still write poor requirements. Reviewers without time, requirement-writing expertise, and domain knowledge compound the problem.

Johnny needs training in writing requirements, but he also needs the help that only you, his manager, can provide. In spite of our culture and education, good requirements are possible if managers allocate resources, define and enforce processes, educate people on requirement definition, include people with extensive domain experience, grade people on requirement quality, and measure the impact of requirements on final product quality. Management commitment will stimulate an individual worker's commitment.

Table 2-1 will help you assess your current requirement definition and management culture. It's intended to get you thinking about the big picture of requirement definition and management and the areas in which you and your organization can improve.

The next chapter will outline practical steps for improved requirements, and Chapters 4–15 will go into detail for each step. Chapter 16 will cover measurement tools to help you quantify your big picture assessment. In Chapter 17, we will return to philosophy and culture. At that point, you will have specific actions in mind to improve your requirements and can begin harnessing cultural forces to get your projects on the right course from the beginning.

> We started out thinking that the main problem was tracking requirements to ensure that they were met, especially on these large projects with many people. We built a software tool to automate requirement tracking. But when I started training people to use this tracking tool, I found that most of their questions had to do with how to write good requirements, rather than how to track requirements. That's when I began offering courses on writing requirements.

> Now, after almost ten years of courses, I have thousands of student course evaluations. Most say, "The major obstacle to applying the things I learned in this course is management" or, "Please make my manager take this course too."
>
> —Ivy Hooks

Table 2-1. Requirement Definition Culture Sanity Check

- What is your current requirement definition process?
- Have you discussed this process with your team members?
- Do you and your team actually follow this process?
- Have you had training in requirement definition?
- How many of your team members have had training in requirement definition?
- How do you choose your requirement writers?
- How heavily do you rely on reviews to catch requirement problems?
- How do you choose your requirement reviewers?
- For what accomplishments have you recently recognized teammembers?
- What documentation is circulating among your definition team members on your current project?
- How are your reviewers educated about the product before reviewing its requirements?
- How much of your product development or procurement resources do you spend on requirement definition?
- If your requirements come from an external customer, how much time do you spend reviewing these requirements with that customer prior to beginning development?
- When in your procurement or development process do you baseline or freeze the requirements?
- How much of your total effort is rework?

Chapter 3
The View from the Top
Steps to Creating and Managing Good Requirements

Requirement definition is hard work, but effort alone isn't enough. Great amounts of energy and emotion are often invested in defining requirements, only to end with a project over cost and schedule because of conflicting, incomplete, excessive, and erroneous requirements. A good requirement definition process, coupled with the training and discipline to follow that process, can prevent the large number of late project changes, frustrated employees, and unhappy customers that result from poor requirements.

In this chapter, we shift gears from the philosophical and cultural concerns to daily practice. We outline a practical requirement definition process and then requirement management techniques. If you already have, and rigorously use, another requirement definition process, great! You know the payoffs of good requirements. Take a look at Table 3-1, a process sanity check, and read this and the relevant following chapters with an eye toward improving parts of your process. If you have a requirement definition process in place, but are unhappy with the requirements coming out of it, consider its enforcement before you

Table 3-1. Requirement Management Process Sanity Check

Does your current process . . .	For information, see these chapters:
Eliminate inconsistencies between requirements?	4
Uncover requirements for the product's entire life cycle?	5 and 6
Reveal gaps in the requirements?	5, 6, 9, and 14
Produce clear, unambiguous requirements?	7
Reveal assumptions underlying requirements?	8
Remove unnecessary requirements?	8
Ensure verifiable requirements?	10
Help you locate specific requirements?	11 and 14
Minimize requirement changes after baseline?	12
Adapt to changes in requirements and resources?	13
Assess requirement change impact?	15
Improve the process?	16

change it. An unenforced (and, hence, unused) process is no better than no process at all. It may be worse. Its existence may give people a false sense of security. Perhaps there's nothing wrong with your existing process, but you need to enforce its use to realize its value.

Why Adopt a Process?

A requirement definition process can help you consistently define good requirements, measure performance improvements across projects, and meet customer demands for a formal requirement process.

Implementing and enforcing a requirement process is essential to achieving better, faster, and cheaper products. If your organization does not already have a well-understood, well-documented requirement definition process, it's unlikely that your people consistently define good requirements. Furthermore, without a common process thread, it's very difficult to measure your progress in improving your procurement or development effort across projects.

The benefits of good requirements and performance measures aside, you may have or want customers who require a well-defined, documented requirement definition and management process. This situation is increasingly the case for large development projects driven by a specific customer. Some customers deal only with providers who meet certain process standards. For example, they may require that suppliers be certified under the International Standards Organization (ISO) 9000, or they may contract for development work only with organizations certified at or above a given capability maturity level in the systems engineering[1] or software engineering[2] Capability Maturity Model (CMM).

We recommend a single, standard process for all of your organization's product development that can be tailored as needed to particular projects. Should you adopt a standard process or invent one? Many people view standardized processes as bureaucratic, too complex, or inappropriate for their particular project. You may feel that your product development challenges are unique, thus tempting you to invent a new, unique process.

This is not a good idea! First, developing a process takes precious resources away from your real mission, your product development. Your job is to develop a product, not a process. You can waste substantial product development resources inventing and proving a new process. Second, it is tough to get a consensus on a new process that fills the same needs as established processes. A debate over the process takes time and political collateral, resources that you need to develop your product. Third, everyone on your project must learn the new process. You must take time to document it and educate them. This feat is not easy if the process is evolving along with the product. Finally, nonstandard or evolving processes make measuring process improvement across projects tough or impossible.

Furthermore, homegrown processes usually start simple, but they grow to be complex and unworkable. Ultimately, they evolve into something that resembles a proven process. Why? Proven processes incorporate many lessons learned the hard way by many product developers. You also will learn these lessons the hard way if you don't have that experience on your team.

Adopting a standard process does not eliminate all of your management flexibility. You can tailor the details of a process to particular projects. Debate and modify only those portions that are overkill for your product. Limit the time spent debating the process to ensure that this investment does not outweigh the benefit or interfere with your product development.

Sometimes politics make it so difficult to adopt a process that the only way to get widespread acceptance and participation is to invent a new one in-house. In general, however, the cost of inventing a process from scratch is far larger than selling and tailoring an existing process.

> Paula couldn't get any of the organizations participating in a large project to agree on a single development process. Members of each group maintained that their own way of doing development was best and the only one that solved their unique problems. Finally, she asked everyone to bring in a diagram of their homegrown processes. She made transparencies of the process diagrams and then laid them overtop of each other one by one. Superimposing them showed how negligible the differences really were.
>
> —Ivy Hooks

Requirements for a Requirement Definition Process

In the past few years, process standards have become fashionable. Your customers are probably telling you that you must meet certain standards in order to continue doing business with them. Many companies have invested heavily in meeting standards such as ISO 9000. Standards are an important part of processes; however, standards like ISO 9000 say what to do, but not how to do it. In true requirement form (as you will see in Chapter 7), the standards writers have left the implementation details to you.

For example, on the subject of requirements, ISO 9001 states: "The supplier shall establish and maintain a documented quality system as a means of ensuring that product conforms to specified requirements."[3] Later, the standard says: "Design input requirements relating to the product shall be identified, documented, and their selection reviewed by the supplier for adequacy. Incomplete, ambiguous or conflicting requirements shall be resolved with those responsible for drawing up these requirements."[4] These statements are requirements laid on your requirement definition and tracking process, not a requirement definition and tracking process. Similarly, the Carnegie-Mellon Software Engineering Institute's (SEI) Capability Maturity Model[5] (CMM) lists "requirement management" as the first step in a software product development organization's path to maturity and repeatable results. The CMM gives two requirement management goals:

1. System requirements allocated to software are controlled to establish a baseline for software engineering and management use.
2. Software plans, products, and activities are kept consistent with the system requirements allocated to software.[6]

Digging deeper into the CMM yields guidelines, such as following written organizational policy for managing the requirements, establishing responsibility for analyzing requirements, documenting the requirements, training personnel in requirement management activities, and providing adequate resources for requirement-related activities. These guidelines are more "what-to-do" rather than practical "how-to" steps for managing requirements. Merely citing these standards does not mean that your organization has a requirement management process.

Other requirement-related standards published by the Department of Defense and various engineering organizations set the form or outline to document a product's requirements. These requirement documentation standards are useful, but they do not constitute a requirement definition process. Even if your customer provides you with requirements, you will need a requirement definition process to ensure that you really understand the customer requirements, to develop lower level requirements, and to control requirements to prevent requirement creep and gold-plating. Does your existing process do this? Evaluate it with our process sanity check (Table 3-1).

What Process?

Until recently, the requirement definition process was only briefly discussed in books that addressed project management, systems engineering, and software engineering. Many texts assume that the requirements are a given and show the requirement definition process as a single step on a waterfall chart. Most college curricula never even address the subject of requirements, much less the requirement definition process. Books devoted to requirement definition are finally beginning to appear.[7] Some outline complex requirement definition processes.[8] More complex is not necessarily better. Most, if not all, of the benefits of a complex requirement definition process come from a few key steps. Overly complex processes use significantly more resources than simple ones do without significant incremental gain.

In your search for a suitable requirement definition process, don't overlook your own organization! If you are in a large organization, a good requirement definition process may already be in use somewhere in your organization. If so, adopting it will capitalize on experience in your own organization and make management across projects easier. It's possible that a requirement definition process from another part of your own organization is already tailored to your product domain.

If your organization does not have a requirement definition process, we provide a simple starting point. From our own experience and research, we have expanded the requirement definition box (Figure 3-1) into a practical process consisting of the following nine steps:

1. Scope the product by defining needs, goals and objectives, mission or business case, high-level operational concepts, customer requirements, constraints, schedules, budgets, authority, and responsibility (explained in detail in Chapter 4)

2. Develop operational concepts (scenarios for how your product might behave and be used), expanding them to cover all phases of the product's life (Chapter 5)

Figure 3-1. Requirement Definition Process

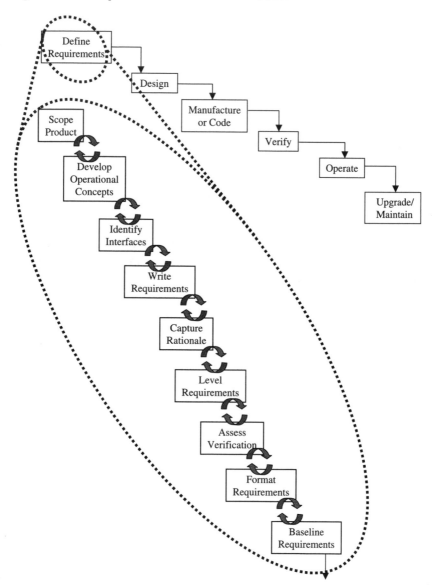

3. Identify interfaces between your product and the rest of the world, clarifying your product's boundaries, inputs, and outputs (Chapter 6)

4. Write requirements to guide product design toward what your customers need and want (Chapter 7)

5. Capture rationale (the reasons for the requirement's existence) behind each requirement and expose potentially dangerous assumptions and incorrect facts (Chapter 8)

6. Level requirements according to system and system subdivisions, ensuring that all requirements are written at the right level and can be traced back to their origins (Chapter 9)

7. Assess verification of each requirement, identifying the verification technique and facilities and equipment required (Chapter 10)

8. Format requirements and supporting documentation to ensure that you have included each of the appropriate types of requirements and that your development team members can find all of the requirements they must meet (Chapter 11)

9. Baseline requirements after validating that they are correct, complete, consistent, meet the project scope, and do not add gold plating (Chapter 12)

In Figure 3-1, we have shown these steps in the context of a product development "waterfall," but they work with other development models.[9] One popular step that appears to be missing from our process is "analyze requirements." Requirement analysis can and will take place throughout the nine steps that we recommend. You need analysis to clarify requirements, uncover requirements, and to prove the feasibility of requirements. You must determine the type of analysis and amount needed, depending on the unknowns and complexity of your project. You can choose from many existing analysis techniques. They range from paper prototypes to operating prototypes. They employ diagramming, software modeling, simulations, and mockups.

Choosing an analysis technique is not the same thing as choosing a requirement definition process. Our requirement definition process does not favor or preclude any analysis technique. A number of books cover requirement analysis for both systems and software.[10] Considering the extensive treatment of analysis by other authors (see Davis's book,[11] for example), and that each project needs different analysis techniques, we will cover analysis only in terms of validating requirements.

We present the steps of our requirement definition process in numbered sequence; however, you may find yourself working some steps out of order and others in parallel. For example, it is common for a product idea to be advanced first as an operational concept, with a dose of implementation mixed in ("We need a program that does X when we do Y") rather than as a pristine need statement. As you consider the proposed operational concept, you uncover the real need.

You will frequently iterate back and forth between steps. You might define a product's scope, including a high-level operational concept, that seems reasonable and within your budget constraints. Then, when you define more detailed operational concepts for all phases of the product's life, you might find that the scope is too large and that you must reduce it. Further downstream, capturing rationale for one requirement may reveal that you need several different requirements. Verification assessment may reveal problems that require a reduction in scope, but better now than after you have invested a fortune in developing a complex prototype!

The important thing is not the order in which you do the steps—this is not a recipe for advanced rocket fuel—but that you do all of the steps completely. Iterating back and forth is fine. Some steps are best done almost simultaneously—writing requirements and capturing rationale, for example. Just make sure that you clean up after the back-and-forth iterations to remove inconsistencies. If you have a complex product that you will divide into subdivisions or subsystems for development, you should repeat this nine-step process for each level of the system.

Even when you reach your requirement baselining milestone with a great set of requirements, you are not finished with requirements. Resource allocations often change, forcing changes in project scope or phasing of capability. The requirements themselves will change. These changes may come as a result of discoveries during design, with new customer needs, or in response to added constraints. You must manage the change process, or you will lose control of your great requirement baseline.

You must keep track of relationships between requirements and other data, from scope to verification. To gauge your progress toward better, faster, cheaper product development or procurement, you must assess the quality of your requirements and your implementation of the process. This assessment requires maintaining and assessing metrics (quality and performance measures).

To effectively manage change and to improve your process, we recommend that you augment the requirement definition process with the following requirement management techniques and tools:

1. Set priorities for requirement implementation and use these priorities to phase development (Chapter 13).

2. Automate requirement management, especially traceability, on complex projects (Chapter 14).

3. Control change to requirements and assess potential change impact before integrating changes (Chapter 15).

4. Measure quality of requirements and your progress toward good requirement management (Chapter 16).

These essential follow-through steps are needed to fully realize your up-front investment in defining good requirements.

What Is the Manager's Role?

In *The Stuff Americans Are Made Of*, Hammond and Morrison point out that "the analysis of the data of over nine hundred separate management practices reveal that there were only three universally beneficial practices."[12] Leading their list of three is "use of process improvement tools." As manager, you are the key player in establishing a new process or refining an existing one. You make the decision to use a process. You must:

- ◆ Choose the process or process modification.
- ◆ Ensure that your people know and understand the process.
- ◆ See that your people have the resources to implement the process.
- ◆ Enforce and reward the use of the process.

You are the leader; your action is key to requirement definition process improvement!

Just the Beginning

We invite you to adopt our entire process (the nine steps for requirement definition) and techniques for postdefinition requirement management or to integrate portions of it into your existing requirement process to strengthen it.

Keep in mind, however, that adopting or improving a process by itself won't create good requirements; you and your team must follow the process rigorously. There is no magic in the process; the magic is all in the discipline. Correct, disciplined adherence to a good requirement definition and management process will result in good requirements and a quality product.

Chapter 4
Creating a Shared Vision
Scoping the Project Up Front

> I was teaching a class of U.S. Marines who have the responsibility of defining the requirements for new equipment. We did several operational concept exercises, and they really got into these, but I still was not absolutely sure that they understood the importance of everyone involved in a project having a shared vision. Then, I remembered they were MARINES!
>
> "You have a vision, a vision of what it means to be a Marine," I proclaimed. "It affects the way you walk and talk and every action that you take. It stays with you even after you have left the Corps. I want you to define the vision for your project and share it with each participant so that the entire team is in step and on the same path."
>
> They got it!
>
> —Ivy Hooks

Too often, projects begin with the assembling of a team to write requirements. People may be chosen for the wrong reasons—for instance, just because they are available or are the only ones willing. They may be given few instructions, perhaps simply told to write requirements for the product by next week. This beginning is not a good one. You will not get faster, better, or cheaper products if you turn people loose to define product requirements without first defining the scope of the project.

The scope of the project constitutes the vision: the need to develop or procure a product; the goals and objectives of the customer and the company; information about the customers and users of the product; and how the product will be developed or purchased, tested, deployed, and used. A project begun with no clear direction will restart many times—and the last start may not produce results any better than the first.

The scope also includes the boundaries and the constraints of the project and the product. A project begun with no boundaries will diverge.

Before anyone writes even a single requirement, you need to clearly define the vision and constraints, which we refer to as defining the project scope. The order of many of the requirement definition steps is not critical to successful use of the process we introduced in Chapter 3, but you must start the process with scope definition. Without scope definition, the other requirement definition steps will be inefficient at best. You must establish a consistent viewpoint of the project for everyone—from customer to requirement author to designers, testers, and end users—to realize better, faster, and cheaper product development.

That's fine, you might think, but what if I am responding to external customer requirements? The same situation exists. Either your customer must give you the scope or you must create it yourself. If you create it yourself, you must validate your viewpoint with the customer, adjusting as necessary to reflect the customer's viewpoint. If you do not have the scope, you will view the requirements from your perspective and risk missing the customer's intent. Worse yet, every member of your team will put their own spin on the requirements and none will have the customer's vision in mind. Your product will almost certainly be a clean miss.

Why Scope?

The earlier you define scope, the more efficient your requirement definition process will be. In our experience, work done before a scope definition is largely wasted effort. An early scope definition keeps requirement writers from diverging, reduces requirement inconsistencies, and keeps the big picture in view. It also shortens the time required for requirement writing and rewriting and reduces debates.

It doesn't matter whether the product is a new toy or an aircraft carrier, a computer center upgrade or a new refinery. If you do not give everyone writing or reviewing requirements your scope definition, they will create their own. Each individual team member's scope definition is likely to differ significantly from yours. No two team members will have the same scope definition. The result will be requirements written and reviewed from very different points of view—different goals, objectives, constraints, assumptions, operational concepts, and (ultimately) systems. Battles will be fought, not about requirements, but about these basic precepts. You will end up with incomplete or conflicting requirements or both. Your project will overrun its budget and schedule, and you will probably not deliver the right product. If you guide your team through scope definition before anyone writes a requirement, you will prevent divergent and inconsistent requirements. You will reduce rework and wasted effort, which translates directly into reduced time and cost.

Defining and documenting scope pays dividends throughout your product life cycle, not just in requirement definition. The scope definition provides a lasting "big picture" reference for you and your team. It prevents you from losing sight of important constraints as well as customer needs. Long after requirement definition is officially complete, the scope definition will provide vision to the customers, designers, reviewers, testers, and maintenance personnel. This vision will enable these people to correctly understand the requirements in spite of their diverse backgrounds and knowledge bases.

What Is Scope?

Scope is a definition of what is germane to your project. It includes needs, goals and objectives, missions or business cases, high-level operational concepts, major assumptions, constraints (including schedules and budgets), and authority and responsibility. The relative importance of these items depends on the product and the customer, but we recommend that you cover all of the items early at some level. On most products, you will need to iterate on these several times before writing requirements, and you can fill in details as requirement definition progress makes the vision clearer.

You can work these scope items in any order. Many great products start with an operational concept based on someone's intuition. For example, someone might say, "We need a company web page." The web page may be an answer to a need, not the need itself. The real need may be increasing exposure to customers or improving internal company communications. You can take this answer and work backward to a need and forward to authority and responsibility. After you have this material defined, you will settle on a documentation or presentation order that suits your project well, but your first priority is getting the material down in any order.

Let's elaborate on each of these.

What Need Are You Trying to Meet?

The need must drive everything else. It is generally a short statement. The need should be related to your business plan or other strategic plan. The need statement should not change much over time. Everything else must trace back to this need. If the need changes frequently within your product development timeline, you cannot build a product to meet it! Need focus is crucial. Given enough resources, it may be efficient to solve several problems at once, especially if the solutions interface with each other. A competition for the most expensive phrase in the English language, however, would end in a tie of "while we're at it" and "might as well."

Consider two examples in which you need an upgrade to an existing computer program that aids you in bidding jobs to U.S. state governments. In the first upgrade situation, you have a need to include a new state law for Missouri in this program. You need this new capability within two months to effectively bid an important job. The requirement writers will write requirements to make your need clear to the upgrade developers. Knowing that your need is specific to Missouri and urgent, they can ask themselves if each requirement they write will aid you in bidding jobs to Missouri and make sure that the requirements can be met within your time constraint.

In the second situation, you want a new computer program for bidding jobs across the United States and in Europe. Your current capability is too cumbersome. It cannot be easily upgraded to incorporate frequent changes in laws and regulations that are different for different states. It cannot handle European bids at all. Stating that you need a new computer program is limiting your requirement writers and developers to this particular solution, which may or may not be the best solution. If your analysis shows that a new computer program is the best solution, state it as your need and state why so everyone will understand. The "why" should include the real need: to bid jobs in Europe and to more effectively bid jobs in the United States. Don't let the real need be forgotten. It is the focus for your investment.

What Are the Goals and Objectives?

Need is the highest level; goals and objectives flow down from needs. Goals and objectives may be related to what your product will do and how the product will be developed (e.g., your project management). A goal states what you want to accomplish on your way to meeting your need. A goal is a broad, fundamental aim that your organization expects to accomplish to fulfill its need. Objectives expand on how you will meet the goals. They are initiatives that implement your goals.

People sometimes struggle with the distinction between goals and objectives. Some see goals and objectives as interchangeable. In some circles (such as government procurement), people distinguish between the two as we have here. Don't get bogged down in these distinctions. They are not important. Capturing the scope-related material is important. Expand on your need, flowing from the most general to the more specific, as necessary.

Let's return to our bid program example. In the first situation (adding the new Missouri law), our customer has a simple problem with a short fuse. Expansion into goals and objectives is overkill.

In the second situation, our customer has a very large new need and it should be further explored. Goals might include handling bid formats for U.S. states and European countries; handling legal data for each state and for each European country; easily updating legal data globally or by country or state; providing all other capabilities that the current tool provides; and generating bids in half the time that is currently required. Objectives might be transferring information from existing system in an automated manner; enabling worldwide access to the new system; having bid capability for U.S. states within 6 months and European bid capability within 12 months; measuring how quickly bids are made and how much time is required to enter and verify the new legal data.

Don't just sit at the table and invent your goals and objectives. It's important to look at what is needed and how the system works now before determining what should be done for the new system.

What Is the Mission or Business Case?

For some products, we need to look beyond the needs, goals, and objectives—we also need to consider the mission or business case. The military may have a need for a new aircraft to replace aging aircraft, but before doing so, it is essential to review the mission of the aircraft. The government may require that a new airplane serve all military branches. Thus, the definition of the missions of the aircraft for all branches must be explored. Defining and restricting the missions will aid considerably in identifying requirements and test cases.

In commercial products, the business case must be considered from many viewpoints. For example, an auto manufacturer's marketing department announces that a new size car is needed to be competitive. The business case for the new car, and for what other cars it may replace, is a major undertaking. This business case must be well understood before starting requirement writing or design.

What Are the Operational Concepts?

The operational concepts are plain-language descriptions of days in the life of your product. During your initial scope definition, you should define the operational concepts at a high level. A few sentences sketching the product's normal (nominal) operation will be enough to start. Once you have a basic scope definition, you will refine and expand these operational concepts beyond the nominal in the next step (Chapter 5) to ensure completeness of requirements. At this point, you need only enough information to create the product vision.

For our bid program example, the scope-level operational concept for the Missouri-only fast program update may be:

> The user will enter Missouri into the user field "state" and the program will invoke the changes caused by the new law with no other inputs from the user. The program will display a message stating that the new law's effect is implemented. The program will also put a note in the bid that states that the new law effect is included.

The highest level of operational concept—the one you do before performing analysis or preliminary design—helps to communicate your vision of the product. This operational concept should enable less involved people to quickly understand what you are going to accomplish so you can gain their support. If you presented the operational concept to your next higher manager, the company president, or the board of directors, would they get it? For government programs, if you presented it to the committee controlling your budget, would they feel confident approving the project?

What Are Your Major Assumptions?

As you define scope, you will have to make some assumptions. Document them explicitly to keep them visible to yourself and your team! Validate these major assumptions early; otherwise, you may find yourself delivering or receiving the wrong product. Sometimes this validation consists of checking the assumption with the customer or user or marketing. At other times, it requires an analysis effort or prototyping by the development team to ensure feasibility. Do not leave assumptions too long without confirming or correcting them, or people will begin to believe that the assumptions are facts. If you cannot validate an assumption before you must move into development, highlight it as invalidated and count it in your risk assessment.

What Constraints Must You Consider?

No one has an infinite budget or schedule. These limits are sometimes painful but always necessary—products with no delivery date never get delivered! Beyond cost and time constraints may be expertise, technology, political, or ethical limits.

Who Is Responsible for What?

Start accountability now. Understanding divisions of responsibility between the customer and supplier are crucial to project success. Responsibility within your company for aspects of the product's development must also be clearly assigned. Fuzzy responsibility assignments will result in people wasting some of their time trying to get approval from the wrong person, or failing to keep the right person informed.

Examples

Tables 4-1, 4-2, and 4-3 present example scope definitions. On a typical project, you will iterate several times between your goals

Table 4-1. An Insurance Industry Project Scope

Scope Item	Example
Need	• Increase revenues from our insurance business.
Goal	• Increase insurance policy sales to our current customers.
Objective	• Make it easier for our agents to know about sales opportunities.
Missions or Business Cases	• Sell automobile insurance to home owner insurance customers. • Sell homeowner insurance to automobile insurance customers.
Operational Concept	• Display complete customer profile (not just current policy information) to policy service agents when customer calls about current insurance policies to alert agent to additional sales opportunity. • Agent suggests additional customer-appropriate insurance options to the customer and arranges purchase of those that the customer selects.
Assumptions	• Automobile insurance customers own homes. • Home owner insurance customers own automobiles.
Constraints	• Use current staff. • Use current computer system.
Authority and Responsibility	• J. Comp of Information Technology department implements customer profile information system. • K. Teach of Customer Service department implements agent training on information usage and incorporating policy sales in routine policy service. • Both report to L. Creech, VP Insurance.

Table 4-2. An Aerospace Industry Project Scope

Scope Item	Example
Need	• Counter Soviet military threat.
Goal	• Demonstrate American technological superiority.
Objective	• Make a decisive move in the conquest of space.
Mission or Business Case	• Transport a man to the moon, and return him safely.
Operational Concept	• Launch crew, lunar lander, and return vehicle on multistage rocket into trajectory for moon. Crew will leave return vehicle in lunar orbit while they take lunar lander to the moon surface. Crew will return to lunar orbit and rendezvous with return vehicle. Crew in return vehicle will land in ocean.
Assumptions	• All technology needs are achievable.
Constraints	• Do it within this decade. • Use American-made components.
Authority and Responsibility	• National Aeronautics and Space Administration has the responsibility to carry out the mission.

and your constraints. Consider the Web page in Table 4-3. The first "we need a Web page" statement was no doubt followed by suggestions that the web page solve internal company communications problems as well as provide a product-ordering interface with external customers. Somebody in production thought that being able to look up inventory and shipping rates on the Web, for example, would help improve production planning. Sales staff wanted to be able to monitor progress on an order all the way through production and shipping. Someone in product support wanted the customer to be able to submit product support requests online. The suggestions continued until the Web page scope was an entire management information system for the company as well as an external sales tool. The development constraints—six months and $50,000—would not support this scope, so management stepped in and quickly pared the project back to an external sales tool before anyone wasted a lot of time writing divergent requirements.

Table 4-3. A Commercial Web Page Project Scope

Scope Item	Example
Need	• "We need a Web page. Our major competitor has one, and we are losing business to them because we only have a paper catalog."[1]
Goal	• To stay competitive.
Objective	• Increase product sales by 10% per year.
Mission or Business Case	• Keep our current customers. • Get new customers.
Operational Concept	• Customer searches for possible suppliers of a product that our company produces and finds our web site. • Customer seeks information about our company online. • Customer views catalog of our products online. • Customer chooses a product and orders it online. • Customer submits payment information online. • System verifies credit card and makes order available to distribution. • Distribution employee fills online orders per current procedures. • Distribution employee adds order status to online data. • Customer checks on order status online.
Assumptions	• A web page is the best way to compete against a web page. • Our customer base is converting to electronic commerce.
Constraints	• $50,000 budget. • Six months to develop. • Use current product order forms and distribution channels.
Authority and Responsibility	• For content and presentation, VP—Marketing. • For development, VP—Engineering.

[1]Some would argue that "web page" is an operations or implementation concept, not a need statement. Because nothing competes with a web page like another web page, and this project is tightly constrained, the web page can be a need.

Defining scope is also iterative for each level of a project. You start by defining scope for the entire product. As you break the project into manageable pieces, such as "subsystems," "hardware," and "software," you must also scope these pieces. You may need to iterate on or refine your high-level scope definition as trade studies and feasibility analyses reveal difficulties. Sometimes external constraints and budget realities change, requiring a change in scope.

How Do You Communicate Scope?

Once you define project scope, it must be documented to ensure that everyone assigned to the job will address the same job. A formal scope document is essential to keeping a project on track. The order that these scope items are covered and the amount of space devoted to each in this document will depend on your project. On small projects, needs, goals, objectives, and missions will often be the same thing, easily encapsulated in a single statement or two. Distinguishing between these things is not important, but establishing a flow from less measurable statements of need to more measurable ones *is* important.

The scope document should be short, succinct, and available to everyone. All of the scope information does not have to be in a paper document. A videotape contrasting current operations with the envisioned operational concept may be more effective than a written description in communicating the vision to the stakeholders.

However you document scope, you must review it regularly to remind you of your own focus as well as bring it up to date. As time goes by and your team conducts design studies, the initial scope definition will need revisiting. For example, your team may be unable to meet an objective; the customer may provide a new objective; you may find that you don't have the budget to meet all of the goals; or new technology may present new possibilities and affect your operational concepts. The revised scope document must be available to everyone on the team to help them stay on the same track.

Once you have defined the scope of your project, and move on to writing the actual requirements, trace the requirements back to your scope definition. (See Chapter 14 for automating traceability.) This trace will help ensure a complete requirement set as well as prevent gold-plating.

How Much Effort Should You Invest in Defining Scope?

Look at your own experience for clues on how big your scope definition effort should be. If large numbers of requirement changes are typical on your projects, it's likely that you have not been adequately defining scope up front. Increasing your scope definition effort and its dissemination may be especially helpful if a large proportion of prior projects' requirement changes have involved fixing inconsistencies or dropping low-priority requirements. If your requirement reviews have been plagued with lengthy arguments about the need for particular requirements, you have fallen short on either scope definition or communicating the scope definition or both. A small increase in your scope definition can streamline the requirement definition effort and save a fortune in product development resources by preventing divergence.

Sometimes people are reluctant to draw boundaries early in a project for fear of limiting the possibility for truly creative "breakthrough" solutions. Much has been made of getting many people together for free-flowing "brain-storming" sessions. At first glance, our scope definition might look very limiting. In fact, breakthrough solutions come not from lots of minds operating without boundaries, but from true understanding of and focus on the real need and constraints. This understanding will free you and your team from breakthrough-limiting mindsets.

What Is the Manager's Role in Scope Definition?

Scope definition can't happen without management involvement. It is your responsibility to ensure that the resources are available

for scope definition and documentation. As the project progresses, you will face tough choices on what is in and out of
scope. You must consider cost and schedule constraints and ensure that the project is doable within the cost and time limita-
tions.

You must also be persistent in disseminating the scope information to all of those involved in development and testing of
the product.

Scoping Success

Imagine that your own manager called a meeting. You are told
that you must give a presentation, but you are not told the date,
place, time, subject, attendees, or intent. No possibility exists for
you to be successful unless you are very, very lucky. Imagine that
this manager did this to a whole group of people. What would be
the result? Either no one would do anything or they would each
do something different. These failures occur when people are
asked to begin writing requirements without knowing the scope
of the project.

Your project scope is to your product what a strategic business plan is to your company. A good investor won't put money
into a company without a good business plan that shows vision
and realistic focus and the management commitment to carrying
it out. Having the plan is not enough. In Chapter 3, we mentioned
Hammond and Morrison's discovery that, after examining over
900 separate management practices, only three universally beneficial practices exist. One of these three practices is "deploying
or communicating the strategic business plans." Unfortunately,
executives of American companies fall short on ensuring that
their people understand the strategic plans. People cannot focus
their effort on attaining a vision unknown to them.[1]

Should your team invest in a project without a strategic plan
to keep them on course? How can they think of creative ways to
develop the product without knowing exactly what the product
must be or do? Whatever you, the manager, do to ensure that
everyone is in sync with the scope—the strategic plan—will pro-

vide incredible benefits to your project. We have provided Table 4-4 to guide you in your project scoping.

I've been asked why the U.S. Space Shuttle program went so much smoother than the Space Station program, which has been under way for over 16 years and is still far from complete. Of the many reasons, the most profound is the difference in how the two programs were scoped. The Shuttle began with Dr. Max Faget, the "father of spacecraft," defining the project to a small team. "We will build America's next spacecraft," he began. "It will launch like a rocket, but return like an airplane. It will be reusable. It will develop low-g levels in comparison to conventional expendable launch vehicles to make it possible to build lighter and more delicate payloads. It will 'shuttle' back and forth to low earth orbit to resupply a space station; carry payloads to low orbits from which they can be boosted to higher orbits; and retrieve and service payloads. It will have a crew of x, weigh y, land at speeds less than z. . . ." He bounded the problem and put a small team to work to assess the feasibility and to flesh out the missing pieces. Dr. Faget was there to guide the program, not manage it, all the way through the first flight.

In contrast, the Space Station program was touted as being all things to all people, begun with a very large team, and had no experienced leader. To compound the problem, everyone wanting to use the Space Station in some way was invited to write requirements. This open-ended program start, without scope, destined the Station for many of the development problems it has experienced.

—Ivy Hooks

Table4-4. Project Scope Sanity Check

Have you:
Identified the primary need?
Reviewed and obtained agreement on the need with customers, marketing, development, and other downstream organizations?
Identified goals and objectives?
Distributed and discussed your goals and objectives with all stakeholders?
Determined if you need a mission statement or business case? Distributed it and gained consensus?
Developed and distributed an overview operational concept to help everyone understand what the product is for?
Identified budget, schedule, and other major constraints?
Determined that the envisioned work can be realistically done within the budget and schedule constraints?
Identified major assumptions?
Done all assumption validation that can be done at this time?
Assigned responsibilities?

Chapter 5
One Day in the Life of a Product
Using Operational Concepts to Improve Requirement Quality

Often, people try to start writing requirements on a blank sheet of paper. Generating requirements this way is an intimidating task at best and fraught with oversights and conflicts at worst. Even if you define and document scope as we recommended in the previous chapter, a big leap from scope to formal requirements still exists.

Operational concepts help writers bridge the chasm between product scope and formal requirements. Operational concepts are scripts describing how a product will be used, manufactured, tested, installed, stored, and decommissioned. You may have seen operational concepts referred to by other names. Software developers call them "use cases." Some spacecraft developers label them "operations plans" or "design reference missions." Other people refer to them simply as scenarios.

Regardless of the label, operational concepts are a simple, cost-effective way to build a consensus among all stakeholders and to discover missing requirements. Operational concepts address two large classes of requirement errors—omitted and conflicting requirements (Figure 1-1). In Chapter 4, we included operational concepts—high-level operational concepts of normal product use—as part of scope definition. Now, you and your team need to further develop operational concepts to lower levels of detail and across all life-cycle phases to support requirements definition.

> For example, consider a few insurance policy claims calls.
>
> High-level operational concept in scope definition: Policyholders can make claims by telephone, fax, mail, or personal appearance.
>
> Lower level concept, telephone claim:
> 1. Customer service representative receives incoming call. Caller ID displays number and transmits it automatically to database manager, which scans for match with policyholder phone number. A match is found.
> 2. Customer service representative: "Hello, this is Hometown Insurance and my name is Betty. May I help you?"
> 3. Customer: "Yes, this is Joe Smith. My hot water heater burst and ruined the carpet. Is that covered on my home owners' policy?"
> 4. Betty confirms that the policy automatically retrieved based on phone call origin is Mr. Smith's policy. She proceeds to review the policy with him.
>
> Alternate concept, another situation:
> 1. Customer service representative receives incoming call. Caller ID displays number and transmits it automatically to database manager, which scans for match with policyholder phone number. No match is found.
> 2. Customer service representative: "Hello, this Hometown Insurance and my name is Betty. May I help you?"
> 3. Customer: "Yes, this is Joe Smith. My house just burned down and I need to know what to do."
> 4. Betty enters "Joe Smith" into the system and finds that 14 customers have this name. "What is your policy number?"

5. Joe Smith replies: "I don't remember. My policy burned up with my house. I'm calling from a pay phone."
6. "How about your home's address? Or your social security number?" Betty asks. . . .

Why Should You Develop Operational Concepts?

Operational concepts are easy to generate and understand, involve everyone, resolve many requirement debates, facilitate completeness of requirements, identify user interface issues, provide a basis for early validation of requirements, and are a foundation for product verification.

Operational concepts are intuitive and easy to generate. Developing operational concepts is like storytelling, and it comes naturally to many people. You simply imagine the operation of the future product and write the steps. People of many different backgrounds can quickly get into creating these scripts with only a brief introduction. They do not need continuing guidance to generate more. It's easy to involve customers and users in operational concept creation and critiques.

Operational concepts are in a language that everyone understands. Operational concepts are effective in communicating with users and developers alike. They bridge the "domain experience" gaps between customers, users, and developers. For example, if your product is a system to track inventory in a grocery store, your customer will be the store manager. Your users will be cashiers and stockers as well as managers and stock buyers. These people are seldom technologists, but their input into the requirement process is essential. Few of your developers have run a grocery store, managed inventory, or checked out customers. The customers, users, and developers don't even have the same vocabulary. They are specialists in different areas, and specialists have domain-specific jargon. The three groups may even use the same words to mean different things.

As requirements become more detailed during the development process, they include more of the developers' language and become harder for the users to understand. At some point, the users can no longer visualize what they are getting when they read the requirements. Their input to reviews will become marginal or useless, or the reviews will become interminably long because each requirement must be explained and placed in some context for each reviewer. Operational concepts maintain the context of a requirement in simple, everyday, informal language. Using operational concepts to get everyone to "buy in" to a product increases the customers' confidence that the future product will meet their needs and the developers' confidence that they are building what is needed. You can use the operational concepts to maintain the customer's confidence throughout the product development.

Operational concepts reduce the debate. We have found that operational concept definitions do not kindle the fiery arguments that requirement definition discussions do; yet these concepts generate good requirements. Why? Most people have an operational concept in mind when they write requirements, even if they haven't documented it formally. They may not even be aware that they are thinking inside an operational concept. Many, if not most, arguments over requirements result from differences in operational concepts in the minds of the participants in the requirement definition process. Unless these operational concepts are spelled out, people can't see these differences.

It's easier to hammer out differences in operational concepts than differences in requirements. People don't invest as much time and energy in the operational concepts as they do in requirements. The level of emotion expressed over a proposed change is often directly proportional to the amount of effort people have invested in the thing that is to be changed. Requirements are much harder to write than operational concepts, so people are far more defensive about the requirements they have written than they are about operational concepts.

Using operational concepts to unite a team to work toward the real goal is not new. During the 1920s and 1930s, debate raged about the proper role for aircraft in combat. Yet the Army procured the B-17 bomber in 1938 with consensus on operational concepts, including remote deployments in the Panama Canal Zone and the Alaskan Territories. The airplane's resulting versatility and long range indisputably shaped the outcome of the second world war.[1]

Operational concepts facilitate complete and consistent requirements. Correcting what you have is easy compared with determining what you are missing. People tend to focus on the normal operation of a product in an ideal environment when they write requirements. In reality, this "normal operation" is only a very small part of the product's life and use! Consider a radar system. What happens to its performance when an ice storm occurs, or a flock of migrating birds selects it for a rest stop? If it needs cleaning or other maintenance, does it have to be shut down? If so, how long can its users survive without it operating? All of these questions assume that someone has manufactured and installed the radar somewhere. How will you manufacture it? Can the assembled radar fit on standard-sized trucks for moving from the factory to the installation site? Will vibration during shipping damage it? Can it be installed without special lifting fixtures? How will you do the postinstallation onsite testing? Will you need to protect workers from high voltage or electromagnetic radiation during the testing?

The requirement definition phase is the time to consider issues in manufacture, testing, user training, installation, maintenance, and disposal. Missed requirements in these areas are, in our experience, a major source of rework and schedule slips. Early identification of requirements associated with all phases of a product's life gives the design team a chance to make choices that minimize all operational headaches downstream. Operational concepts are an ideal medium for finding problems outside the basic usage area.

Operational concepts identify user interface issues early. Human user interfaces are often the greatest challenges a product development team faces. Too often, their implementation is just fallout from the rest of the design effort. Operational concepts will show you how human beings must interact with your product. As your concepts develop, you will see where your product might need data entry fields, buttons and levers to push, handholds and straps for carrying, warning bells, safety labels, information displayed on screens, and monitoring windows. Well-developed operational concepts expose human interface issues early and guide you to requirements that ensure the right emphasis and solutions in design.

Operational concepts offer inexpensive opportunities for early validation. You can take operational concepts to a wide variety of customers, users, dealers, testers, builders, and maintainers to get feedback on what is feasible. This feedback will help fill holes, find inconsistencies, and correct your course. Operational concepts also lend themselves well to quick validating simulations.

Operational concepts form a foundation for testing scenarios in product verification. Scenario-based testing is one of the best ways to flush out operational problems before products are put in service. If the verification team marches through verifying the requirements in the order they appear in the requirement specification or an order that minimizes verification time and resources, they will check off all of the verification boxes but risk missing problems associated with transitions. Operational concepts can become realistic test scripts to guide the verification team.

How Do You Develop Operational Concepts?

Begin the operational concepts with the routine, "everyday" use of the product. Normal operation is the natural starting place for most people and will give you and your team familiar territory to learn how to develop useful operational concepts. You probably already have some normal operational concepts for your product in mind. Document them with your team to start the process.

Be sure to include all aspects of "routine." For example, a product used outdoors in a particular region must operate through the weather extremes there. People from different cultures or with different needs use a product differently. Men and women do as well! If your product will have human interfaces, imagine yourself using the product.

> Every public building contains an example of how different people (in this case, men and women) use the same product differently: the condition of the partitions around the toilets in the restroom. Men seldom think about these parti-

tions. When men do use the partitions (not on every restroom trip), they just walk in the stall, close and latch the door behind them, hang their jacket on the conveniently placed hook above the latch, and use the toilet. Men don't have to think about these partitions because the door nearly always works and the latch holds it shut in all but the seediest establishments.

The scene is very different in the women's restroom! Women must deal with these partitions every trip to the restroom. They start by inspecting the doors of all stalls not in use, trying to determine if the door will close and latch at all. Next comes a lengthy struggle to latch even the best-looking door after entry. Women then hang coats and purses—both heavier than a man's sport coat—on the hook on the back of the door, because there is no other place besides the dirty, wet floor to put them. If a woman is blessed with small children, the diaper bag and children's survival gear also go on that hook. Is it any wonder that the hinges of these doors soon sag under this repeated loading and unloading? To make matters worse, while Mom is supervising child one through toiletry 101, child two and child three are running about, trying to push open every door and swinging on those that they succeed in opening.

After decades, we are finally seeing some improvements, such as moving the hook off of the door and occasionally a shelf for bags.

—Kristin Farry

Your approach to operational concept development will depend somewhat on whether you are on the product developing or procuring side of the fence.

Product Developer

If you are a product development manager, you traditionally receive a set of requirements from customers, ask customers to provide product requirements to you, or ask marketing what your broad base of customers need. Unless the customer or the marketing department has some education in producing requirements, you end up struggling to interpret bad, ambiguous, and incomplete requirements. We recommend that you not ask for formal requirements. Ask for operational concepts instead. If they have already given you requirements, ask for their operational concepts also. These concepts will help both you and your customer communicate and identify holes in the requirements.

You and your team may need to help your customer develop the operational concepts. We suggest that your team begin by meeting informally and documenting the customer's use of existing products that they wish to improve. Let the customer review your team's documentation of their current operational concepts to ensure that you have understood them. Sharing this assessment with your customers also shows them that you are listening to them. This first document must be approachable and coherent to build their confidence in you and convince them that you are not wasting their time.

In the process of working with your customer to develop operational concepts, your team will develop valuable sensitivity to the customer's investment in the ways they are already doing business and what they understand their problems to be. The way the customer is doing something now may not be the best way to do it, but it is important to understand why they are doing it that way. Their "why" may contain important requirements, and not just functional ones—it may hold clues about special training and deployment needs, for example.

If the customer initiated the dialogue for an improved product with you, they already have some specific ideas for improving their existing equipment and processes. If so, your next step is developing the operational concepts supporting the customer's ideas.

As you document the customer's current and desired operational concepts, you will see opportunities for improving their operations that they have not noticed. Outsiders sometimes see ways to improve existing processes that people immersed in them cannot. Outsiders can also elevate good ideas from low-level working troops to management visibility. When you find such ideas, develop the operational concept with enough detail to ensure that the ideas are solid improvements. Introduce the "new idea" operational concept to your customer as iterations on the original concepts.

These rework and replay iterations with customers will give them opportunities to "buy in" to the product incrementally. It will also give you valuable insight into what needs early prototyping for customer review and how to phase in the product's capability. This iterative process takes time. Maintaining and disseminating professional documentation to customers and developers throughout the requirement definition process also requires valuable resources. This investment will pay off in the long run, because it will take less time to write and get consensus on the requirements and you will have a better set of requirements to begin design. The resulting requirement quality improvement will reduce rework later in development.

Product Procurer

As a customer, you can define operational concepts for many aspects of the product you need, long before you communicate with the provider. It doesn't matter whether the development organization is internal or external to yours, or whether your product is purchased or must be developed. The more you know about what you want the product to do, or not do, before you talk with a provider or write requirements, the less time the total process of obtaining the right product will take.

If you deliver requirements to your providers, also give them the operational concepts that drove the requirements. Then, your providers will be viewing your requirements from the correct perspective. In some circumstances, you may only give them the operational concepts and they will write the requirements for you.

No one else has the exact perspective that you have. No one else has the domain knowledge that you have. This is a great way to share that knowledge. Remember that you will be living with the product longer than the provider, so it's essential that the provider understand your perspective and domain!

Beyond Basic Usage

Once you have routine usage concepts, consider the other phases of the product's life. We suggest that you next develop concepts for normal manufacturing, testing, storing, shipping, installing, upgrading, and disposing of the product, where relevant.

The importance of specific life-cycle phases depends on the product and whether you are the customer or the provider. In some instances, the customer will not develop these concepts. For example, only the provider can develop concepts for manufacturing. If you are the customer, you may have some manufacturing requirements, such as those related to industry standards or environmental concerns, but you do not have the knowledge or need to develop manufacturing operational concepts.

Operational concepts for some phases cannot be developed in any detail until some design work is complete. If, while working on operational concepts, you find yourself developing multiple operational concepts for different design contingencies, it may be time to stop and wait for the design to progress.

Let's explore each phase of a product's life cycle.

Manufacturing

Consider manufacturing concepts to identify facility, raw materials handling, inventory management, intermediate product storage, tooling, and personnel requirements. These manufacturing concepts can imply a development effort parallel to your product's development, one that must be finished before you can start manufacturing your product. You can also impose manufacturing-related requirements on the product (e.g., require that it be manufactured with existing tooling or use a particular material). If quality-critical processes appear in the manufacturing concepts, the product may need test connections so your manufacturing people can verify that an intermediate stage of the assembly is done correctly.

One of the best ways for a product development manager to incorporate manufacturing requirements is to go directly to your manufacturing people before writing any requirements. Talk with experts. Ask them how they currently manufacture similar products. Then, ask them what they would do differently to save time and money. Describe the new product, and ask them for other manufacturing objectives or constraints that you should consider for this product. You will get valuable information that will result in requirements that will in turn drive the design to a product that is cheaper and faster to manufacture. You will also get buy-in from a stakeholder.

Software is not a manufactured product, but software developers need to consider concepts for finalizing and distributing code. Compilation of large software packages might require large computer resources. Pressing, labeling, and packaging CDs with manuals is a significant effort.

Verification

Before shipping, you must verify that the product meets every requirement. Review your operational concepts to identify product functions that are hard to verify. Highlight the functions that will require expensive facilities or equipment to test. Consider introducing new requirements that might reduce these verification costs, such as an extra connector on a wiring harness to tap into some otherwise sealed module or brackets that allow existing fixtures to hold the product for tests. Test concepts can also identify places and times where and when your product might have to operate outside its normal envelope, thus requiring extra power (either in amount or duration) and cooling. Properly identifying and preparing for verification is so important that we devote Chapter 10 to it.

Storage

Nearly all products spend some time in storage, before first use or at intervals during normal operation. The storage environment might differ considerably from the normal operations environment. For example, electronics installed in an aircraft for navigation spend much less time guiding a pilot through the air than they do getting baked and frozen while the plane is parked on an airport ramp.

During World War II, Howard Hughes started building the biggest seaplane in the world. His objective was a large cargo transport plane made of nonstrategic material (birch wood) that could take off and land on water instead of runways vulnerable to bombing. The seaplane, which critics dubbed "The Spruce Goose," did not fly until 1947, long after World War II ended. It reached an altitude of only 70 feet on its only "flight"—not high enough to qualify technically as true flight but high enough to swing public opinion to Hughes's side in a congressional investigation of the project.

Howard Hughes surprised everyone by making this flight himself. He did it immediately after the plane was put in the water and months before the first flight was scheduled. Howard Hughes then declared the plane a success and sealed it in a special air-conditioned hangar. It remained there, unseen by the public, for the rest of Hughes's life. [2]

Some say that Hughes simply lost interest in the project; others believe that his hiding the plane was a symptom of his descent into paranoia. An aeronautical engineering legend, however, says that Hughes failed to consider the high moisture levels (humidity as well as seawater) in the seaplane's storage environment when he designed it. The wood absorbed so much water that the plane became too heavy to fly. Hughes apparently figured out the water absorption problem just in time—another few weeks and the plane would have never lifted itself out of the water at all.

Legend, perhaps, but it is curious that Hughes felt an air-conditioned, dehumidified hangar (quite a novelty in 1947 Los Angeles) was necessary to store the plane.

—Kristin Farry

Shipping

Unless your operational concept involves completely manufacturing and testing the product on the site where it will be used, you must consider moving the product, which drives requirements for transportability, partial disassembly for moving, compatibility with standard trucks and forklifts, and survival through shipping hazards. If shipping is a small portion of your product's life cycle, your operational concept for protecting your product during shipping may be some combination of packing it in cushioned containers, covering it with temporary coatings, and requiring handlers to use removable lifting attachments. You must define requirements for these strategies early enough to enable their development in parallel with your product.

"Shipping concerns really shaped our product [modular housing]. Each module of our houses—we call them 'boxes'—has to be within the "over-the-road" size. We typically make these up to 60 feet long and 14 feet wide.

"The boxes have to fit under all the highway overpasses, so for the roof we make a truss system with hinges. We attach the roof at the factory, including the shingles, then fold it down for shipping. This limits the interior ceiling height to 8 feet on a ranch home. We can do 9-foot ceilings on two-story homes.

"People have some attitudes in the housing industry. Say "modular home," and they think "mobile home" . . . but we build a lot of custom homes. People bring us plans that they want to build—maybe something they got out of Better Homes and Gardens—and the first thing we do is overlay these plans with our shipping templates. Some of those fancy rooflines get modified . . . but we've done some big houses. It's not uncommon to do a house with 12 or more boxes.

"Size isn't our only shipping concern. There is tremendous vibration on the road. We do many things in construction that you don't see in site-built or "stick" homes. . . . We joke that we "pre-settle" our homes by driving them down the highway. After we set a house on its foundation, there's a little touching up required to hide the effects of the shipping, but then our houses don't have the settling problems of site-built houses. The actual installation of the house takes only hours. We can roll in at 6am with our trucks and have the house done by 3pm on the same day."[3]

—Rob Ebbets
Vice President of Marketing
Excel Homes Inc., Liverpool, Pennsylvania

Installation

Product installation ("introduction" in some circles and "deployment" in others) is difficult when no interruption or downtime can occur in the service that the product provides. Your installation problem is compounded if you have a distributed product or a safety-critical product. Upgrading the air traffic control system, for example, must be done without increasing any aircraft collision hazards and without shutting down aviation. Developing product installation operational concepts will reveal requirements for speed of installation, simultaneous operations for old and new to build customer confidence in the new to support a final "buy" or changeover decision, training users on the new system, and reverting to the old temporarily in case a problem appears in the new.

It doesn't matter what your business is. Replacing a system that must operate continuously is tougher than building the original system. The transition from the old to the new drives the design as much as the long-term operation of the new system.

A prominent insurance company tackled the "Y2K" problem early. In 1994, they decided to use fixing the year 2000 date bug as an opportunity to upgrade all of their point-of-sale service. They developed excellent operational concepts for the future interaction of their customer service representatives and customers, all the way down to possible scripts for policy change and claims calls. These concepts made the requirements for normal operations of their system clear.

An independent review conducted before they started building the new system revealed that they hadn't thought about how they were going to install the new system and start using it. Portions of this insurance company's customer service department must respond to calls at any hour of the day or night. A natural disaster can make the calls flood in, and no one can control the timing of these events. They couldn't just flip a switch from the old system to the new system and expect everyone to start using the new system without training. They also could not shut the business down for a month

or two to install the new system, work the bugs out, and train
all of the customer service representatives.

—Ivy Hooks

Upgrading

Consider concepts to increase your product's capability when
new needs or new technology appear. These upgrading concepts
can suggest requirements that will extend its life. For example,
isolating certain functions to one component or software module
can enable inexpensive field upgrades later. Perhaps competing
standards exist, and you must launch your product before knowing which one will ultimately prevail—modem manufacturers
faced this situation in 1997 and 1998. Other products used in
conjunction with yours will be upgraded, and yours must continue to work with them.

Disposal

Decommissioning or disposal is especially difficult when biologi-
cal wastes or noxious chemicals are involved. For instance, a
requirement for safe containment of surgical blades after a medical operation or chemical disposal after a paint-stripper is used
might be necessary. A satellite cannot be allowed to break up in
orbit and create space debris. For aircraft parts, a requirement
to keep worn-out parts from being reused without proper recon-
ditioning might exist.

Even if carting away a useless eyesore is the only motivation
for the disposal, it may lead to requirements for onsite disassembly and hauling.

"Some 3,800 [offshore oil] platforms now line the Gulf
of Mexico—6,500 world-wide. . . . Some are in water over a
half-mile deep. One in four is over 25 years old. Most production equipment sits on the deck of an underwater tower until

the oil below is gone. Then what becomes of that huge structure?

"A few platforms could possibly be used by marine scientists. Several have been toppled onto the ocean floor where they continue to shelter marine life—growing coral and forming artificial reefs. . . . But most towers have to be cut loose, turned on their side, and floated off to land for recycling. It's in that removal process that trouble arises. . . . The worst problem is cutting the tower away from the ocean floor. The cuts must be made well below the mud line—below water—so currents that scour the bottom won't expose the stumps. Protruding steel can threaten fishing—especially shrimp nets.

"The policy has been to cut the legs off 15 feet below the mud line. That can be done by a diver inside the legs of the tower, or by digging a great pit around the footings—then cutting the legs off from outside. The cleanest way to sever the metal is with oxyarc cutting torches. But that's also the most dangerous. Divers have died from oxygen explosions, and they work in fear of shifting mud.

"It's far safer to lower explosive charges down the hollow legs and fire them from above. It's safer, but it's also far messier. On the wrong day, thousands of fish might be killed by the blast—the very fish that make their habitat in the tower structure. So engineers, out of the political limelight, work to save people and fish alike. They ask, 'How far into the mud should we really cut the legs? Can we shape explosive charges so they won't send killing shock waves through the water?' . . . All the while we wonder if we'll ever learn to consider the death of a machine—as well as its life—when we first design it."[4]

—Dr. John Lienhard
Professor of Mechanical Engineering
University of Houston, Houston, Texas

The Abnormal

After outlining the normal use in each life-cycle phase, begin asking "what if?" to expand your concepts into abnormal operations.

Failures

Start at the highest level: What if your product fails to work as advertised? Will it merely lead to a disappointed user, or will it hurt that user? Even if your product can't hurt someone by itself, look at how it will be used. If the customer relies on the product for information to make decisions involving safety, you will have reliability requirements and requirements to warn the user of performance degradation. It may be cost-effective for the user to distinguish between minor failures with which the product can still be safely used and major failures requiring a shutdown or switchover to a backup. Otherwise, the user will have to stop using the product with every failure, no matter how minor, which could signal a requirement for built-in test capability or automatic backup mode.

What if someone makes a mistake in operating the product? If your product will use external inputs (user commands, power, or data from other products such as sensors), reliability requirements for your product's output may lead to requirements for the product to check its inputs for accuracy. Operational concepts involving input failures will show you the necessary accuracy checks. For example, what degradation in the power supply to your product will cause degradation in its performance? Operator failure concepts may expose requirements to make your product tolerate operator error. What will happen if someone distracts the operator during a command sequence? What if the operator reverses two inputs?

As your product takes form, you should iterate on these failure response concepts to find requirements for your product's subsystems and components. Operational concepts will help you see which parts of your product are the most failure-critical, because a part is "critical" only in the context of the product's use. That is, a bolt is just a bolt until you use it to hold a half-ton weight above someone's head or attach a wheel to a truck.

Failure operational concept development is not a replacement for failure modes and effects analysis (FMEA) that many industries employ. FMEA's are done after design, not before. These operational concepts are to aid you in defining requirements so that the FMEA will reveal few or no problems.

Maintenance

A customer's requirement for a certain reliability or availability level may also lead to requirements for maintainability. It's often impossible or too expensive to make a product 100 percent reliable. A customer may accept lesser reliability coupled with maintainability requirements to balance cost and availability. For instance, the customer may require that certain maintenance operations (such as changing an ink cartridge, shear pin, or igniter) be performed within a specific time and with no training.

Maintenance operational concepts must also consider the environment. Will special difficulties occur getting spares to the maintenance site? Rain or dust or wind might add requirements for protective equipment during repairs. Your operational concepts for troubleshooting an inoperative product might lead you to requirements for the product to isolate its own failures to subassemblies, or you might require separate test equipment, the development of which must begin before your product is complete to be available when your customer needs it.

Training

In every phase when people must install, test, use, handle, or maintain the product, you must consider the burden of training them. Users need to practice their role in time-critical, dangerous, or material-wasting operations (such as fire drills or missile launches) without actually having the product complete the operation. Perhaps the product must be available for use by some people while others are training. Training operational concepts will expose needs for simulators, special training modes, instructor control mechanisms, and trainee evaluation tools.

"When World War II started, no one had given pilot training much thought. People didn't understand what a gigantic step it was from those little biplanes that we had for basic training to the new multiengine monoplanes. Our class was assigned to A-20s. It had over ten times the horsepower of our basic trainers. The landing speeds must have been twice as fast. But there were no 'trainer' versions of the aircraft with two sets of controls and instructor seats. The instructors just handed out the aircraft manuals and said, 'you have one week to make your first flight.' "

"Half the class died that week in Mississippi, thousands of miles from the war. After my combat tour was over and I was assigned to the Pentagon, I found out that more pilots died in training than in combat. The worst was during my training. Six thousand aviation training casualties in one month! These numbers were classified then—the American public would have been outraged if they knew the truth."[5]

—Lt. Colonel A. B. Farry, Sr.
U.S. Army Air Corps and U.S. Air Force Pilot
1942–1968

Human Interface Detail

Even after training, human beings are variable and unpredictable. Designing a human interface requires a careful design effort to increase the probability that people will routinely do the right things. Unfortunately, no guarantees exist that all people will interact with a product in the same way. Simplicity and consistency in human interfaces reduce the variability as well as training and operations costs, although they may increase development costs. In the requirement definition phase, be alert to operational concepts that reveal many or very complicated user interactions. Identify who these users will be and what their experience and education will be. The customer may have some unstated requirements on the users by virtue of being unwilling to spend much on training them! Include maintenance and your own customer support personnel in this assessment.

In this requirement stage, we urge you to check for existing appropriate human interface standards. Adopting them for your product capitalizes on extensive human factors research and experience. They also reduce the detail needed in your operational concepts and, ultimately, your requirements. In products replacing products in wide use, a huge investment in human capital has been made—training all these users—and any changes in user interfaces (even those not codified in a standard) must be weighed carefully against this investment and people's comfort with the existing interfaces. Citing existing human interfaces on other products is an effective and efficient way to communicate between customer and developer. For example, you can say, "Make it look and act like the MSWord menu." Specifically stating that you want the help menu on the right or that you want pull down menus isn't necessary.

Some people worry about specifying too much detail in user interfaces, thinking that they are leaving requirement definition and getting into design. It is true that some user interface details are shaped by product design decisions and detailed operational concepts must be postponed until these design decisions are made; however, the user interface details are still requirements, not design. For example, a computer screen on a factory machine is the result of some high-level design decisions. How information gets to the screen is design, but what information the user must see on the screen is a requirement. It is not enough to say, "Make it user-friendly" or "graphical." People define these terms in the context of their domain knowledge and experience. Developers seldom have experience in the environment where the product will be used. Thus, don't be afraid to get into the user interface details. To prevent wasting time on premature detail, however, consult Chapter 9 on writing requirements to the appropriate level.

Look beyond the obvious buttons, levers, and display screens for human interface requirements. Review your operational concepts for subtle needs, such as safety interlocks. High-speed assembly line machinery, for example, may require sensors to detect a person entering the work cell and controls to stop operation.

Assessing Completeness

How many operational concepts do you need? Your goal is a good set of requirements, not a complete operations manual. Table 5-1 will help you review the product's operational concepts for completeness from a requirement definition perspective.

The list may seem overwhelming, but remember that you need representative coverage, not exhaustive coverage. No one can anticipate and script every possible situation that a product might face. People are creative. If the product offers options, they can work out ways to make the product meet their needs. For example, none of the operational concepts that drove the design for the B-17 aircraft in the early 1930s exactly matched its eventual role in winning World War II in the 1940s, but the concepts led to requirements and ultimately a design versatile enough to perform that role.[6]

Some parts of Table 5-1 will not apply to some products. Some items cannot be filled until the product design is under way. Revisit this table regularly to see if a previously "not applicable" item has become important. Going through this table item by item will also give you an idea of who needs to be reviewing your operational concepts for correctness and feasibility.

Early Validation Opportunities

Reading the operational concepts that your team is producing is a start on early validation of them. You can provide them on paper to different stakeholders to read and request written feedback. You can put the concepts on a Website and hold discussions online. You can present the operational concepts in meetings to obtain verbal feedback. Informal group readings of the scripts around a conference table can expose gaps or problems. Take turns having potential users play the "users" and the "product." Give developers a chance to be the "users" as well as the "product." This exercise will start you and your team thinking about product requirements in ways that merely reading the concepts by yourselves never will. If you feel slightly ridiculous doing this, remember that "paper sims" like this played an important role in getting the United States to the moon and are still used during Space Shuttle mission development.

Mockups and simulations of product functions based on the operational concepts can help everyone better understand the requirements.

Table 5-1. Operational Concepts Completeness Sanity Check

Questions	Coverage Assessment
Have you looked at each phase of the life cycle?	• Development • Manufacturing • Verification • Shipping • Storage • Installation • Training • Operations • Maintenance • Upgrading • Disposal
Have you considered the viewpoints of all stakeholders?	• Developers • Manufacturers • Verifiers • Purchasers • Handlers for packaging, storing, shipping, and disposal • Training personnel • Users during training, operations, and upgrades • Logistics personnel • Maintenance personnel
Have you covered nominal operations and environments?	• Who will use the product? • Why? • Where? • When? • Under what conditions? • How?
Have you covered the "off-nominal" operations and environments?	• Hazards to users • Hazards to others • Hazards to the product • Hazards to other products if product fails • Potential misuse of product • Extreme conditions
Have you considered all interfaces?	• Inputs expected • Outputs expected • Input does not occur • Output does not occur • Wrong input occurs • Wrong output occurs

> By asking its customers what they wanted and then giv-
> ing it to them—giving it all to them—-Griffin Hospital radi-
> cally reformed its culture in a change-allergic industry. . . .
> [T]he [state hospital] commission literally laughed in [Griffin
> Hospital CEO] Charmel's face when he told its members how
> he wanted to spend some of the money. But the commission
> finally agreed to let Griffin do what it wanted, as long as it did
> it for no more than the average cost of adding on a similar-
> sized conventional hospital building—about $145 a square
> foot. . . .
>   The design not only had to meet patient demands for
> a homey, nonthreatening feel but also had to accommodate
> medical equipment. . . . [They] sketched ideas, then employed
> a computer-aided design system, then played around with
> cardboard models, and finally built a full-scale mock-up of a
> hospital room in a warehouse across the street from the hospi-
> tal. Hundreds of patients, staff members, technicians, builders,
> and board members paraded through the room, each one car-
> rying a "ticket" with which to submit ideas for modifications.
> "We must have moved the sink six times," recalls Charmel.[7]
> —David H. Freedman
> "Intensive Care," Inc., February 1999

What Is the Manager's Role in Operational Concepts?

As manager, you must ensure that operational concepts are
timely. Developed too late, the operational concepts cannot influence requirements. Endless development of operational concepts is not the right answer either. It takes acumen and
judgment to know how much to do and what to ignore. Managers
have more data than most of the team about costs. If manufacturing is not a big cost driver, nor is it affecting product quality in a
negative manner, you may not want to look at operational concepts for manufacturing.

You can't please everyone—you must settle disputes and
keep the requirement definition process moving forward. You
won't get consensus on everything, and you have to make the
hard decisions.

You must also ensure that all of the team has access to and understands the operational concepts. If the concepts are not documented in some manner, if you do not require that people review them, and if you do not check to make sure that they did, you will have developers and testers interpreting requirements to their own operational concepts.

Follow-through is important. You must have your team update and maintain the operational concepts as they update and maintain the scope and requirements. You must continually relate these operational concepts back to your needs and scope and forward to your requirements. Downstream, in reviews of the requirements being defined, take the lead in asking questions. Ask how specific requirements being proposed relate to the operational concepts. In design, ask how the proposed design meets the requirements and how it relates to the operational concepts. The word will get around that you care, which will make your people care.

Operational Concepts Have High Return on Investment

Good operational concepts lead to good, complete, and consistent requirements for the entire product life cycle. They enhance communication among customers, users, and developers and can increase the customer's confidence in you and the future product. They give you a head start on developing good human interfaces, which are so crucial to user satisfaction.

As the requirements mature and product development proceeds, you can develop the operational concepts to finer levels of detail. This refinement helps focus your product developers. Just as important, these concepts give the nondevelopers, such as customers, the information they need to follow the development and enable them to provide useful input throughout the process. This practice also prevents customer expectations from drifting away from the formal requirements. The developer will assess the product's quality by the requirements, but the customers will measure it against their expectations.

Chapter 6
Collision Course
Identifying and Managing Interfaces

The [Atlanta Olympics] Games competition began the morning of Saturday, July 20, with, among other things, gymnastics and basketball. Information about events, competitors and winners was supposed to instantly flow through IBM's system to a computer that then formats and feeds the data to newspapers around the world. But it wasn't working. The data in the feed, called World News Press Agency (WNPA), started backing up, not getting out. . . .

By later that day, the press was engaged in tense meetings with IBM. Almost no agate, the tiny type that shows detailed results, was coming in for Sunday newspapers. To sports fans, that's like leaving out stock listings in the financial section. Sportswriters weren't getting results for their stories. Deadlines loomed. Tempers flared.

Caught in the middle was Bob Neal, director of technology for the Atlanta Committee for the Olympic Games (ACOG). . . . "In hindsight, we obviously didn't test as much as we should have," says ACOG's Neal. "But mostly, I wish it had been something less visible, to be honest."

Still, the problem was clearly IBM's mistake. Several members of the Atlanta team had gone to the 1992 Olympics in Barcelona, Spain, to observe and prepare. They worked on the Atlanta system for four years. Many of the WNPA problems were a case of programming a computer to format a certain sport's information one way, while newspapers were expecting it another way. IBM just didn't see it coming and never tested the whole system until the Games started.

So IBM was stuck fixing unbelievably complex technology on the run.

—Kevin Maney
"IBM: The mad scramble—Olympic crucible tests corporate giant's mettle"
USA Today, August 2, 1996

Many projects neglect to detail and control the interfaces until testing. The first encounter with this oversight often occurs when people find out that they cannot plug test equipment into the product to perform the tests. Some projects neglect interfaces until operations.

We recommend that your team identify the product's external interfaces very early—preferably, before you write the first requirement.

Why Define External Interfaces So Soon?

Missing or incorrect interfaces are often a major cause of cost overruns and product failures. Identifying external interfaces early will clarify your product scope, aid risk assessment, reduce product development costs, and improve customer satisfaction.

Identifying interfaces will clarify your product scope with the boundaries imposed by their product. Does your product have its own power supply or plug into someone else's? Does it contain a database or use someone else's? If you define external interfaces early, who owns what will be clear to your requirement writers. If it is not clear, you can resolve the issue before you begin writing. The result will be fewer requirement rewrites. An early study of the interfaces will eliminate development rework due to bad interface assumptions.

If your product must interface with existing products, you cannot change the external interface to your liking, but you can write requirements to simplify the interface from your product's viewpoint. Good external interface requirements are essential to ensuring a successful mating between your product and others when you reach integration testing.

Identifying interfaces aids risk assessment. An important part of your risk management job is identifying those interfaces that are known and unchanging and those that may be in question or volatile. Early knowledge of external interfaces, and their volatility, can reduce product development costs. For the nonvolatile interfaces, early definition will prevent rework resulting from a misunderstanding or lack of knowledge. For the volatile interfaces, you must first understand the existing interface and how and why it might change, or understand why no well-defined interface exists. Then, you can write requirements that will make your product less vulnerable to interface changes.

For interfaces with products still in development, an early interface assessment gives you the option to open dialogues with product users and developers of interfacing products to clarify and simplify interfaces before anyone does serious design work. The concurrent development of interfacing products presents the hardest and riskiest interface problems. If your product is complex enough to have multiple levels (Chapter 9), you will face this challenge internally as well as externally.

Identifying interfaces early reduces product development rework and improves customer satisfaction. On some systems, the interface requirements are a significant percentage of the requirements. Furthermore, interface requirements often have consequences far beyond what their actual percentage might suggest. Many requirement omissions that we see are interface requirements, and these omissions are crippling. If you miss a functional, performance, or maintainability requirement, your product might not be as useful as you had hoped, but it may still be useful. If you miss an interface requirement, your customer may not be able to do anything with the product until you fix it.

How Do You Identify Interfaces Early?

From the highest-level perspective of a product, two categories of interface exist: external and internal. External interfaces are the boundaries between your product and the rest of the world. Internal interfaces are the boundaries between parts of your product. Before design start, you are concerned with external interfaces. After system architecting begins, you will address internal interfaces.

The External Interfaces

External interfaces fall into two broad categories: those interfaces involving an animate or live (usually human) user and those that involve everything else, which we'll call inanimate external interfaces. User interfaces include buttons and levers to push, handholds and straps for carrying, warning bells, safety labels, information displayed on screens, monitoring windows, and so on. Inanimate interfaces include structural support or anchor, power supply, storage container or toolbox, shipping system, test equipment, computer host, maintenance tool, data supply and destination, and existing equipment used with your product.

We separate these external interfaces into two categories because animate users are variable and uncontrollable. Well-developed operational concepts are crucial to developing the requirements for, as well as the design of, these human interfaces. The scope of this book is requirement definition, not design, so we emphasized the importance of Chapter 5 (operational concepts) in developing user interface requirements and focus the remainder of this chapter on inanimate interface requirements.

A product's inanimate interfaces are more consistent than human interfaces. They can also be controlled. For example, if your product needs power from an external source, you can choose a power supply interface from those controlled by industry standards, such as 115-volt alternating current at 60 cycles per second or 208-volt three-phase. Perhaps your product must interface with another product not controlled by industry standards. If that product already exists, you may have no choice but to make your product fit it—especially if the other product is widely used, such as a particular word processor or database. In these situations, specific interface requirements are imposed on your product. Check to see if an industry standard, an application programmer's interface (API), or an interface control document (ICD) is defined for the existing product. The standard, API, or ICD will detail the requirements that your product must meet.

If no existing interface document can be found, your team may have to research the interfacing product and create an ICD substitute. In the process of filling this gap, get as much information about the other product as possible directly from the developers of that product. "He said, she said" is an expensive game when it comes to interfaces! You must also consider the risk of changes in that other product that will affect the interface. Your team must monitor the other product for such changes.

Sometimes you can influence another product's external interfaces. When your product and another product are being developed in parallel, your team and the other product team can jointly define interfaces that are logical, simple, and most cost-effective. This process sometimes presents a challenging management problem. What is logical, simple, or cost-effective for your team may appear as illogical, complex, or expensive to the other product development team. Expect to do some give-and-take to resolve all but the simplest interfaces. When you and your counterpart on the other project have agreed on the interface requirements, you should jointly write an interface requirement specification (IRS) or interface requirement document (IRD) that you both will approve and abide by. After this document matures and both organizations accept it, place it under change-control.

We recommend that you and your counterpart jointly define an interface operational concept (Chapter 5) for your products' interactions. As you develop this operational concept, maintain awareness of all other events surrounding the interface. Avoid focusing so much on the interface that you forget to look at everything that leads to the interface and away from it.

While you develop this interface operational concept, you should also develop an ongoing relationship with people from the other product's organization. It's prudent to follow-up on the agreement periodically to ensure that the other organization is on track to meet the agreed-to interface. Even if it is their fault that they fail to meet the interface, your product won't be useful until they comply.

Requesting ICDs or writing IRDs assumes that you have identified the interface. Many people identify the obvious interfaces like power supply for use during operations, but they miss interfaces for other parts of the life cycle, like the power supply needed during testing and maintenance. How do you ensure that you have identified all of the external interfaces? First, make a brief list of the potential interface areas. For example, you may have:

1. Structure or physical
2. Power
3. Data or signal
4. Command

Next, consider each of these areas throughout the product's entire life cycle. Table 6-1 gives an interface identification matrix. Go through this checklist for each of the above interface candidates. For example, what kind of physical support does your product need during manufacturing and testing? Can it sit on a bench during assembly, or will it require a jig or an alignment fixture? Do tooling or test fixtures exist that you can use if you design the product with the correct interface? Even if you can get it through manufacture and testing using nothing fancier than a bench, will a bench be in its operational environment, or will another type of support be needed in the field? Will it need a special container or structural supports to protect it from vibration and drop damage during shipping? How about during storage?

Note that if you are developing a totally new product, you may not know some of the answers to the above questions until the product is in design. You must still consider the questions and note what you do not know for resolution. For example, you might require that the new product interface with existing equipment, or you might not want this constraint. If you write no interface requirement, you are driving toward development of new equipment and tooling to build and test the product. Is this new equipment and tooling part of your product, or is it part of an

Table 6-1. Checklist for Individual Interface Exploration

(Interface type)	Manufac-turing	Verification	Deployment	Operations	Disposal
Normal Use					
Failure and Abnormal Use					
Maintenance and Logistics					
Storage or Stand-by					
Shipping					

external product? Who is going to pay for its development? Who is in charge of it? These issues must be resolved. If it is part of your product, what is needed will evolve with the design of the product. If it is external, you now have to work with another manager to resolve the interface issues.

Tables 6-2 and 6-3 provide an example interface exploration for a prosthetic (artificial) hand controller, which consists of a computer on an electronic circuit board (to be embedded in the artificial hand) and controlling software. In this example, the product must interface with existing electrical equipment, so much interface detail is known before development. This level of detail won't exist at this early stage for products that will interface with products in parallel development. If that is your situation, simply identify where the design will fill in these details.

Ask yourself the following questions at each boundary and product life stage (Table 6-2):

1. What does my product do to the world?
2. What does the world do to my product?
3. What is the worst thing that can happen across this interface?[1]
4. Is this interface likely to change during the development of my product?
5. Is this interface likely to change after my product is in use?

Asking these "interface five" questions about the power interface for the artificial hand controller (Table 6-3) during the operation life-cycle phase yields the answers and insights in the example below.

1. What does my product do to the world? My product draws 4 milliAmps of current at ± 9-volts DC when processing a command.
2. What does the world do to my product? The world supplies up to 100 milliAmps of current at ± 7.5- to ± 10-volts DC, per plot 1 in reference A.
3. What is the worst thing that can happen across this interface? The NiCad supply voltage peaks at

Table 6-2. Example Interface Identification Matrix for Physical Interfaces: Artificial Hand Controller

Physical (Interface type)	Manufacturing	Verification	Deployment	Operations	Disposal
Normal Use	Jig holding board during component insertion and soldering	(1) Jig holding board during test (2) Connector(s) for power, test software download, data, and command	(1) Mounts to hold controller and allow multiple removals and reinstallations (2) Connector(s) for operational software download, test data, and command	(1) Mounts holding controller through routine use of hand (2) Connector(s) with strain relief for power, sensor input, and command output	(1) Mounts to allow easy removal of controller
Maintenance and Logistics		(1) Jig holding board during repair (2) Connector(s) for troubleshooting software download, data, and command		(3) Mounts to hold controller and allow for many removals and reinstallations	

(continues)

Table 6-2. Example Interface Identification Matrix for Physical Interfaces: Artificial Hand Controller (continued)

Physical (Interface type)	Manufacturing	Verification	Deployment	Operations	Disposal
Failure and Abnormal Use			Emergency grasp release button to override controller and open hand	(1) "Breakaway" mounts in hand that free controller from high loads encountered during a fall, protecting controller hardware (2) Emergency grasp release button to override controller and open hand	
Storage or Stand-by	Antistatic container				
Shipping	Antistatic container		Container for shipping to customer		Container for shipping to recycling

Table 6-3. Example Interface Identification Matrix Power Interfaces: Artificial Hand Controller

Power (Interface type)	Manufac-turing	Verification	Deployment	Operations	Disposal
Normal Use		115 volts AC	(1) 115 volts AC (2) ±9 volts DC from artificial hand's battery pack	±9 volts DC from artificial hand's battery pack (max 200 milliAmps)	
Failure and Abnormal Use				(1) ±12 volts DC, max 500 mA, for overcharge state (2) 0 volts DC when batteries are drained	
Maintenance and Logistics		(1) 115 volts AC from test equipment (2) ±9 volts DC from battery simulator	(1) 115 volts AC (2) ±9 volts DC from artificial hand's battery pack	(3) 115 volts AC from battery charger or test equipment (4) ±9 volts DC from artificial hand's battery pack	
Storage or Stand-by					
Shipping					

$\pm$ 12-volts DC when a battery overcharge occurs. The supply voltage goes to zero when batteries are exhausted. When NiCad batteries age, current-voltage profile changes, per plot 2 in reference A.

4. Is this interface likely to change during the development of my product? The two major battery pack suppliers have tentatively scheduled increases in their products' battery milliamp-hours to accommodate additional motors in prostheses. The impact on our controller from such an increase is good—it will increase the time our users have before they must recharge the battery pack—without requiring any change to our controller. A possibility exists for change in the battery pack connectors used which would require a different connector on our controller.

5. Is this interface likely to change after my product is in use? Yes. NiCad battery technology appears to be giving way to nickel-metal-hydride (NMH) and lithium ion (LI) technologies. These battery technologies have higher energy densities but different current-voltage profiles, per reference B (NMH) and reference C (LI).

Data and signal interfaces are particularly messy. It's often easy to identify the nominal situation, such as data or signal inputs from sensors, but what happens if one of those inputs is incorrect or disappears? If you do not account for these scenarios, your product's behavior in the face of interface troubles will be unpredictable and perhaps dangerous. The supplier of the interfacing product may change that product; thus, you should try to anticipate some interface change, adding requirements to design for it. You will want to avoid having many internal components driven by external interfaces. That is, write requirements to limit the internal components that actually can be affected by an external interface. For example, you might require that developers define a buffer module through which all external inputs pass rather than allow the external inputs to go directly to many different components of your product. Then, external interface changes impact only one module, the buffer module.

Another defense is to determine if the volatile requirement can be bounded. Perhaps the product on the other side of the interface can use only two possible connectors. Can you write requirements that enable you to switch between the connectors late in the design or manufacturing process? A requirement to design for change can simplify your world in situations in which you have little or no control and must proceed in order to meet schedules.

> Because the Sprint spacecraft's flight would be very short, no one would recharge or replace the spacecraft's batteries in orbit. So, those advocating rechargeable batteries and external power interfaces early in the spacecraft's design got squelched. "We'll just have the battery supplier make some extra battery packs to get us through testing and replace them as needed," the program manager answered their concerns. "We don't have time and money for all this fancy stuff like rechargeable batteries or power ports just to support testing." He didn't have time for thorough requirement definition either.
>
> The structures group also knew that the spacecraft would never be opened when it was in orbit. They designed the battery compartment cover with over 100 screws that had to be removed to replace the battery pack.
>
> Testing time was over a 100 times the length of the spacecraft's flight and much longer than the program manager anticipated. The added time was partially caused by the lack of effort in requirement definition, but the half-day delay to remove and reinstall those 100-plus screws every time the batteries went dead contributed a lot to the delay. Of course, the original order of batteries was exhausted before the testing was even complete. Lithium-ion batteries are expensive, build-to-order items requiring rigorous testing for failures that can release poisonous gases, and getting new ones caused more delays. Finally, cheaper and less dangerous battery packs were made for testing, but the project spent thousands of dollars on batteries before the spacecraft ever left the ground.
>
> —Kristin Farry

The Internal Interfaces

As you proceed into system design and product architecting (Chapter 9), you must consider the internal interfaces between product subdivisions or subsystems. Examples of internal interfaces include software to hardware, power converter to device powered, engine to chassis, and doll's head to doll's body. Internal interface choices have large budget and schedule impacts. You can control internal interfaces, and the guiding rule is to keep them simple. Simplicity of development, product phasing possibilities, testing ease, maintenance effort, and manufacturing effort should drive internal interfaces. As with external interfaces, well-developed operational concepts are crucial to dividing your product in ways that improve its manufacturing, deployment, and operation, and reduce development headaches. Others have written excellent books on how to do system architecting. See, for example, Eberhardt Rechtin's *Systems Architecting: Creating and Building Complex Systems* and Jeffrey Grady's *System Requirements Analysis*.[2] In this book, we restrict this discussion to converting these internal interface choices into unambiguous requirements.

Where do you put internal interface requirements? The requirements for internal interfaces must be documented just as the requirements for external interfaces are documented. Remember that, to the perspective of your subsystem or component developers, these interfaces are external, not internal. Thus, the rules for external interfaces apply. Some of the internal components will be existing off-the-shelf items, and these will have an ICD or an API. This ICD or API will be used to define interface requirements for other to-be-developed components that must connect to them.

Because you have control over the internal interface requirements, you can put them in your product's highest (known in some circles as the "system") level specification (detailed in Chapters 9 and 11). This is a good place for them, because you must control these interfaces and this system specification controls your product development. You don't know what these internal interfaces will be until you have begun design, however, because dividing a system into subsystems is a design task. You must leave a hole in the system-level specification for these internal interface requirements. Your team can then come back and fill this hole when far enough into design to know where these interfaces should be. Once your team has identified these internal interfaces, you must go through a requirement definition phase for each of the subsystems, so backing up to fill this hole in the systems specification is not as messy as it sounds. We recommend that you use the higher-level document for these requirements, even though you will have a postbaseline change. The document will exist anyway and will control all of the system components. An alternative is to develop an IRD for each of the interfacing components. This process adds another document, and you will have to set up the authority and control of the document.

> Preliminary findings by an internal peer review at NASA's Jet Propulsion Laboratory indicate that a failure to recognize and correct an error in a transfer of information between the Mars Climate Orbiter spacecraft team in Colorado and the mission navigation team in California led to the loss of the spacecraft. . . . [O]ne team used English units while the other used metric units for a key spacecraft operation.
> —NASA Press Release: 99-117
> "Head of Mars Climate Orbiter Investigation Team Named"

Document, Document!

For both external and internal interfaces, early comprehensive documentation is important to avoid rework and unpleasant surprises late in development. A word of caution: Your team should document each interface in only one place. Multiple documents containing what is supposed to be the same interface information will get out of synchronization at some point even on the best-run project. Avoid this problem by not duplicating interface information between documents. An exception to this rule might be appropriate when referencing a large ICD from which only one or two items are needed. Duplication of these one or two items inside your document makes it much easier for those using your document; however, someone must keep an eye on the ICD for changes. Be sure to show the ICD as the source of the interface data. Use common sense.

Include diagrams of the interfaces in your documents. If you restrict your interface definition to words alone, everyone reading the document will draw their own diagram as they read. A large number of people will do the same work—drawing the diagram that you could have included—over and over. Furthermore, it's unlikely that all these reader-generated interface diagrams will be identical and correct.

Drawing diagrams for inclusion in the specification is an excellent interface definition validation exercise for your team. If you can't draw it, you can't build it. Separate drawings for external and internal interfaces will reduce misinterpretations of what is inside versus outside your product. As a test, do a diagram of your internal components as they interface to external products and systems. If any of these external interfaces are replicated (e.g., a command can come into two different components), you need to rethink the interfaces. A single interface change affects multiple parts of your product.

What Is the Manager's Role with Interfaces?

Your most important role related to interfaces is ensuring that all are identified. Next, you must get involved wherever you must provide the conduit to the other product. External interfaces often need to be negotiated, and these negotiations may require a manager's authority.

You also must ensure that external interface definition is clear before your team completes its architecture of your product. If you do not, you may find that your product's architecture (as it relates to external interfaces) is a nightmare. You will then be redoing the architecture and will probably experience a cost and schedule hit.

At each design review, you will want to ensure that everyone understands the impact of interface requirements on the design. You will also identify any problems that require your involvement with an external product manager.

Ignoring Interface Issues Makes Them Bigger

It's easy to forget about interfaces until they become a collision with major casualties in testing or beyond. How do you keep interfaces from becoming collisions? Use the product interface identification sanity check (Table 6-4) to stay on top of the interface issues. Identify, simplify, control, document, communicate, and monitor your interfaces. This process requires an investment of time and resources plus discipline. The alternative is much more expensive. After all, if the interface is wrong, your product won't work, no matter how good it is.

Table 6-4. Product Interface Identification Sanity Check

Have you identified all product interfaces?
Have you located interface control documents for interfaces to existing products?
Are you monitoring interface change outside your control?
Have you involved people from the other side of external interfaces in the interface definition effort?
Have you simplified interfaces as much as possible?
Have you documented all product interfaces?
Have you distributed the product interface documentation?
Are you tracking the interfaces through development to ensure that reality matches the documentation?

It takes two people to time the ignition on most aircraft piston engines, which has nothing to do with the complexity of the task. The length of the cables on the timing box and the timing box's shape make it a two-person job. The box is a cube, made to sit nicely on a bench, but an aircraft's engine compartment contains no flat surfaces! The cables aren't long enough on any of the timing boxes to allow you to connect it

to the magnetos and set it on a bench where you can see the
display while you move the propeller (which is always on the
opposite side of the engine) from a safe place. The box has an
audio signal that helps a little—it tells you when you have a
timing problem—but it doesn't tell you which side of the ignition system has the problem. So, you wedge the box somewhere in the engine compartment where you can see it while
you move the propeller and try to keep from being clobbered.
The timing box doesn't stay put. After the box hits the hangar
floor four times or so, you find someone else to hold the box
and tell you what lights are on when while you move the propeller and tweak the magneto, or vice versa.

—Kristin Farry

Chapter 7
Be Careful What You Ask For
Writing Good Requirements

Jackie, my 10-year-old granddaughter, asked for a lesson on how to write requirements. I began by asking her to name something she wanted me to get her.

"A lollipop," she said.

"That's fine, but what kind of lollipop?" I asked.

Jackie thought for a moment. "Oh, you mean like a flavor, like cherry."

"OK, cherry. Now what size lollipop would you like?" I prompted her.

"Humongous!" she replied.

"That's not a good requirement," I countered. "What you think of as humongous and what I think of when I hear that word might be very different. I need a size that cannot be misunderstood, like the size of a golf ball."

We went through some more of this and then she started throwing in extraneous information, like what kind of lollipop her brother likes.

"No, don't add that, it will only confuse me," I told her.

Abruptly, Jackie smiled and said, "I've got it, Grand-

> mother. You want to make requirements real simple and spe-
> cific, so that everyone can understand them. And you don't
> include anything that doesn't matter."
>
> —Ivy Hooks

What is a good requirement? We started this book by telling
you that good requirements are essential to developing better
products faster and cheaper, but then we devoted five chapters to
discussing processes (Chapter 3), scope (Chapter 4), operational
concepts (Chapter 5), and interfaces (Chapter 6) instead of ex-
plaining what we consider a good requirement. Why? Attempting
to write requirements without defining, documenting, and disseminating scope, operational concepts, and interfaces leads to
inconsistent and incomplete requirements. Now that you have an
understanding of these areas, you and your team are prepared
to write the actual requirements—requirements that will lead
you to a quality, useful product. In this chapter, we cover writing
a draft of the requirements. A good draft will put your team halfway down the road to a good set of requirements. The second
half of the requirement definition process (chapters 8–12) will
complete, validate, and refine this draft into your baseline requirement specification.

Why Are Individual Requirements So Important?

Good requirements give you control over your product's development and prevent rework throughout development. The individual requirements for your product are where the rubber hits the
road. The requirements are your control over the product development outcome. They are usually contractually binding, and
your team must verify that the product meets each and every one
of them. If something isn't spelled out in the requirements, the
development team will make the decisions on it. If the developers
lack customer domain knowledge, which is usually the case, their
choice won't be the same as the customers' or users' choice. The
development team will probably choose the easiest development
path. In any case, the result will not be verified and, hence, may

be useless to the customers. Unfortunately, someone will wind up paying for it somewhere.

Ambiguous or poorly crafted requirements tie up development resources in resolving their ambiguity at best and cause rework when the real need becomes clear at worst. All too often, the real meaning of the requirement doesn't become clear until the product enters testing or later. If the bad requirement is a high-level requirement in a complex product, all requirements derived from it will be flawed, and the resources involved in fixing this requirement cascading downstream will be huge.

How Do You Recognize the Good?

A good requirement clearly states a verifiable and attainable need.

Need

A requirement is a statement of something that someone needs. The something is a product that performs a service or function. The someone may be a company, user, customer, maintainers, testers, or another product. For example, a company needs a manufacturing machine that stamps out widgets, or they need a certain plastic to feed a manufacturing machine that they already have. A bank must process debit card transactions. Alternatively, a requirement is a statement of a characteristic of something that someone needs. In the same vein as the above examples, a machine must stamp out 60 widgets an hour. The raw material must be formed in sheets, or it must be red in color. A bank must process at least 1,200 debit card transactions in one hour.

Generally, you must distinguish between needs and wants. Even if it is verifiable, attainable, and eloquently stated, a requirement that is not necessary is not a good requirement. The definition of need will depend on the context or circumstances. For instance, if you are spending taxpayers' or shareholders' money, need will be narrowly defined. For commercial products, a consumer want is a need for your product when it tips the consumer's buy decision in your product's favor.

Verifiable

A requirement must state something that can be verified by inspection, analysis, test, or demonstration. As you review a requirement, think about how you will prove that the product meets it. Determine the specific criteria for product acceptance, which will ensure verifiable requirements. Because verifiability is so important, we devote an entire chapter to it (Chapter 10).

Attainable

The requirement must be attainable—within your budget, schedule, and technically feasible. A moving company might want an antigravity pack to float furniture from one place to another, but physicists have yet to understand what gravity is, let alone how to cancel it. A set of dollies, lifts, and trucks are technically feasible and more likely to be within the budget of a typical moving company. Try not to write a requirement for something that cannot be built or that you cannot afford.

Many feasibility questions will not be as clear-cut as our furniture-moving example. You may not have the expertise to judge whether a requirement is technically feasible. If so, be sure to include members of the development team in the review process to foresee technical problems. Your team may need to conduct research to determine a requirement's feasibility before it is added to the product baseline. If this research still leaves you uncertain about the feasibility of what you want, consider stating the need as a goal rather than as a requirement. If you can't back off to a less demanding but obviously feasible requirement, you will have to identify the requirement as a risk and needing frequent reviewing. See Chapter 12 for risk assessment before baselining the requirement.

Clear

A good requirement cannot be misunderstood. It expresses a single thought. It is concise and simple. Remember that there is no requirement for a requirement document to be a literary masterpiece! Leave the long, eloquent sentences and clever word choices to James Joyce and William Faulkner or save them for your future best-selling novel. Use short, simple sentences with consistent terminology for requirements. For instance, decide on specific names for your product and refer to it by that name alone in all your requirements. As you define subsystems, name them also and use only those names. If you can't make the names short, define standard acronyms for everyone to use.

State your requirements positively whenever possible. It is easier to develop and test a product that does something specific than one that does not do something specific. It is extremely difficult, if not impossible, to test that something does not happen. This type of testing is expensive and may break your budget.

Make your requirements grammatically correct. Good grammar is essential for understanding. Good sentence structure ensures that the implementer and tester understand what thing should do what task—it makes the lines of responsibility obvious. Use the "who shall what" standard form to prevent misunderstanding: The (service provider or product) shall (do, perform, provide, weigh, or other verb, followed by a description of what).

For example, consider:

The painting system shall coat Widget X with a 1-millimeter thick ($\pm$ 0.2-millimeter) coating.

The customer service management tool shall store model number, serial number, and problem description for each problem reported.

The component tester shall weigh less than 40 pounds.

The transaction management system shall print 1,200 or more transaction summaries in 1 hour.

If writing is a struggle for your team, this standard form presents a less painful alternative to directly writing requirements. It lends itself well to bulleted listings, which you and your team can develop and discuss in brainstorming sessions. Once you have agreed on the content of the bullets, a competent writer can convert them into specification sentences with little guidance.

We recommend that you use standard requirement terminology as well as form. Terminology is especially important if your requirements go outside of your organization to an external provider. Government agency and industry conventions require that you use:

* *Shall* in requirements
* *Will* in statements of fact
* *Should* in goals

Grammar teachers might quibble with this usage, but in this case, disagreeing with your schoolteacher makes a document more useful and understandable. The *shall* serves as a flag to identify the requirements that must be verified. Every *shall* is contractually binding and drives your development budget. Using other words can confuse developers. In today's increasingly electronic environment, people bidding on product development or performing product testing will often simply search for the word *shall* and ignore every sentence in a requirement document that does not contain *shall*. You will have a contractual problem if someone has used words other than *shall* (such as *must* or *will*) in a requirement.

If your organization is one that does everything from requirement definition to product testing internally, you may wonder if you need to use these terms. Your organization still needs to use something that is consistent across all internal development efforts. Because you hire people from other companies or from schools where the above terminology is the convention, why make things more difficult by inventing new terms? Use of the standard terms will also make it easier for your organization to review its own requirements. Consistent application of this terminology saves time and effort by "keying" the reviewer to statements that are meant as requirements. Keep it simple, and devote all of the resources on determining the requirements, not fiddling with vocabulary.

A lively Internet discussion took place on the Software Requirement Engineering reflector about the use of the terms "shall," "will," and "should" in requirements.

One contributor said, "We don't need to do that any more because that was U.S. Department of Defense terminology and they threw out those standards."

The response from an Australian contributor was, "Your DoD may have thrown out those standards, but here is a list of international standards that mandate use of these terms."

A computer science professor at a not-to-be-mentioned university wrote, "This is too difficult. What we need is a simple symbol or icon for requirements."

The prompt response was, "We have a simple symbol for requirements. It is the word 'shall.' "

—Ivy Hooks

The Bad and the Ugly

Common mistakes in this stage of the requirement definition process include:

1. Making bad assumptions
2. Writing implementation instead of requirements
3. Describing operations instead of writing requirements
4. Using incorrect terms or sentence structure
5. Writing unverifiable requirements
6. Missing requirements
7. Overspecifying requirements

Making Bad Assumptions

Your previous work in defining scope and operational concepts exposed many bad assumptions before you and your team began writing, especially if you were able to involve customers; however, the requirement-writing process will expose additional gaps in your thinking, gaps that requirement writers will fill with assumptions. To aggravate the problem, someone may be writing requirements without studying the scope and operational concept material. Documenting assumptions when requirements are written can further expose bad assumptions early in the process and eliminate serious problems later. Chapter 8 will show you how to do this.

Writing Implementation

Requirements should state what you need, not how to provide it. Put another way, the requirement should state the problem, not the solution.

For example, in an Air Force request for proposals to develop a requirement management tool, the first requirement was to "provide a database." A database is one possible implementation of a requirement management tool, but it is not a need. The real needs for this tool include (1) provide traceability between requirements and (2) sort requirements. A database implementation might be the best implementation, but this is a choice best left to the tool developers. Besides, do you really want to verify that you have a database?

Two major dangers lurk in stating implementation instead of need in requirements. The first danger is that you will force the developers to use a particular design or solution that may not be the best way to meet the need. You are, after all, "requiring" this solution, and the product will only meet all of your requirements if it embodies this particular solution.

The second danger is more subtle and insidious. Stating implementation may lull you into believing that you have covered all of the real requirements or needs. In fact, important requirements may be missing. The product developers will deliver what you requested, but it may not be what you wanted. Consider the requirement management tool example: A "database" is literally a store of data. The developers would be compliant if they gave you a tool that simply lists your requirements. Having that store or list does not automatically mean that you can find which of the requirements in it contain errors or are causing your developers problems. This simple list would be an unwelcome surprise if you envisioned the term "database" to include all of the input display screens and output reports that would make managing requirements easier!

To screen implementation out of your requirements, ask why you need each requirement. If this question takes you back to a more fundamental requirement, you are stating implementation, not need. Another beneficial question to ask is, "Is the requirement really what I want to verify?" If you have stated implementation, not a requirement, this question will reveal the problem. For example, if the requirement states that you need "a switch," ask, "If I verify that I have a switch, which can be done by inspection, will I be satisfied?" Perhaps what you really want is a product that can be manually switched on and off, possibly with some frequency, within some time period, and over a certain lifetime. Simply verifying that you have a switch is not going to prove that you can do these things with the switch. Chapter 10 will delve more into verification assessment as a requirement validation tool.

Describing Operations

Similar to the implementation description trap is the operation description error, which occurs when the writer blurs the distinction between operational concepts and requirements. Operational concepts are an important part of understanding what the requirements must be, but they are not the requirements. For example, "The operator shall be able to turn the machine on and off."

This description of the operations (what the operator will do) is not a requirement on the system. The real system requirement is "the system shall provide a manual on/off switch." Table 7-1 contains more examples. You must be especially alert for this error in environment- and user-related requirements.

Two dangers exist in stating operations instead of the true requirements. First, the operation statement may be unverifiable.

Table 7-1. Operations Description versus Requirement

Incorrect (Operations Description Instead of a Requirement)	Correct (True Requirement)
The life vest shall be worn by individuals the 5th ranging from percentile female to 95th percentile male.	The life vest shall float individuals ranging from the 5th percentile female to the 95th percentile male (Reference 2).
The operating instructions shall be understood by operators with only fourth-grade level reading skills.	The operating instructions shall meet the National Education Association's fourth-grade reading skills standard (Reference 4).

Second, the developers may misunderstand your intent when they translate this operation statement into a verifiable requirement. Giving the developer the operation description (in the form of the operational concepts of Chapter 5) in addition to the requirement will reduce the risk of misunderstanding the requirement. You may also find that, if your requirement writers have some place (the operational concepts) to describe the operations that they envision, the requirements that they write will not have operations descriptions in them.

When screening requirements for this problem, ask, "Do I or the product developers have control over this?" No one has control over operators (human or animal) and what they do to a product! Also ask, "Is this a need my product must meet or an activity involving my product?" Consider how you will prove that your product meets the requirement. For the second example in Table 7-1, verifying the incorrect version of the requirement might involve finding operators with fourth-grade reading skills to operate the product after reading the instructions. This process would be expensive, and you would probably not be able to conclusively prove that the instructions are appropriate for all operators with a fourth-grade reading level. It would be a lot simpler and cheaper to check the vocabulary, average word length, and average sentence length against a published standard.

> Someone wrote a requirement in the mid-1980s for the Space Station program that said: "The monkeys shall not bite the astronauts." The developer could not have solved this problem because he was not delivering and had no control over the monkeys. Requirements that state, "The crew shall . . . ;" "The pilot shall . . . ;" or "The operator shall . . . ," are almost always operational statements, not real requirements.
>
> —Ivy Hooks

Using Incorrect or Ambiguous Terms

A number of words and phrases can cause budget and schedule problems. For example, what do *support, but not limited to, et cetera* or *etc.*, and *and/or* mean? People use these words and phrases in requirements when they don't know exactly what the product will need to do. We often see "support" used like this: "The ABS system shall support the teller in processing customer transactions."

This statement is a stick of dynamite. It has a long, slow fuse, but it is dynamite nonetheless. Given this requirement, the product developers will define support, and chances are neither you nor your customer are going to be happy with their definition unless the developers happen to know as much about the product's use as the customer does. When you find a requirement like this, return to your operational concepts. They will reveal the real requirements, which in this case might include "the ABS system shall scan the account number from a check" and "the ABS system shall display to the teller the amount on deposit in the account."

If your operational concepts also say "support," you must develop them further to find the real requirements hiding behind "support." The only time that the word "support" doesn't introduce ambiguity is in requirements for structure, as in "the structure shall support loads up to 100 pounds."

People include "*et cetera*" or "but not limited to" in a requirement when they suspect that they have missed a need, or an unanticipated need will develop later. They want product flexibility to handle that now-unknown need. Consider the following:

> The customer service management tool shall store model number, serial number, problem description, etc.
> The customer service management tool shall store data concerning each customer problem, including, but not limited to, model number, serial number, and problem description.

Putting these terms in requirements will probably not give you a product that includes the unknown. These terms can be expensive when you are contracting the product development. They cannot be priced in any uniform, meaningful way. Each bidder knows that you are likely (and perhaps obligated) to choose the lowest bid. They won't take the risk of adding cost for these ambiguities when other bidders probably won't. After the contract award, a contractor may use these terms as an excuse for doing additional work for which you must pay extra. If you cannot convert these terms into explicit requirements before hiring a contractor, consider adding tasks to the contract for analysis of these ambiguities, with options to increase the scope of the development effort to include any essential requirements uncovered in that analysis.

Another way to deal with the unknown is to add requirements that the system be modifiable. For example:

> The customer service management tool shall store model number, serial number, and problem description for each customer problem reported.
> The customer service management tool shall provide four user-definable fields for each customer problem.

This second requirement will spawn many lower level requirements. In this case, including some rationale for the requirement (i.e., give us flexibility to expand our data records to include other data items in the future) can guide developers as they expand this requirement downward. The next chapter covers the use of rationale in detail, and Chapters 12 and 15 revisit writing requirements for growth.

Terms like "and/or" are also ambiguous. For example, consider:

> The customer service management tool shall store model number, serial number, problem code, and/or problem description for each customer problem reported.

A developer who implements only the "or" as in:

> The customer service management tool shall store model number, serial number, problem code, or problem description for each customer problem reported.

has technically met the requirement. The result is a tool that stores only one of the four items listed. The requirement writer might have meant:

> The customer service management tool shall store model number, serial number, and either the problem code or problem description for each customer problem reported.

This requirement would result in a tool that stores three items for each problem report. Alternatively, the writer may have intended:

> The customer service management tool shall store any of the following combinations of items for each customer problem reported: (1) model number, serial number, problem code, and problem description; (2) model number, serial number, and problem code; OR (3) model number, serial number, and problem description.

This requirement would make developers deliver a tool that stores up to four items for each problem report.

We can't leave the subject of terminology without a caution about jargon. Some everyday words take on different meanings in groups of specialists. Developing operational concepts with both your customer and developer helps you find these jargon traps early.

Even if your requirement management tool is only a word processor, you can find the dangerous words with simple word searches on every draft of your requirements.

> In industry, "increasing productivity" means increasing production of something per dollar spent. In the military, it means increasing the number of objectives accomplished per dollar spent. The community responsible for planning activities during space flight uses "increasing productivity" to mean increasing tasks done per launch. For space operations, there is no "per dollar" in "productivity."
>
> —Kristin Farry

Using Bad Grammar

Poor writing can obscure the most necessary requirement. If you can't understand it, your developers probably can't either. Major grammar problems cannot occur within the simple "who shall what" form we recommend above. Rewriting a confusing requirement into this form will clarify it.

Writing Unverifiable Requirements

If you can't prove that your product meets a requirement, how will you sell it to a customer having those requirements? Requirements that contain subjective, unquantifiable words (such as "easy" or "portable" or "fast") are not verifiable. What is easy or adequate to one person may be hard or insufficient to another. "User-friendly" is particularly troublesome. The product developer, comfortable enough with technology to choose a career developing technical products, is almost guaranteed to have a different threshold for "user-friendly" than the customers going outside their organization to acquire a technical product.

Agreeing on standards that a product must meet in verification reduces ambiguity in requirements. If you can't define a verification technique or standard, but still want to send a message to your developers, you can make it a goal, as in:

The control system should be easy to operate.

A good way to find unverifiable requirements is to search for the words in Table 7-2 and "-ly" and "-ize" endings on words in your requirements. The latter search will catch fuzzy words, such as easily, clearly, slowly, optimize, and maximize.

Chapter 10 explores verifiability in detail.

Table 7-2. Unverifiable Words

flexible	fast
easy	portable
ad hoc	light-weight
sufficient	small
adequate	large
user-friendly	quickly
useable	easily
when required	clearly
if required	other "-ly" words
appropriate	"-ize" words

Missing Requirements

People tend to focus on product function and performance. Unless their area of expertise or responsibility includes maintenance, training, or safety, they miss requirements in these and other areas listed in Table 7-3. As you review your requirements, remember that failing to mention a detail is tantamount to telling the product developer to make the choice for you. If you do not specify the color, you cannot complain later if your product turns out to be pink.

The first defense against missing requirements is well-developed operational concepts (Chapter 5). The second is using standard formats for your requirement document. We will discuss these in Chapter 11. Your final defense is review by people with knowledge of the products domain (Chapter 12).

Overspecifying

Unnecessary or overly stringent requirements are a major cause of cost overruns. People asked to write requirements will write

Table 7-3. Checklist of Requirement Areas*

Functional
Performance
Interface
Environment—development, manufacture, test, transport, storage, operations
Facility—manufacturing, test, storage, operations
Transportation—among areas for manufacturing, assembling, delivery points, within storage facilities, loading
Training
Personnel
Reliability
Maintainability
Operability
Safety
Appearance and Physical Characteristics
Design

*Table 11-1 expands on this list

everything that they can think of, both what is necessary and what would be nice to have. They will include requirements that they have seen elsewhere, perhaps because the organization has always done it that way, with no knowledge of the need for those requirements in the new product. This problem has escalated since the introduction of word processors, which make it easy for people to cut and paste whole sections out of existing requirement documents.

You must review your writers' requirement inputs for necessity before you create the baseline for the requirements. If any doubt exists about a requirement's necessity, ask: "What is the worst thing that could happen if this requirement were not included?" If the answer is "nothing of consequence," you don't need the requirement. Because you must implement and verify each requirement, deleting the unnecessary ones saves both development and verification time and money. Fewer requirements result in a simpler product that will be cheaper to use and maintain.

Evaluate any tolerances specified in the requirement for necessity. Precision costs money in development: Asking for 100 meters exactly (which you do by default when you omit tolerances) is more expensive than 100 meters plus or minus 10 centimeters, which in turn is more expensive than 100 meters plus or minus 10 meters. Requirement writers will often specify overly tight tolerances to avoid having to determine the real tolerance required. Ask, "What is the worst thing that could happen if we doubled the tolerance or tripled it?"

What Is the Manager's Role in Writing Requirements?

As a manager, you probably don't write the requirements, except perhaps management-related or programmatic requirements. You generally are the first reviewer, however, screening the requirements for acceptability as your team writes them. Hence, you must be able to distinguish good requirements from bad, so you can send the bad ones back to their authors for more work. Unless your team has had training in requirement writing, you must be able to give the authors of unacceptable requirements some indication of what is wrong with their requirements, to help them find the right direction.

If you are a product development manager, you may get the requirements from another party, such as your marketing department or customers. You also must be able to spot bad requirements and help their writers fix them before your team is deep in product development. Otherwise, you cannot do the product development job well.

If you feel that you are unable to review the individual requirements adequately, you must arrange for someone else—perhaps a technical person with training in writing requirements—to do it. You must then ensure that your writers address the problems identified in the review. Chapter 12 will expand on reviews.

In any case, you, as manager, will set and enforce the standard for requirements!

A Review Mindset

Product quality and development cost hinge on the quality of individual requirements. Small requirement errors can become black holes consuming project development resources. In Table 7-4, we leave you with a list of questions to identify problems in individual requirement statements. The best way to prevent requirement errors is at their source.

Table 7-4. Individual Requirement Sanity Check

Requirement:	Characteristic
	Is it necessary? • Is it a needed function or characteristic? • Are the tolerances defendable and cost-effective?
	Is it verifiable? • Does a means exist to measure its accomplishment? • Can you state the criteria required for verification?
	Is it attainable? • Is it technically feasible? • Is it within your budget? • Is it within your schedule?
	Is it clear and understandable? • Is there only one thought per requirement statement? • Is it in the form "who shall what?" • Is it grammatically correct? • Is it simply and concisely stated? • Is the terminology consistent? • Is it positively stated? • Are the words unambiguous?
	Is it free from: • Implementation (ask, "Why")? • Operations (ask, "Do you or the person developing the product have control of this")?

Chapter 8
Theirs But to Reason Why
The Value of Recording Rationale

In an experiment, five monkeys were put in a cage. A bunch of bananas was hung above a ladder in the cage. When any of the monkeys climbed the ladder and tried to take the bananas, all of the monkeys were drenched with ice water. After a while, when any monkey started up that ladder for the bananas, the other four would drag him away and beat him up.

Then the experimenters began replacing the monkeys in the cage, one by one, with new monkeys. Of course, each new monkey would try to climb the ladder and the old-timers would drag him away from it. Eventually, not one of the original monkeys who had been doused with cold water remained in the cage. Yet, if any one of the new monkeys tried to climb the ladder, the others would drag him away from it. None of them knew why they did that, but if they were asked, they would say, "Because we've always done it that way."

—Circulating on the Internet

Of all the things you can do to improve your requirement management process, none can be done cheaper or faster or have more impact than capturing the rationale for each requirement. Rationale is simply an explanation of why a requirement exists, any assumptions made in writing the requirement, relevant findings of design studies, or other information useful in managing requirements over the life of the project. If the only reason for the requirement is "we've always done it this way," the requirement rationale will record that and people will no longer assume that some important but unknown reason exists for the requirement.

No requirement should be put into a specification until the rationale behind it is well understood. You may already require rationale later in your requirement management process. When someone proposes a change to a baselined requirement document, you ask for justification. Why do they need the requirement change? What is the impact of implementing the change? What is the impact of not implementing it? You know that changes are expensive and allow only the justifiable changes. Do you also require that the original requirement writers document their rationale from the start? You need rationale for the original requirements as well as proposed changes. Your effort to get the right requirement at project start will be wasted later if others make a change without understanding the "why" behind the requirement.

Why Record Rationale?

Recording rationale reduces the total number of requirements, exposes bad assumptions, removes unintended implementation, improves communication between team members, shortens the review cycle, maintains corporate knowledge, reduces risk in defining a derivative product, and supports maintenance and operations.

Rationale reduces the total requirements count. If the requirement writers must submit a reason for each requirement along with the requirement, they will invest more in justifying the requirement before submission. When they try to state its reason for inclusion, some writers may recognize that their requirement is not necessary and drop it before submission. Even if the author doesn't recognize that the reason is weak, you or your reviewers will. Reviews of requirements and their rationale together will also identify requirements that should be consolidated.

The Global Positioning Satellite (GPS) system, used on Earth for locating all sorts of things from airports to taxi cabs to semis on the interstate, helps locate the Space Station as it circles the Earth.

Detailed requirements for a GPS receiver were included in the original Space Station system requirement specification. The people responsible for the GPS receiver procurement were having trouble finding any existing "off-the-shelf" receivers that would meet these requirements. No rationale existed for the requirements, so I suggested that they challenge the requirements.

When they located the author, his response to "where did you get these requirements?" was "I made them up." He said that the guidance and navigation people would not tell him what they needed, so he derived the requirements from what he thought were specifications for commercially available receivers. Unfortunately, he did not understand these specifications. Not only were the values he chose wrong and not, in fact, commercially available, but they were not the values needed. He also had too many requirements. No one except him knew how weak the requirements were because no one had asked him.

—Ivy Hooks

Rationale exposes bad assumptions. On a typical project, the largest group of requirement errors stems from incorrect facts (recall Figure 1-1). Many of these errors begin when someone writing a requirement makes a bad assumption that is not obvious from reading the requirement. Because the requirement is at least one step removed from the original assumption, no one finds the error until testing or operations. Capturing requirement rationale makes the requirement writers' assumptions obvious to reviewers and designers, greatly increasing the chances that a bad assumption or incorrect fact will be caught before the product development proceeds very far.

Anyone can make incorrect assumptions when producing requirements. Customers may ask for something because they believe that is the best technically feasible solution available today. It may be, but it may be much more expensive than they realize and more than they can pay. It may also be possible to do much better technically. Either way, if you document the customers' assumption, and it proves incorrect, a discussion can quickly resolve the problem. If you have no idea of why the customers asked for what they asked for, however, no discussion will occur at all.

Requiring a reason for each requirement will also expose some very interesting reasons for requirements, including "because we have always done it this way." Sometimes this statement is a very good reason for a requirement, because retraining people is expensive and disruptive. In other cases, it's a poor reason and these words should raise a flag for further investigation. You may still decide to do things the way that they have always been done, but if you record the reasons that you uncover to support this decision, change proposers or the next-generation product developers will understand the "why" as well as the "what" of your decision.

Rationale removes unintended implementation. Many poor requirements are not requirements at all but are a candidate implementation. The authors are thinking in terms of solutions, not in terms of the problem to be solved. When you ask the authors of these requirements to tell you "why" the requirement is necessary, you will find the problem that they want to solve— the real requirement.

In 1932, Trans Continental and Western Air (later to become Trans World Airlines) began looking for replacements for the aging Ford Trimotor fleet. Their original requirements read:

"an all-metal, *trimotor* monoplane, maximum gross of 14,200 pounds, fuel capacity for cruising range of 1000 miles at 150 miles an hour, carry a crew of two and at least 12 passengers."[1]

By stipulating that the new aircraft had to have three engines like the Ford Trimotor, they were stating implementation, a solution to a problem. Asking why they wanted three engines revealed their real requirement—an aircraft that would fly safely after one engine failed. Once Douglas Aircraft engineers understood this, they produced a two-engine plane that could fly safely on one engine: the DC-1. This aircraft and its DC-2 and DC-3 derivatives were the first that could pay for themselves carrying passengers only.

Note that, if Douglas had put three engines on the plane per the customer's original request, but two engines did not provide safe flight after one engine failed, the customer's real requirement would not have been met, even though the stated requirement would have been.

—Kristin Farry

Rationale improves communication between stakeholders. Sometimes even the best requirement writers find it difficult to state a requirement unambiguously. At other times, the requirement might be precise but include language from the customer's domain that confuses developers. Rationale clarifies these requirements, preventing misunderstandings. Rationale gives developers additional insight into the customer's needs and can guide the product design choices toward a more satisfying solution. Requirement rationale can also help the verification team design appropriate tests to prove that the product will meet the customer's needs. Plus, documented rationale never takes a vacation. Recorded rationale makes team members more productive because it answers many questions that would otherwise require finding and interrupting someone—or perhaps many "someones," if the requirement's origin is unknown—for questions.

Rationale shortens reviews. Imagine you have ten people reading and reviewing a requirement specification. For many of the requirements, each of these people has the same question or concern. Out of the review will come ten redundant responses or critiques for each of your questionable requirements. These ten reviewers will read, reread, and possibly debate the reason for including this questionable requirement. Because reasons for even very good requirements are often not obvious, the reviewers will expend this energy for every requirement, not just the questionable ones! Reviewers may attack good requirements because they are unaware of a particular need, and you must respond to every critique. This effort could be applied to producing your product.

Now imagine the same review in which each reviewer has rationale for each requirement. When the ten reviewers read the rationale, they will grasp the reasoning and assumptions behind the requirement, which will make it easier for them to understand the requirement's validity. They will be able to immediately proceed to a critique, instead of delaying the review with requests for more data. We have participated in reviews of documents with and without rationale and can assure you that the savings from including rationale in reviews are considerable. Rationale eliminates redundant questions and data requests. In addition, reviewers can quickly find the incorrect assumptions before any serious design, coding, manufacturing, or verification takes place.

Rationale maintains corporate knowledge. Has your team ever had to reverse-engineer someone's work because that person was no longer there to explain what had been done and why? Even if the person is there, how do you know who it is? Does he or she even remember? Corporate memory seems better before a retirement, death, or job offer from a competitor than after, doesn't it?

In the not-too-distant past, the original development team stayed around throughout the product's life cycle. Many people stayed with programs for 20 or 30 years and could mentor new people. It is rare today to see people stay with programs throughout the life cycle. Products with development cycles longer than the average team member's tenure are particularly vulnerable to waste from relearning important lessons. If you have rationale recorded for each requirement, the remaining team members can carry on without losing time on reverse engineering or ill-advised requirement changes.

When Ed, the senior engineer of a NASA project, was diagnosed with cancer, his division chief asked us to document the rationale behind all of Ed's decisions on the project. I suggested that we capture the rationale behind everyone's decisions, not just those of the senior engineer, but management didn't want to spend the money at first. My recommendation finally prevailed, and we documented rationale for all of the requirements and design decisions.

A few months later, project personnel were mourning not only the passing of their senior engineer, but also the tragic, totally unexpected death (in a plane crash) of the young engineer who had developed the requirements for the crew interface. Both people were irreplaceable, but the data we captured made it possible for the other team members to complete the project.

—Ivy Hooks

Rationale reduces risk in defining an improved derivative product. "Improving" a product implies changing it. When you make changes—adding a new requirement, or deleting or changing an existing requirement—you take risks. If you do not understand the original requirements, you may make a change that will make your product unworkable or even dangerous. Software-intensive products have special risks. It's often easier to change software than hardware because no retooling is involved. The risks may be greater, however, because the complexity and inter-relationship of the parts is often not as clear. Recording rationale is especially important in helping you identify the impact of proposed changes. It will prevent you from frivolously changing any of the important original requirements.

Rationale supports maintenance and operations. What makes maintenance and operations hard? Sometimes, it is hard because the developers missed important maintenance and operation requirements. At other times, safety or environmental cleanliness requirements (for example) may have driven the product design toward more complex operations. If the maintainers and operators don't know why the product is built the way it is, they will be frustrated by difficult tasks that seem pointlessly difficult to them. They may modify operating procedures, skipping steps or doing them out of order. They may also modify the product itself—removing guards or filters—to make their life easier. Doing this modification without understanding the "why" behind the product's design is risky. Requirement rationale makes an excellent foundation for operational rationale.

The space shuttle's aft reaction control jets, aft RCS, are rocket motors that are mounted on the aft pod of the space shuttle orbiter and are used to control the orientation or attitude of the orbiter. In the vacuum of space, jets pointing outward, when fired, will cause a yawing motion of the orbiter. Jets pointing downward (on both sides), when fired will cause a nose-down pitching motion. When a paired set of up-firing on one side is combined with a set of down-firing on the opposite side, a rolling motion of the orbiter will result.

This control scheme is more complicated during atmospheric flight. The RCS jet exhaust gases mix with the flow of the air over the space shuttle. Firing the jets changes the aerodynamic effect over large areas of the orbiter and the resulting effects are not always what one would expect. There exist cases where the actual jet firing response is reversed from what one might expect: the as-designed RCS jet thrust logic appears to be contrary to any logically thinking engineer's opinion.

Two eager and properly motivated engineers have seen the "illogical" jet logic and have initiated change requests to correct the "mistake." Fortunately, the paperwork crossed the desks of persons who had enough cause for concern to contact the original designer. We were lucky: it was retirement, not the fabled Beer Truck that caused the loss of corporate knowledge. The original engineers were contacted and the control reversal phenomenon was explained.

Much time and quite a few dollars would have been saved if the requirement was "tagged" with the information that would have explained the requirements that appeared illogical.[2]

—Barney Roberts
Program Manager
Risk Management Center of Excellence,
Futron Corporation

What Should Rationale Include?

Along with each requirement, you should capture the reasons, assumptions, relationships with the product's expected operation, and design decisions behind the requirement. Each of these items helps improve requirement quality as well as project management.

Reason

Sometimes the "why" behind a requirement is obvious. If the requirement is derived from a higher-level requirement, that link may completely explain the reason for the requirement's existence. More often than not, however, the reason for the requirement is not obvious and it may be lost over time. Documenting the "why" as part of the rationale for the requirement will pay off in reviews, during development and test, and in managing changes over the product life cycle (Chapter 15). The "why" is not always technical. It could be mandated by public law, government or corporate regulations, or public relations concerns. Technical or not, document it.

Assumptions

Collect the assumptions made by the requirement's writer along with the requirement itself. Presenting requirements, with their assumptions, to reviewers and developers will enable your team to identify bad assumptions. It will also enable you to assess risk before baselining, because risk is partially a function of unvalidated or volatile assumptions. You may not know the quality of the assumptions when compiling the requirements but identify them in the rationale so that you can explicitly validate them.

Operational Relationships

Expectations about how customers will use a product drive many requirements. Include these key operational relationships with the rationale to help you tune the requirements and the product to changing operational concepts. Otherwise, your product may be in operation before you find divergence between requirements and operation conditions. If you are manually tracking operational concepts, you can number each concept and refer to its number in the rationale. You can use a requirement management tool (Chapter 14) to link the requirement and operational concept so that you do not need to put any operational information in the rationale.

Design Decisions

High-level design choices drive low-level requirements. You may conduct trade studies to select among alternatives. Reference these trade studies or other design-related data in the rationale for these lower level requirements. In addition to protecting your product from ill-conceived changes, this history of the product's current configuration saves time and money when considering product upgrades.

How and When Should You Capture Rationale?

You need complete rationale recorded in black and white, but you do not need to keep a novel-length manuscript for each requirement! Your rationale can be concise and still provide a wealth of data. Consider the examples at the end of this section. Concise rationale is easier to maintain and more likely to be read than long rationale.

Capture rationale as you and your team write requirements. Make providing the rationale a requirement for including the requirement in the baseline! Yes, this process takes time, and it's tempting to postpone it. The effort to capture rationale when the requirement is being written is minuscule compared with the time that you will spend trying to reconstruct the requirement's lineage later, perhaps when considering a change late in development. Even short-term projects will have some personnel turnover. On long-term projects, even those people staying with the project will forget the real reason for some requirements.

It is possible to use a paper form for each requirement, stating the requirement and its rationale. It doesn't take very many requirements, however, to make files of these forms hard to manage and maintain. You can't search a paper file quickly and accurately for key words and phrases. If it is hard to find what they want, people will skip the rationale review when a change is proposed, thus wasting some of your rationale capture investment.

Word processors have features that allow you to capture rationale in the same document as the requirements. You may also elect to use a comprehensive requirement management tool to automate rationale capture (Chapter 14). Unfortunately, no automation exists for developing the rationale itself! It takes hard work and discipline.

Recording rationale should not become a substitute for writing good requirements. It should enhance good requirements. Rationale is not contractually binding; only the requirements are. Even very good requirements, however, often need some supporting data to keep everyone on the same sheet of music (Table 8-1).

Requirement Rationale Examples

Requirement: The claims support system shall retrieve individual customer's insurance policy files in response to the customer's name and any two of the following data inputs: (1) the customer's birth date, (2) the customer's social security number, (3) the customer's automobile make and model, (4) the customer's address, or (5) the customer's insurance policy number.

Reason: Customers sometimes need to make a claim from locations where they do not have policy details, such as from the scene of an accident or a shelter after evacuation from their homes. This requirement will enable the claims representative to assist them with easily remembered information.

Assumptions: Name plus any two of the listed items uniquely identify a customer.

Requirement: The claims support system shall retrieve and display a customer's insurance policy files in less than 20 seconds.

Reason: Surveys have shown that customers filing claims by telephone become impatient if answers to their questions about coverage are delayed more than 20 seconds.

Assumptions: The claims representative will need to see the customer's policy files to service a claim.

Relation to operations: Some customers will use the telephone to file claims (operational concept 4).

Requirement: The truck shall have a height of no more than 14 feet.

Reason: Ninety-nine percent of all U.S. interstate highway overpasses have a 14-foot or greater clearance.

Assumptions: The truck will be used primarily on U.S. interstate highways for long-haul, intercity freight in the United States.

What Is the Manager's Role in Rationale?

You, as manager, probably won't be writing the rationale; however, it is up to you to ensure that every one of your product requirements is accompanied by complete, readable, and logical rationale before proceeding into product development (Table 8-1).

Because the savings are phenomenal when rationale is captured early and the costs of not capturing the rationale are high, you need to read the requirements and rationale as they are being developed and show interest and concern. If you ask the questions and keep the focus on doing this job well, everyone will benefit. If you praise the good rationale and ask for clarification when bad rationale is given, the writers will be motivated to do the job.

Table 8-1. Requirement Rationale Sanity Check

Have you:
Instructed your team on the importance of rationale?
Provided guidelines and examples for your team to help them understand how to write rationale?
Recorded reasons for each requirement's existence?
Captured assumptions behind each requirement?
Identified those assumptions that are unvalidated?
Recorded each requirement's relation to operations, if pertinent and not handled elsewhere?
Recorded each requirement's relation to design, if any?

The Rationale for Rationale

Recording rationale is an investment with huge returns. It improves requirement quality and reduces the total number of requirements. It shortens reviews and enhances communications between team members. Rationale is essential to understanding change impact. It makes handovers between life-cycle phases easier. Because it captures your project's corporate knowledge, it reduces the impact of a person leaving the team.

Collecting and maintaining requirement rationale takes extra effort at the beginning of the project, but it more than pays for itself before development is complete. In today's world of high employee turnover and complex, long-lived products, well-documented rationale is essential to better, faster, cheaper product development.

The U.S. Standard railroad gauge (distance between the rails) is 4 feet, 8.5 inches.

Why do we use that fractional spacing instead of a nice round number? Because that is the way people built them in England, and English expatriates built the U.S. railroads.

Why did the English build railroads with that spacing? Because the first rail lines were built by the same people who built the pre-railroad tramways, and that is the gauge they used.

Why did THEY use that gauge then? Because the people who built the tramways used the same jigs and tools that they used for building wagons, which used that wheel spacing.

Why did the wagons use that odd wheel spacing? If they tried to use any other spacing, the wagons would break on some of the old, long-distance roads, because of the spacing of the old wheel ruts.

Who built these old rutted roads? Imperial Rome for the benefit of their legions built the first long-distance roads in Europe. The roads have been used ever since.

And the ruts? The initial ruts, which everyone else had to match for fear of destroying their wagons, were first made by Roman war chariots. The chariots were to specifications set by Imperial Rome, so they all had identical wheel spacing.

Thus, the U.S. standard railroad gauge of 4 feet, 8.5 inches derives from the original specification for an Imperial Roman army war chariot. So, the next time you are handed a specification and wonder what horse's rear came up with it, you may be exactly right: the Imperial Roman chariots were made to be just wide enough to accommodate the back ends of two war horses.

—Circulating on the Internet

Chapter 9
Everything in Its Place
Levels, Allocating, and Tracing Requirements

If your product is a complex system to be built by many people, you must exercise diligence to prevent your requirement writers from introducing low-level requirements into high-level documents. As the system is designed, you must also be alert for higher-level requirements that are not implemented by lower-level requirements or design, and lower-level requirements that cannot be justified by higher-level requirements.

These problems can add to development costs and time. They complicate management and control of development. Missed features will have to be added after design is under way. At the other extreme, "gold plating" (unnecessary capabilities meeting low-level requirements not justified by high-level requirements) will introduce unnecessary development risks and excess maintenance costs. Sometimes, when the developer writes the requirements, he includes design as part of the requirement. Design in the requirements almost always drives unnecessary verification, which increases cost.

If you have only one person designing and building your product, you generally don't have these problems. Because most products being built today involve teams of people and often multiple organizations, you need to confront the problems of levels of requirements, allocation of requirements, and traceability.

What Are Requirement Levels?

Products have many parts. Depending on the type of product, these parts might be hardware and software; structure, electrical, and propulsion components; and operating system, application modules, and objects. The architecting process breaks a product into its parts, defining the parts to a level that can be built or purchased.

We generally refer to the highest level as the system. We first try to define all of the requirements for the system as a whole, not for its parts. The requirements for parts are not defined until we really understand what the system must do. The system architecture then defines the parts of the system, which may themselves be very large systems. If so, each of these parts will need further architecting, defining more parts. If the system is small and simple, only one level below the system may exist and all else may be design.

Figure 9-1 shows levels for a large, complex system. Each of these levels evolves. System requirements evolve into system architecture and then system design; system design yields segment requirements, which evolve into segment architecture and then segment design, which evolve into element requirements, and so forth. The names you give these subdivisions, segments, elements, subsystems, blocks, units, or components will depend on the number of levels in your system, as well as your industry and corporate culture. The number of levels depends on system complexity and how the design and development will be managed. The complexity will drive the architecture. The management approach will drive the documentation needs.

Why Is Writing Requirements to Levels Important?

If a small team is going to do all of the development work, you will only need one requirement document. You may not need to

Figure 9-1. Levels

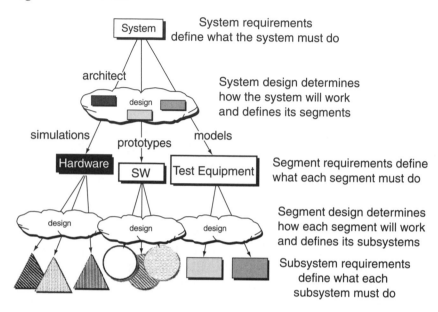

separate requirements by levels, either, but the discipline of writing requirements to levels will help you build a better product. For complex products built by a team, imposing the discipline of levels helps maintain awareness of the big picture, decreases development problems, and prevents administrative gridlock.

Separating requirements by levels helps everyone keep the proper focus on the Big Picture. People's expertise tends to make them start at the bottom and work up. The discipline of writing requirements for specific levels balances this tendency. It will help your team separate the big picture from all of the little pictures. One outcome will be a "big picture" summary to refer back to throughout product development, to yank everyone out of the trees and show them the forest at critical times.

Backing off to the big picture (the top-level requirements) opens the door to a whole new approach. People tend to approach new product development with what we call the "delta mindset." They get bogged down in thinking about what products they have now and what specific things they don't like about them. They end up designing products that are only a small "delta" change from the existing products. Asking "which requirements are the top-level requirements?" and "can we state the requirement without any implementation or architecture implications?" can show you and your team the mindsets that trap you into refining existing products instead of making breakthroughs. Failing to think top-down has a high probability of locking you into constraints that no longer exist.

This top-down viewpoint is especially important today, because a rapidly changing technology base enables many breakthrough opportunities and capitalizing on them quickly is essential to surviving in competitive industries. For example, consider data storage products: A CD-ROM is a large departure from floppy disks, and those who introduced the CD-ROM had to step way back from their floppy disk requirements to people's basic data storage requirements to see the potential of the technology. Floppy disks were, in their heyday, a huge advance over magnetic tapes. How many magnetic tape storage system manufacturers are still in business? How many are now producing CD-related products?

A group at a heavy equipment manufacturer was developing its next product, a paver to lay asphalt. The group's members came to my requirement workshop with lists of engine requirements, vibrator requirements, and so forth, thinking they had captured their paver requirements. They had, after all, built a lot of pavers.

Once we started talking about levels of requirements, I asked them fundamental questions like "what does a paver have to do?" They suddenly realized that they had lists of paver subsystem requirements, not paver requirements. These lists were constraining their development effort to be a minor refinement of existing pavers. The large performance gains that would put them ahead in today's competitive marketplace were not possible inside that mindset.

Within a half-hour of this realization, they had identified the top-level paver requirements and were tossing around revolutionary paver ideas. Even a small investment of time in stepping back to the big picture can open the door to a whole new "breakthrough" architecture.

—Ivy Hooks

Writing requirements to the right level can decrease development problems. If you define low-level (part, not system) requirements at the system level, you force the developers to comply with the part requirements and constrain their system design options. There is almost always more than one way to "skin the cat." High-level requirement writers should not be making the decision about which way to skin the proverbial feline, only stating that it must be done. If you improperly limit the designers' choices, they may not be able to reach an optimum solution or even a feasible one. Consider the massive overruns on California's State Automated Child Support System, a computer-based system to find deadbeat parents: California was forced to model the system on designs meant for Maine and New Hampshire. California's child-support caseload (2 million) is 17 times that of the combined caseloads of both those states, and the system couldn't handle the numbers.[1]

Sometimes, however, high-level constraints or knowledge dictate that requirements limit the designers' choices. These limits should be clearly understood and explained in the rationale. For example, if you are a system integrator, you have already made a number of design decisions to market your systems. You will be calling out lower-level requirements in higher-level documents, because no options exist. If you are designing a large, complex system, you will investigate many concepts and narrow the options to proceed. You will then impose the design element of these concepts in your requirements. If you are modifying an existing system, you may have a number of constraints that will drive the design. All of these situations cause confusion because requirement writers are told to only state "what" and not "how." It is not possible in all cases. Use common sense, and document the rationale for the requirement to prevent problems later.

Writing requirements by levels can also prevent administrative gridlock. Your customers (if you have specific customers contracting for the product), more senior managers, or the head of your marketing department may need to sign off on top-level requirements and approve changes. They don't need to approve of internal architecture or design decisions reflected in derived requirements. If you mix these low-level requirements with the high-level requirements in the document requiring these external approvals, you have in effect given these outsiders veto power over what should be internal development decisions, which is especially messy when the requirement document is contractually binding.

Separating requirements into more than one document may also reduce administrative delays and problems associated with change traffic later in the project. If more than one organization is involved, separating the requirements into separate documents for each group may help clarify lines of responsibility. Change traffic in one area won't distract people working in other areas or desensitize them to all change traffic so that they miss a change important in their area. Interface change traffic, of course, must go to everyone affected.

In the name of "better, faster, cheaper," a program manager that I worked with decided that we would save money on documentation by having only one requirement document. Unfortunately, the top-level requirement document (and the only requirement document on our project) had to be approved two offices above our program manager. Keeping all of the requirements in one document meant that three levels of management had signature and redlining privileges on our low-level, design-specific requirements as well as our top-level requirements. Because all of the senior managers in that division were originally engineers who had been reluctantly drawn into management, they had a field day redesigning our product every time we sent that requirement document up the line. We had to send it up even for small low-level changes. Because they didn't have the time to get intimately acquainted with the product details, a lot of their well-intentioned input actually caused problems. Worse, we didn't have a stable, approved requirement document until we were into testing. Developing to a fuzzy, moving target swamped any savings we might have had from limiting the number of requirement documents. It was chaos.

—Kristin Farry

What Is Allocation?

You or your customer will first develop the system requirements and then you will architect the system, which will identify the parts that must be constructed or purchased to fulfill the system requirements. One or more of the lower level parts must meet each system-level requirement. The process of assigning each system level requirement to the part(s) that must accomplish the requirement is called allocation. Consider a fabric-cutting system composed of hardware, software, and test software. The system's hardware—shears, perhaps—will actually cut the fabric, but software may be the best choice for determining when the shears should move, based on quality control and safety requirements. Allocation is performed from higher to lower level throughout the requirement definition process.

Why a Top-Down Requirement Allocation?

The architects of the system—system engineers and other primary system designers—have the knowledge of what system requirements should be allocated to which part or parts. Having these system personnel perform the allocation from the top down can reduce the workload at the next lower level and prevent errors. This process will ensure that the people responsible for defining part requirements know exactly which system-level requirements apply to their part.

If a formal allocation is not done from the top, people assigned to each of the parts must interpret the system requirements and design documents to determine which requirements are pertinent to their part. If three parts exist, as in the fabric-cutting system, this bottom-up effort will take at least three times the effort that a system team might have expended on a top-down allocation. The parts specialists have to learn the system requirements and the architecture—things that the system team already knows—before doing the allocation. All three sets of part requirement writers will be reading all requirements and then making decisions about what is relevant. The parts specialists bring three different specialized viewpoints versus the system team's interdisciplinary viewpoint. It is unlikely that these three views will coincide with the system team's view.

If the part requirement writers misinterpret the higher-level requirements and architecture, they will introduce errors that may not be found until late in development, causing rework. For example, if system requirement X should be allocated to hardware alone, but software and test software specialists believe that it is their requirement, both software areas will do implementation work that is ultimately wasted. If the hardware specialists don't think that requirement X is applicable to their part, work that should be done will not be done and the product will be delayed while they catch up later. If requirement X should apply to both hardware and software, each specialist may view it as the responsibility of the other. In that case, neither specialist will do anything!

What Is Traceability?

Each parts specialists will write requirements for their deliverable. As each part requirement is written, its lineage should be traced to its origin, a parent requirement at the system level. Each part requirement should show the system-level requirement or requirements that drove it. This process is requirement traceability. Proper requirement tracing upward can then be viewed top-down to ensure that all requirements are flowed from the top, through all requirement levels, and into design and testing.

Why Start Tracing Requirements Now?

Early requirement tracing saves tracing time, reveals opportunities to save development resources, and reduces change-related risk.

Capturing requirement tracing as the part requirements are written saves tracing time. The data are fresh in the writers' minds; reconstructing it later will take more time. The longer you wait, the greater the possibility of errors in the reconstruction.

Early tracing analysis can save development resources. A report that traces the system requirements to part requirements and vice versa can be an eye opener. This report will expose system requirements not reflected at the part level or even contradicted at the part level. It will show part-level requirements that seem to have sprung from nowhere—that have no relation to the system requirements. You will have the opportunity to correct these omissions, misunderstandings, and gold platings before effort is wasted.

Failure to record and track relationships between levels of requirements, between requirements and design, and between requirements and verification will almost always result in problems that must be corrected late in the life cycle and that will drive up the cost or reduce the desirability of the product.

> On several FAA projects, we linked the FAA Mission Need Statement (MNS), to the FAA Operational Requirements Document (ORD) to the System Requirements (prepared by a contractor). We generated reports containing the statements of need that showed related ORD requirements side by side. When read in this way, as opposed to just reading two separate documents from beginning to end, it was obvious that many of the stated "needs" did not "flow down" to the ORD. Further, there were requirements in the ORD that were not derived from an identified need in the MNS.
>
> When a similar task was performed linking the ORD to the System Specification (SS), there were numerous requirements in the SS that could not be linked to ORD requirements, and many ORD requirements that had no further specification in the SS.
>
> When these results were brought to the attention of FAA managers, they were somewhat shocked. The fact that there were such major disconnects in the traceability did not necessarily mean that the requirements were not valid; however, it did imply that each one had to be reviewed and a determination made regarding its validity. This lack of traceability in

requirements was of such concern to FAA management that they instituted requirements traceability as part of their requirements definition process.

Lack of traceability and validation of requirements may have been a leading cause of cost overruns and schedule delays in major automation projects.[2]

—William E. Rice
Director of Engineering and Development
Adsystech, Inc.

Traceability between levels of requirements and between requirements and verification is important, but so is traceability to design. Design reviews should address how the design meets every requirement. Periodic checks to ensure that requirements are actually implemented in the design before integration and verification can eliminate many late-breaking problems.

Good traceability throughout requirement definition, design, and verification phases reduces change risk. Traceability can enable rapid assessment of proposed requirement changes and prevent approval of changes that look like cost savers but in fact will cost more (Chapter 15). Traceability can preclude disasters in which one part is changed but a related part is left unchanged. It helps you to see the changes needed in verification associated with a requirement change, which might dramatically drive up the cost of the change.

In 1993, I was assigned the task of managing the requirements for a sonar system program. I worked for a leading aerospace company located in California. Initially, the program was using a spreadsheet to track the systems requirements. My preliminary review of the requirement spreadsheet revealed an error percentage of approximately 50 percent. This was a result of personnel turnovers and using a spreadsheet with a 240-character limit per cell. Each engineer interpreted the original requirement text so it would fit the spreadsheet cell limit. After four iterations it was nearly impossible to determine some of the requirements' source or the original requirement. There was no tracking mechanism to tie the source documents to our system segment specification (SSS) requirement text.

The company and the customer selected a requirement management tool to perform traceability of requirements. The program traced from the source requirements to the design of the systems engineering development model as well as to our subcontractor's design derived requirements. We traced SSS to System Software Specifications (SRSs), and these SRS requirements to the Computer Software Code (CSC) and as applicable to the Computer Software Units (CSU). We took one step further and traced the CSC/CSU to their associated test procedures. This provided the visibility of where all the requirements were to be implemented and tested.

Unfortunately, our subcontractor in Europe wasn't included in this traceability effort. A month prior to the delivery of the hardware and software we loaded the subcontractor's hardware and software specifications into the tool and performed this same tracing of requirements. The best we came up with was about 72 percent compliance.

The subcontractor's products arrived at our plant on schedule; however, they didn't work as planned. We had to burn new PROMS and the subcontractor had to fly his programmer from Europe to California to fix the problems. Most of these problems were uncovered using the tool in the tracing of the requirements in the subcontractor specifications. That trace only consumed about 24 man-hours, a mere pittance compared to what it cost in time and money to fix the problem. The problem could have been identified months earlier if the subcontractor used the same tool, allowing time to correct the problems.[3]

—Buddy F. Webb
Systems Engineer

How Do You Get Every Requirement in the Right Place at the Right Time?

Requirement levels, allocation, and traceability are architecture issues. Careful attention to levels, allocation, and traceability often reduces the total number of requirements that you must carry into implementation. After you have a handle on levels, allocation, and traceability for the product, you should address the document tree, which is driven by project management concerns and the architecture.

Levels

Many people struggle with writing requirements to the proper level. Simply saying that "requirements are always the what, never the how" makes it hard to understand writing requirements for different levels in a complex product. Similarly, trying to draw sharp-edged, straight lines between requirement definition and design also leaves people confused. In fact, iteration between requirement definition and design is inevitable in all but the simplest products. Ideally, you would define and baseline your requirements. Then, you would perform preliminary design, architecting the product. The result would be a definition of your second-level subdivisions. You would next allocate your top-level requirements (now "parent" requirements) down to these second-level subdivisions and derive their "children," the second-level subdivision requirements. You would repeat this process all the way down to component requirements (Figure 9-2).

In your real world, the trip down the requirement pyramid is not so straight, nor is it one way. First, we rarely know enough to write the requirements without exploring concepts, building models and prototypes, or performing analysis and trade studies. The more complex the system, the more of this preliminary design work you must do before you write requirements. Furthermore, at each level, the child requirements may need the same attention and refinement (scope definition, additional operational concepts detail, interface definition, verification assess-

Figure 9-2. Allocation of Requirements

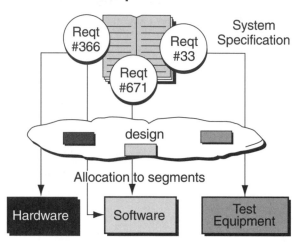

ment, baseline reviews, and so on) that the parent requirements did. Thus, you are simultaneously doing design for a level and requirement definition for the next level down. You may find yourself revisiting a level as you discover problems in the scope of a segment or an awkward interface. If you've identified an area as technically risky, you will direct your team to delve into the design of a particular segment far enough to drive the risk down to an acceptable level. Your team may have to start design on long lead items earlier than you would like to meet an externally imposed schedule. Thus, real-world product development is a struggle to balance the top-down approach with risk and re-source constraints.

A complex product will have many levels of requirements. As you move down each level, you will make decisions that will constrain the next level of requirements and, hence, the next level of design. This is what is supposed to happen. If your system is a component of a much larger system, your options are going to be constrained to fit within the larger system.

As a system integrator, you will define a system and many of its parts, with options and customization for different customers. When you work with a customer to determine their requirements, for their particular system, you and the customer are constrained by the design that you have created.

The line between requirement definition and design is a jagged one, and writing design-free requirements can only be done relative to the level of the requirement. Even so, most of the requirements should be written before your product is in detailed design. If your people are still writing requirements at the end of the design stage, they are simply documenting the product "as designed" rather than defining its requirements.

Many people can't help but write requirements for more than one level at a time—a typical product developer's career starts in detail design. Developers only move to higher-level design after proving themselves in the nuts-and-bolts department. Thus, it's natural for developers to include requirements that address their pet peeves dating from their nuts-and-bolts days along with the high-level requirements. The resulting level-mixed list must be sorted. In fact, you will probably receive more low-level requirements than top-level requirements on the first few go-rounds, especially with untrained requirement writers.

Screen your writers' requirements for level appropriateness as they come in. To identify top-level requirements, ask, "Why do we need this requirement?" This question will take you up a level. When the question takes you back to your needs statement in your product scope (Chapter 4), you have a top-level requirement. Another good test to sort out the top-level requirements from the rest is to think of more than one way to architect the product. Then, check the requirements that you believe are the top-level requirements against all of these architecture options. If you have a conflict between a requirement and any of the architecture options, that requirement may not be a top-level requirement.

Consider a management information systems example. Let's say you have a directive to automate payroll processing, personnel records, training records, tax accounting, sales reports, and cash flow analysis. Enough data overlap exists in these functions to consider an integrated system rather than totally separate solutions for each function. Your top-level requirements will consist primarily of function descriptions, input and output data, response times, and uptime. You can separate lower-level from top-level requirements by considering at least two product architectures, say, a monolithic database architecture or existing independent software packages integrated with a custom user interface (Figure 9-3). Any requirement that precludes one of these straw man architectures may not be a top-level requirement.

This "multiple design option" test also works at lower levels, with the proper perspective. At any given level, level-appropriate requirements will permit more than one design approach to get down to the next level. An airplane's top-level requirements should not limit the designers to a particular shape or number of engines or type of engine. Similarly, requirements for the flight control subsystem of the airplane should not preclude implementing its control with manual, hydraulic, pneumatic, or electric techniques, or some mix of these potential solutions.

Don't become obsessed with striving to keep architecture options open. You probably won't be able to write even your high-level requirements without some limits to architecture. If you succeed, you most likely will have simply restated your need statement (Chapter 4). Although this process would be a nice crosscheck on your need statement, it won't advance you very far down the road to developing your product, your ultimate goal. Sometimes you must make some decisions constraining options to focus the development effort. For example, when President

Figure 9-3. Level Test Via Architecture

**Architecture A:
Monolithic Database**

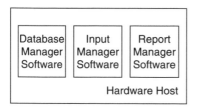

**Architecture B:
Integrated Off-The-Shelf
(OTS) Applications**

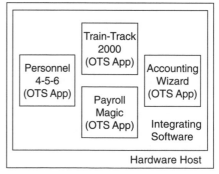

Kennedy challenged NASA to put a man on the moon and return him safely, NASA did not just write a requirement to go to the moon. NASA considered many options and finally wrote "system" requirements that constrained the development effort. The preliminary design team showed what was feasible, including trans-lunar injection and a separate lunar lander and lunar orbiter. The requirements reflected these decisions. On very large or complex projects, a preliminary design team will narrow the options before any requirements are written. High-level goals, objectives, and operational concepts will guide this team. The team will evaluate different concepts and eventually select one to narrow the options. Then, they will write requirements for a system that will meet the selected concept.

Another good level screen is asking, "Would something in the level below this requirement cause it to happen anyway?" If you will be driven to this solution no matter what, you can delete the requirement. It's not necessary and will only waste verification time. Verification assessment (which we will visit in more detail in Chapter 10) offers additional clues to a requirement's proper level. The highest verification level is often the customer acceptance test. If a specific customer contracts for the product or integrated system, a top-level requirement document based only on what the customer will test for acceptance can be contractually binding. Make sure that these things the customer wants to test are written to the highest level and included in your top-level requirements document. Sometimes, the customer requires you to use a particular solution—in other words, levies a constraint on your product. This constraint will become a low-level requirement, but it shapes your high-level architecture choices. You must include the requirement constraint at all levels above its natural level, even if it violates the level criteria. Often, political or practical reasons exist for constraints like this: budget or purchasing rules that make using existing equipment the only option; government regulations or widely used standards; or a need to incorporate other company products into your product to increase company sales.

Table 9-1 summarizes requirement-level considerations.

Table 9-1. Requirement Levels Sanity Check

For each level:

Does "why do we need the requirement" take you back directly to the
level above?
Does the requirement allow you more than one architecture or design
option for the next level?
Would something in the level below cause the requirement to be met
anyway?
Does it make sense to verify the requirement at this level?

In my requirement writing classes, I form teams of students to write requirements for a robotic system to light candles. I, acting as the "customer," have "hired" the students to write the system requirements. The requirements writing teams often fall into the trap of designing the robot system instead of writing the requirements for it. The students aren't intentionally doing this—they don't intend to state implementation—but it's a common trap, especially when the customer imposes a low-level constraint on the solution, as I do in this exercise. I impose the constraint that the robot must use a match to light the candle. Because they know that the robot will have to find the candle, they often write a requirement that the robot shall have a sensor to locate the candle. They have stated a solution—a sensor. Sometimes they even state that the robot shall have a visual sensor. In fact, many possible solutions exist, which may or may not include a sensor, and selecting a solution needs to be left to the design team.

Some student teams will state only that the robot shall locate the candle. This requirement does not seem to drive implementation, but it is still dictating some aspect of the design. You can go one step higher and simply require that the robot light the candle within the documented constraints for timing and location of the candle. This action is what needs to be verified to meet the customer needs. All else is design.

If the designers decide that the robot must locate the candle (as opposed to move to a specific position, which has a high probability of containing the candle), a lower level requirement will be to locate the candle. If further design analysis determines that this process is best done by a visual sensor,

> requirements will exist for a visual sensor with certain performance parameters written at an even lower level.
>
> —Ivy Hooks

Allocation

The process of allocating your requirements to subdivisions and eventually components of your product involves architecting and eventually design (Figure 9-1). Entire texts have been written on architecting—see books by Rechtin, Grady, Blanchard, and Fabrycky for examples.[4] Here, we will stick to requirement issues. Your team must choose an architecture that addresses all requirements. Thus, the allocation of requirements is a great test of a candidate architecture. Some parts will implement multiple requirements, whereas some requirements will be allocated to multiple parts (Figure 9-2). Certain requirements, such as product reliability and resource-limiting requirements, will affect every part of the finished product. Analysis will convert a 30-year product life requirement into a 30-year life for some components and easy replacement for others. For resource-related requirements, the allocation process will involve analysis to assign target resource allowances to parts.

Check your allocations to each level as your product design evolves for coverage, completeness, gaps, overlaps, and interface correctness and simplicity (Table 9-2).

Traceability

Each requirement must have at least one "parent" at the next higher level. Using automated tools (Chapter 14), it is easy to link

Table 9-2. Requirement Allocation Sanity Check

Is every requirement allocated?
Are there any duplicate requirements in different areas?
Can the area to which you have allocated the requirement do it alone?
  Or should it be allocated to more than one area?
Is an interface implied? If so, is it simple and controllable?

the related requirements to show that one is the child of the other. With a tool, you can view all children of a parent requirement or you can view all parents of a child requirement. Without automated tools, traceability is usually shown in a matrix. Each requirement of a part, for example, would have listed its parent requirement(s) at the next higher level. The manual approach does not show the reverse trace—from parent to child—that can be easily done using a tool.

More and more customers are requiring that developers show requirement traceability.

Requirement traceability is more than checking a square to keep these customers happy. It ensures that you and your team understand the higher-level requirements above each requirement. Requirement tracing is also a valuable check on requirement placement. If your tracing check reveals a requirement that simply repeats at a lower level, and it isn't an externally imposed constraint, something may be wrong. Perhaps a low-level requirement is masquerading as a high-level requirement. A trace check can also identify requirements for a part of the system traced to a parent requirement that was not allocated to that part. At a minimum, you will need analysis to discover whether the error exists in the linkage or in the allocation. One of them is wrong, and a hidden problem may exist.

Tracing can identify low-level requirements that have no link back to a high-level requirement. These orphans may be gold plating, but they may also signal that a high-level requirement is missing. If the orphan shows up in more than one place at a lower level, it's likely that it should be elevated to the higher level. When you elevate the orphan, you will write it at a higher level, as a new parent requirement. Then, you will allocate the parent to the lower levels, which will then link back their former orphans to the new parent requirement. This process will ensure that you can properly assess the impacts of proposed changes to the parent and its children. When performing tracing checks, be careful how you react to uncovering an orphan. If your team members get in trouble for having an orphan requirement, they will make certain that they don't have any. They may force some unsuitable adoptions to eliminate the orphans and hide expensive problems in the process. Just having traceability is not enough. Checks must be made to ensure that the traceability is correct and complete. Just because every part requirement has a parent, doesn't mean it has the right one, or that it fully answers the parent requirement(s). Validation of the requirements should assure that the requirements do flow down and do so correctly.

At each level, you should validate that your requirements are indeed incorporated into the design. It is very difficult to do this validation with automated requirement management tools, except at extremely low-level software requirements. You cannot use automated tools to trace many of the requirements, especially the quality requirements such as reliability, maintainability, or portability. To trace to design, include in each design review a presentation and a discussion of how the design meets the requirements. Failure to validate during design will undoubtedly lead to problems during verification or operations because all requirements were not met in the design. It will be much easier to fix the problem during design than later.

Tracing requirements to verification—and this is a task that automated requirement management tools do well— can improve your efficiency in a number of ways. Each requirement must be verified. For example, as each requirement is traced to specific verification tests, the quality and test personnel can often find ways of combining and aligning the testing to accomplish the most for the least effort. Traceability will also provide you with a rapid verification impact assessment should a requirement change.

Table 9-3 gives questions to guide your team's requirement tracing. Beyond validating requirements before baselining, trace-

Table 9-3. Requirement Tracing Sanity Check

Have you:
Put a requirement tracing system in place?
Traced each requirement back to requirements (or scope, for the top-level requirements) in the level above them?
Resolved duplication between levels?
Eliminated orphan requirements?

ability will prove crucial later in change impact assessments (Chapter 15).

Documentation

The architecture of your system will determine its components. The complexity of your program will determine the number of levels needed to develop or acquire the system. This pyramid does not necessarily dictate a document tree for requirement specifications.

On simple projects, you may only need one document that contains sections for the system and each of its parts. You will simply place the system-level requirements in their section of the document and add the parts requirements as they are derived or created. On other more complex projects you may need more documents but, again, not aligned with every part of the system. The reasons to create separate documents are driven by two major concerns: size and control.

If you have one part that is very large and all of the others are very small, you can put all of the small parts in the system specification but produce a separate document for the large part. This separation makes document updates easier and can make change control less traumatic.

You may be having different organizations or companies build or supply part of your system. A separate requirements specification should be created when the control of a part is delegated to a separate management entity. If the part will be developed by a different unit in your company, is contracted to another company, or is purchased separately, it needs its own specification (Figure 9-4).

Resist the temptation to demand a documentation tree on day one of your project. If you create a document tree too early in a project, you run the risk of having a system architected according to the document tree. The document tree has a powerful influence on your design team's mindset.

Table 9-4 summarizes documentation tree decision considerations.

Figure 9-4. Creating a Document Tree

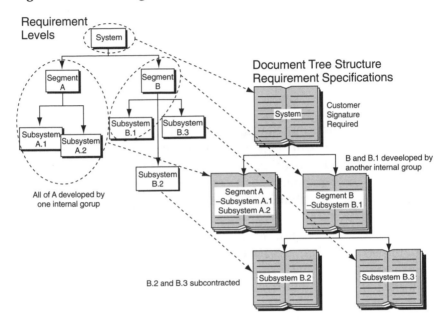

Table 9-4. Documentation Tree Sanity Check

Have you:
Identified approval levels and segregated requirements accordingly?
Identified external contracts and segregated requirements that will be contractually binding to each outside party?
Segregated requirements that may be revised frequently?
Segregated requirements into manageable document sizes?

What Is the Manager's Role in Levels, Allocation, and Traceability?

Your role in defining requirements to the correct level depends, of course, on your management level as well as your span of control: customer, systems engineering, system architect, or developer of system, hardware, or software.

If you are the customer, you want to make sure that your

requirements don't include implementation that can and should be left to the developers. You also need to carefully review the next level of requirements, whether written in-house or by a contractor, to ensure that all of your requirements have been answered by the next level requirements. You will want to request and review traceability between your requirements and the next level.

If you are managing in the product development organization, you must question any requirements inappropriate for your level. You will supervise your designers' architecting and requirement allocation. As your team writes its lower level requirements, you must check the validity of the lower level requirements, seeing that inconsistencies, gold-plating, and omissions are eliminated.

Ben Franklin is still right: An ounce of prevention is worth a pound of cure. Make certain that your people understand that requirements must be written to the correct level, allocated, and traced. Follow through with checks to see that the work is done and done properly. It will make a world of difference in the cost and quality of your product.

Wrapping Up with Neat Packages

Levels, allocations, and traceability—getting the requirements to the right place—should be concerns from the first requirement's writing to the last requirement's baselining. These concerns, along with structuring documentation, are management control issues as well as technical and product architecture issues. If you architect something you cannot control, you cannot build it! On the other hand, consideration of requirement placement during requirement definition will help drive your team to an architecture that makes management sense as well as technical sense.

Chapter 10
But Will It Work?
Thinking Ahead to Verification

"Quality: The degree to which a system, component, or process meets specified requirements; or the degree to which a system or process meets customer or user needs or expectations."

—CMM
Software Engineering Institute
Carnegie-Mellon University, Pittsburgh, Pennsylvania

Many people talk about and even perform "V&V" or *validation and verification* as though they are one and the same, but these activities are separate. Validation is the process of confirming the completeness and correctness of the requirements. Verification, consisting of tests, inspections, demonstrations, and analysis, is the process of confirming that the designed and built product meets the requirements. To prevent rework, you must validate your requirements before design and during detailed design. Otherwise, you will be doing requirement validation and product verification together, during what was supposed to be only verification. Because verification is guided by the requirements, the effort may not expose invalid requirements. If you verify that the product meets the requirements, but the requirements are invalid, the product will fail to meet customer needs and expectations.

Because this book is a guide to ensuring requirement quality, we focus on requirement validation techniques rather than product verification techniques. Having said that, however, we believe that a verification assessment while you are developing the requirements is a key step in validating the requirements. In Chapter 7, we touched on verifiability as a key attribute of a good requirement. Now that your requirements are maturing, it's important to revisit verification in depth.

Why Look at Verification during Requirement Definition?

Assessing verification as you develop your requirements improves requirement quality, ensures that your requirements support verification, provides a basis for estimating verification cost and schedule, and reduces verification cost.

Early attention to verification improves requirement quality. Asking "how will we verify this requirement?" before you baseline a requirement is an important step in validating that requirement. An unverifiable requirement is an unnecessary or bad requirement. If you can't verify it, you may not be able to design a product that will meet it. For example, how do you verify "the product shall be safe?" How will designers make it "safe?" If you can't verify a safety-related requirement, you may not be able to convince your customers to use the product.

Early verification assessments help identify additional requirements needed to support verification. Your product may need features dedicated to support verification, especially tests and demonstrations. Extra connectors on the wiring harness to connect to test instrumentation or external power, extra data on a display or in a database to give you visibility into an internal process, an inspection portal, or a bracket to hold a part in a test fixture are examples of features that can make verification possible in some cases or reduce its cost dramatically in others. Knowing these requirements before starting design avoids late rework of the product to enable verification. It will also reduce delays in product development while you await delivery of test support equipment or software, which could have been on a parallel development track if you'd known that you needed it earlier.

> *The major problem with the THAAD [Theater High Altitude Area Defense] missile was it was not designed to do an end-to-end ground test by putting a simulated target on the top end and watching the system respond to the motion of the target. . . . If they could have done that with THAAD, they might have caught some of the problems before a flight test.*
>
> *We cancelled the last flight because the missile still has a flawed design. We are doing a new design, and we are confident that it will work. . . . the major [design flaw] being the lack of ability to do end-to-end ground testing. . . .*
>
> *I think it was optimism, and trying to get things deployed early. Larry Welch, in his report on the THAAD program, said it seemed to be like a "rush to failure."[1]*
>
> —Dr. Hans Mark
> Director
> Defense Research and Engineering, U.S. Government,
> Washington, DC

Considering the verification approach before development provides a foundation for estimating the cost and time required for verification. Proving that product meets the requirements is a major cost element in product development, often as much as 50 percent. You will go a long way toward avoiding schedule slips and cost overruns by considering verification of each requirement when you build your schedules and budgets. What test support equipment must be purchased? You may need a special test facility, such as an extreme environment simulation chamber. Will it be available when your product is ready for the test? Perhaps you are developing a medical product. What verification requirements will the government and medical insurers place on your product? What extra reviews from outside experts and liability insurance will be required before your tests involving human or animal subjects? Many consumer products require outside experts in the verification process. Does yours need, for example, Underwriter's Laboratories (UL) certification? If so, have you budgeted for both your internal verification and the UL verification?

If you are the customer acquiring a product, or a developer producing a product for a particular customer, you will have a contract including the requirements. This contract typically includes an agreement on verification approach and scope. If the product is complex, testing every possible case or path may be cost-prohibitive. Vague or open-ended verification plans can overrun the developer's budget or leave the customer without confidence in the product. Clear statements of verification expectations—generated by an early verification assessment—protect all parties in the contract.

During development of the Space Station, someone suggested using a different tank than the one in the baseline design. The substitution was authorized when the potential savings were estimated at $150,000. No one considered the impact on verification, however, and later it was discovered that NASA did not have a building suitable for testing the new tank. Building a new facility might have cost $100 million. The problem was eventually solved. NASA and the Air Force agreed to swap buildings at neighboring facilities. The building swap was a lot cheaper than constructing a new building, but it more than cancelled the $150,000 savings that had made the tank substitution attractive.

—Ivy Hooks

Making verification assessment part of requirement definition reduces cost. You can identify the requirements that will be the most costly to verify and rewrite them to reduce the verification cost while still meeting your product's goals. You want to do this assessment before investing in designing to the verification-intensive requirements.

How Do You Address Verification during Requirement Definition?

Three aspects of verification should be considered during requirement definition: need, how, and when.

Need

In Chapter 7, we recommended that you ask, "Is this requirement needed?" when reviewing each requirement. If it isn't needed, you can delete it; however, in some cases, the answer to this question is not obvious. For these requirements, ask, "Do we want to verify this requirement?" instead. If the answer is no, you don't need the requirement.

How

If you do need the requirement, ask, "Is this requirement verifiable?" Screen each draft requirement for subjective words that are unverifiable, such as those in Table 10-1. You may be able to eliminate a rewrite cycle by giving your writers this list of "words to avoid" and their alternatives before they start writing. Search for words ending in "-ly." For example, "the system shall move the arm quickly" is unverifiable. "Quickly" is a subjective term. It must be replaced with a measurable speed to make this requirement verifiable, as in "the system shall move the arm at 50 ± 2 centimeters per second." Table 10-2 expands on Table 7-2 with example requirement rewrites to improve verifiability. Note that a single, unverifiable requirement often unpacks into more than one verifiable requirement.

For each requirement, ask yourself and your team, "How will we verify that the product meets this requirement?" Pick one or more of the methods of verification (inspection, test, demonstration, and analysis) for each requirement. A requirement may have single or multiple verification methods. Develop the operational concept for verification far enough to uncover interface, facility, and instrumentation issues. Will the product require different power or cooling during a test or demonstration than it will require in field operations? Will it need simulated data streams? What data must be recorded and how fast will the product output this data? Who must observe the test, perform the analysis or demonstration, or inspect the product? The verification (a.k.a. "test") engineers will ask these questions when be-

Table 10-1. Certain Words Flag Unverifiable Requirements

Unverifiable Words	Possible Substitutes
flexible	• Add bending threshold or spring constant • Features that will cover anticipated changes from operational concepts
easy or user-friendly	• A maximum number of steps to perform an operation • An educational standard reference • A list of features found on similar popular products • Menus or prompts to guide user
accomodate	• Precise definition of accomodation from operational concepts
ad hoc	• List of features that support all uses anticipated in operational concepts
safe	• List of features that prevent harm from operator errors anticipated in operational concepts • References to specific safety standards
sufficient or adequate	• Quantities or other dimensions
useable	• Exact features needed
when required or if required	• Exact circumstances • Triggering events from operational concepts
fast or quickly	• Minimum acceptable speed
portable	• Dimensions and weight • Description of desired carrying means • Operating systems that the software must run on
light-weight	• Maximum acceptable weight
small	• Maximum acceptable dimensions
large	• Minimum acceptable dimensions
easily, clearly, or other "-ly" words	• Quantitites appropriate for the verb that the "-ly" word modifies (i.e., replace "fit easily" with "fit in X by Y by Z space")
maximize, minimize, optimize, or other "-ize" words	• Limits, greater than or equal to, less than or equal to

Table 10-2. Rewrites for Unverifiable Requirements

Unverifiable	Verifiable
ABC shall support ad hoc queries.	• ABC shall retrieve up to five user-specified data items per user query. • ABC shall retrieve those records meeting the criteria in any legal Standard Query Language user query.
The ZZ database shall be flexible.	• The ZZ database shall have eight user-definable fields per record.
The sorting arm shall be flexible.	• The sorting arm shall elastically deform under loads of 0-75 pounds.
PQR shall clearly display safety warnings.	• PQR shall display safety warnings in yellow letters 1″ ± 0.05″ high and 0.5″ ± 0.05″ wide.
The power supply shall be portable.	• The power supply shall weigh 25 pounds or less. • The power supply shall be less than or equal to 20″ in each dimension. • The power supply shall have a carrying handle of the dimensions in drawing 12 of reference 4 (Human Factors Standards).
The case shall accomodate contingency maintenance tools.	• The case shall have maintenance tool storage to hold all tools in drawing A.
The TMS shall handle deposits quickly.	• The TMS shall scan and record customer account number and amount from a single deposit slip in 2 seconds or less.

Table 10-2. Rewrites for Unverifiable Requirements (*continued*)

Unverifiable	Verifiable
XYZ shall be user-friendly.	• XYZ shall have controls labeled with their purpose in letters 0.3″ ± 0.03″. • XYZ shall have controls positioned in the order (from left to right) of their use. • XYZ shall display menus of control options. • XYZ shall display prompts to remind the user of the next step. • XYZ shall use the display convention of product PQR. • XYZ shall have emergency stop controls colored red.
MNOP shall be safe.	• MNOP shall stop operation if a person comes within 10 feet of any moving component. • MNOP shall stop heaters if the vat temperature exceeds 100 degrees Celsius. • MNOP shall meet UL 544 Section 3.4 standards for temperatures on external surfaces.

ginning their work. Because these questions must be answered sooner or later, try to answer them now, before you have unknowingly spent project resources on designing or building an unverifiable requirement. Some of these questions cannot be answered before product design. Requirements, however, are an ongoing task. Even if you cannot answer these questions before some design effort, you can certainly do so during or after design but before manufacture, code, or build.

Make certain that your requirements include the appropriate industry standards and any other standards mandated by regulatory agencies. For products targeted for the United States, chemical containment requirements from the Environmental Protection Agency, operator protection requirements from the Occupational Safety and Health Administration, clinical trials requirements from the Food and Drug Administration (FDA), materials flammability requirements from the Federal Aviation Administration, or accessibility requirements mandated by the Americans with Disabilities Act may exist. If you have been developing similar products for a while, you will know who has jurisdiction over your product line; however, you should still make a practice of checking to make sure that you have the most current regulations before you baseline your requirements. If you are expanding your market internationally, or launching a radically different product on otherwise familiar turf, you must find and incorporate the relevant regulations in your requirements. Your verification planning must include producing the data required by the regulatory agencies.

In the United States's litigious climate, you may find that liability concerns from your legal department and your product liability insurer also shape your requirement verification. Even if no regulations exist for your product (a rare occurrence), marketing to customers may require a statement of reliability or other performance claims. Your verification must substantiate these claims. If you will offer a warranty or laws in your market area imply a warranty, your verification should prove that the product is as good as the warranty to keep your enterprise solvent.

If you have customers doing their own acceptance testing, check your requirements against their acceptance test plan. Are you missing requirements that are obvious in the customer acceptance test plan? If you are a customer, your acceptance test plan must be comprehensive enough to satisfy your organization that the product will perform as advertised or contracted for. Make sure that your acceptance test plan reflects the requirements and does not introduce previously unstated requirements.

When

Once you have laid out the verification "how," consider verification timing and develop a "when" strategy. Balance component and higher level (subsystem and system) verification. You may be tempted to save verification time and money by doing only system-level verification, testing the product only after final assembly. This strategy is risky. You won't find your product's problems until very late in the development process. It may be hard to trace the problem to its source in a complex system. Once you find the source of the problem, it will be a mess to fix, especially if more than one component is involved. If you have manufacturing tooling on a parallel development track, your product changes will require late changes to that tooling. All of these changes will enter the development process very late, which further increases risk. A single problem emerging during system-level testing may cancel all savings projected from eliminating component and subsystem verification.

On the other hand, verifying every component-level requirement may be cost-prohibitive and unnecessary. When looking for requirements to verify early, ask, "Is there a cornerstone requirement that may be difficult to meet?" Consider verifying that requirement early, either whole or in part, to give your team more time to respond to design shortcomings and thus manage technical risk.

For example, you may identify the difficulty of verifying a totally new product's user interface because the requirements are poorly understood. A high risk of customer dissatisfaction exists with the entire product if they don't like the user interface. This is requirement risk, not technical risk. Smart risk control might involve prototyping the user interface during the preliminary design effort. This prototype might be electronic, a mock-up, or simply a paper drawing. Have the customer evaluate the prototype and then you can write clear requirements based on their response.

Failing to test the integrated system or failing to test the system with its external interfaces can result in major embarrassment when the delivered system fails to perform. Even though you may have tested every part or component, you need to ensure that they work as a whole and that they work with other external interfaces before your provide the product to your customer. Verifying internal and external interfaces very often requires test, as opposed to other forms of verification. The cost of this testing can be high, but failure to test can lead to major, and even catastrophic, problems.

Once you have a verifiable set of requirements and an approach to verify them, document the verification assessment in a way that you can consult frequently and refine with greater detail as development progresses. As you assess each requirement's verification, tag it with:

+ Method (test, inspection, demonstration, analysis)
+ Level (component, subsystem, system)
+ Phase (design, manufacture, verification)

of verification. Capture the assessment in a verification matrix of requirements versus phase and method or requirements versus level and method. Automating the matrix with a requirement management tool (Chapter 14) allows you to sort requirements by verification method. This sorting capability can make it easier to assess the resources required for the most expensive verification methods. A good map between the requirements and verification can show you duplication or other inefficiencies in your verification approach. It also reduces your verification tracking workload later.

In all verification documentation, avoid the format that leads to "fill in the squares" by simply repeating requirements. That is, avoid rewriting each requirement as a verification statement, as in:

"The product shall do X." => "Verify that the product does X."

This is a money-waster. It tells you nothing that the requirements don't already tell you. It also creates a documentation maintenance nightmare. Every time you change the requirement, you must find and change the verification statement.

> In one of my requirement classes, a student mentioned a verification plan that he was compiling. He said, "I have been told to write the plan so that I repeat every requirement after the words 'verify that. . . .' Then, I'm supposed to add any other data needed to make the requirement verifiable."

> "From this class, I've concluded that, if the requirement is written correctly, I don't need to add anything. If it isn't, I need to get the requirement changed, not rewrite it in the verification plan."
>
> —Ivy Hooks

What Is the Manager's Role in Assessing Verification?

Risk management is one of your primary responsibilities, and ensuring that you begin development with verifiable requirements is key to reducing risk. You, the manager, make the decision to consider verification during requirement definition and direct your team to submit verification suggestions along with their requirement inputs. You will review incoming requirements and verification suggestions to screen out totally unverifiable requirements or request rewrites on those that are unverifiable as first written. You must ensure that a good map exists between requirements and verification.

Because verification costs are a significant part of a development or procurement budget, you must also be on the lookout for requirements whose verification will require expensive facilities, extensive time, hazardous procedures, or unfeasible tests and ask for alternatives that will keep your customers happy.

You must also assess your team's verification suggestions to balance the cost of verification and the risk associated with the level and type of verification. You will make the final decision on the how and when of verification. It may be safest to verify that every component in a product meets their component requirements as well as verify the product as a whole, but it may not be possible to do such a thorough verification within your budget. Then again, no budget may be big enough to fix problems that slipped through verification into operations, and the pressure on you and your team to fix these operational problems will be greater than any development pressure.

Verifying Your Assessment

Table 10-3 summarizes the verification-related questions you should be asking during requirement definition and reviews. Per-

Table 10-3. Verification Assessment Sanity Check

Have you:
Screened out or rewritten unverifiable requirements?
Identified all verification stakeholders (customer, regulatory agencies)?
Decided how each requirement will be verified?
Decided when each requirement will be verified?
Written requirements to cut time, cost, and special equipment required to verify your product?
Built a verification matrix?

forming an early verification assessment on a set of requirements benefits your project beyond providing a foundation for estimating verification costs and schedule. It's a crucial step in identifying invalid and incomplete requirements. It augments other requirement validation steps, such as interacting with the customer, developing operational concepts and simulations, and interface analysis.

Frequent verification assessment should become a habit beyond the requirement definition stage of a project. As the product takes specific form in design, new verification-driven requirements will appear. Visiting verification early and often will keep the rework created by these to a minimum.

When I began developing a new artificial hand, I thought that amputees were my customers. I assisted with a survey of hundreds of people missing one or both hands to get a better idea of their requirements for a prosthetic hand. My team developed operational concepts for the prosthetic hand and reviewed them with a focus group. The fact that we must have human subjects participating in our verification of the hand forced us to do a thorough verification assessment early. It was an eyeopener.

A lengthy standard exists from UL covering medical equipment safety. The FDA has jurisdiction over medical devices. In theory, FDA approval is not necessary to market an artificial hand, but in practice some health insurers require it on everything that they provide an individual.

Liability concerns and the search for ways to reduce liability insurance premiums for our experiments led us to make arrangements to perform the clinical trials of the new hand in a hospital with experience in amputee rehabilitation, under supervision of a team, including a doctor and therapists. We developed clinical test concepts and reviewed them with the clinical professionals at the hospital. Their questions and comments led us to expand the verification scope further. Medical professionals and insurers must be convinced that the new hand was needed, not just that it met the requirements from the amputee users. Beyond their concerns about the well-being of their patients is worry about acceptance by "payors." We discovered that we needed additional performance monitoring capability in the artificial hand, plus separate monitoring equipment.

In other words, the hand users are seldom, if ever, our customers! Our real customers are the doctors prescribing the hand, the insurers and charity foundations authorizing payment for it, the prosthetic specialists actually purchasing and fitting it, and the therapists certifying that the treatment outcome is acceptable. Our verification effort must be acceptable to these people plus regulatory agencies, liability insurers, and, almost as an afterthought, the ultimate user.

Thanks to an early verification assessment, we are beginning our development effort with a much bigger verification budget and a much better idea of what our requirements are and whom our customers are.

—Kristin Farry

Chapter 11
A Needle in a Haystack
Formatting Requirements

I was trying to find someone on a U.S. Army post. I knew her name but not her location on the post or her organization. No problem, I thought, I'll just borrow a post phonebook and look her up. To my dismay, I discovered that the post phonebook did not list people's names in alphabetical order. Instead, the book was arranged by organization. Finding anyone in there without intimate knowledge of the post's organization was hopeless.

Think of how much time we would all spend looking for people if phonebooks weren't standardized in alphabetical order!

—Ivy Hooks

In Chapter 7, we presented a structure for individual requirements that ensures clear communication of the individual requirement. Because we insisted that you restrict each requirement to a single thought, you now have a large number of these individual requirements. It's time to organize them into a specification and look for holes.

What's Wrong with Just a List of Requirements?

Organizing your requirement list into a standard specification format will reveal requirement omissions, prevent loss of requirements, save time during development, and capitalize on a broad industry experience base.

A standard specification format will reveal omissions. As long as your requirements remain in an unorganized pile, it will be tough to check for completeness, no matter how clear each individual requirement is. The second largest class (31 percent) of requirement errors on our sample program (Figure 1-1) was omissions. These omissions are not only failures to spell out needed product functions. William Perry, executive director of the Quality Assurance Institute, observed that "the failure to spell out the quality attributes—maintainability, reliability, ease of use, portability—of software are causes of more problems than are caused by functionality characteristic." [1]

Your first line of defense against requirement omission is a set of operational concepts (Chapter 5) covering all of your product's life cycle. The second line of defense against omissions is a comprehensive format for collecting the requirements into a document. A good requirement document outline is a checklist for completeness during requirement definition.

A standard specification format will prevent loss of requirements. A well-organized, familiar requirement document outline is the ticket to finding requirements throughout the development. Misplaced requirements account for another 2 percent of requirement errors in our example (Figure 1-1). Two percent may not seem significant, but this number includes only the lost requirements that surfaced at the end of the development cycle. The requirements that people lose forever are no doubt padding the 31 percent requirement omission statistic. How much development time gets wasted looking for the requirements that people know must be somewhere, but are not easy to find? How much time do reviewers spend plugging holes that really don't exist? How many of the "plugs" result in duplicate or conflicting requirements? Organizing your requirements in a standard format can save time throughout the product development.

A standard specification format capitalizes on a broad experience base. We say "standard format" here because standards exist for requirement specifications (also called requirement documents). Starting with a standard format almost always saves time, even though you may tailor it (i.e., modify the format to meet your needs) to your particular products and organization. It's easy for your people to forget that their job is to build a product, not a process! A requirement document outline is not your product.

> I see large efforts expended to develop many different document formats within a single company. The stated reasons usually are (1) we are unique and we need something different from everyone else and (2) we can't find a standard that is easy to use.
>
> I've begun to suspect that some people just like to fiddle with processes and do not want to face the hard work of building the product. I find that most managers are not aware that their employees are spending large amounts of time on this effort and so are not aware that they need to do something to stop this effort. Simply tailoring standard formats and processes helps people concentrate on developing a quality product instead of inventing processes.
>
> —Ivy Hooks

If you do business with others—perhaps a prime contractor or government organization—using a standard specification format, you may be required to use their outline. Even if no one is requiring you to use standard format, we recommend that you review the existing standards to determine if one or several of them might be applicable to your product and organization. You can tailor these standards to create your own corporate standard and still increase your overall productivity. Incoming employees, your customers, and other stakeholders will probably already know the standard from other projects, so adopting a standard format will reduce training time as well as product development time.

If your specifications never go outside your company to others, you can invent your own outline from scratch. The benefits of a custom outline may outweigh its costs in some cases. If your company does decide to develop a new outline, we recommend that the same outline (at least at the top level) be used for all of your company's products. A "company standard" enables managers and other cross-project discipline experts, such as quality engineering and safety, to quickly find specific information for a number of projects. Thus, the savings go beyond any single project's budget.

What Are the Requirements for a Requirement Format?

Whether you start with an existing standard or build your own format from scratch, keep in mind why you have the document in the first place. Your top-level requirement document provides communication between the customer and the developer. Requirement documents must communicate what is to be developed and how it is to be verified. Major tests of the top-level requirement document include: Can the customer read the document and understand what will be provided? Can the developer read the document and understand what to provide? Can the quality monitoring person understand what is to be verified?

Below the top level, your requirement documents must communicate between the levels of development (e.g., system to subsystem). The customer may not need to understand the lower tier specifications, but certainly development and quality personnel must do so.

After communications, the next driver for outline selection is its contribution to completing requirement definition. Is the requirement document outline simple but complete? If it is not simple, people may not use it. If it is very complex, people will waste time trying to decide where in it to put each requirement. Yet, it must be a complete checklist for your product's requirements. Completeness is relative to your product and industry. Different products need emphasis on different types of requirements.

Outline completeness is more than a comprehensive list of requirement categories. The specification must do more than list requirements in some logical order. It needs to set the stage by providing background information about the purpose of the item being developed and other information discussed under scope (Chapter 4), plus operational concepts (Chapter 5). The specification needs guidance for reading sections so that no one gets lost and misinterprets the requirements. Unless you use a separate database, the specification should also contain the rationale (Chapter 8) for each requirement or set of requirements. When it is necessary to reference other documents, these must be clearly defined so that no confusion develops about their purpose, version, and accessibility. The specification must also contain or reference the requirement verification matrix (Chapter 10).

Table 11-1 is a shopping list of items for your specification outline choice. We have simply listed them rather than put them in outline form for you because the nature of your product should drive the final arrangement in a specification outline. For example, consider safety. For some products, safety concerns will be consistent throughout the life cycle, and, hence, safety should be a major, all-encompassing section of the document. For other products, safety concerns vary considerably between phases of the life cycle, and it may be best to make safety a subsection under each life-cycle phase.

In addition to the list here, you may have other regularly occurring requirements. If you build equipment for airplanes, you must meet Federal Aviation Administration standards plus standards for other countries where the planes may fly. If you build medical devices in the United States, you must meet FDA requirements. Other countries' governments levy their own requirements on medical devices. If requirements like this occur for over 50 percent of your organization's products, consider inserting them into your organization's standard requirement document outline so that they will not be forgotten. If you include them in your standard outline, however, you must make certain that these special requirements are deleted from the specifications of products where they are not applicable, or they will waste resources. You must also ensure that these requirements are kept up to date. Incorporating these requirements by reference to their source documents avoids these headaches.

If you do reference another document to incorporate requirements—a regulatory document or an international stan-

Table 11-1. Items Your Specification May Need to Cover

Scope
Applicable Reference Documents
System Definition
Missions
Operational Concepts
System Diagram
Interface Definition (External)
Interface Definition (Internal)
Customer-Furnished Property
Organization and Management Relationships
Functional and Performance Requirements
Physical Requirements
Environmental Conditions and Survivability Requirements (Environment
    on Product)
Induced Environment Conditions (Product on Environment)
Reliability Requirements
Maintainability Requirements
Availability Requirements
Serviceability Requirements
Transportability and Mobility Requirements
Logistics Requirements
Usability (Human Operability) Requirements
Security Requirements
Reuse and Refurbishment Requirements
Safety Requirements
Testability Requirements
Electromagnetic Interference Requirements
Materials, Processes, and Parts Use Requirements
Labeling Requirements
Design Requirements
Interchangeability Requirements
Workmanship Requirements
Manufacturing Cost and Affordability Requirements
Producibility Requirements
Disposability Requirements
Packaging Requirements
Support (Manufacturing, Test, and Use) Equipment and Facility
    Requirements
Verification Matrix

dard, for example—cite the document by name, number and version, and the exact paragraph. The document number and paragraph must be in the associated requirement, and the other information must be in the reference document list. It will prevent confusion if you also include the list of paragraphs that are applicable along with the reference document information. Just as the requirements that your team writes must have rationale for inclusion, each of the requirements incorporated by reference must have rationale. If you don't have rationale for them, you will wind up with many of these references simply because someone else suspects that they might apply or because someone else used them on another product. Keep in mind that requirements incorporated by reference must be met and verified just like any other requirement. If they are not truly needed, this is very costly and wasteful!

If you are in a large organization, consider the possibility that someone else, somewhere in the organization, may have experience with an outline that will work well for your project. If so, try that outline. If there is no in-house precedent, Table 11-2 lists some requirement document standards that you will want to consider for your products. Some of these standards are military, but they may still be suitable for your commercial products; many industry standards around the world have their beginnings as military standards. In the international arena, long-standing standards for software-only products exist, but standards for systems involving hardware are relatively new.

Table 11-2. Specification Standards and Sources

Standard	Source
IEEE/EIA 12207.1 Software Life Cycle Processes-Life Cycle Data	The Institute of Electrical and Electronics Engineers, Inc.
MIL-STD-961: Standard Practice for Defense Specifications	Military standard and the origin of many other standards
MIL-STD-498: Software Development and Documentation	Military software standard, replaced by IEEE 12207.1, but available at no cost.

How Do You Tailor?

If you choose to use a standard outline, you will probably tailor it for your product. We recommend that your company first tailor it at a high level so that it will have sections in common for all of your organization's products. This high-level tailoring would add items that your company uses on all or most products and delete section headings that are not applicable to any of your product lines. We believe that an organization should have an organization-wide standard. Then, the organization should allow each product line to tailor the standard to fit their products. The tailoring will probably focus on things like environment or functions and performance related to a particular product line. The high-level standard will save the time of senior management and cross-discipline professionals (e.g., quality and safety) in reviews. It will also keep people from reinventing the documentation wheel on every project.

Below the top level, tailoring is often necessary to ensure that requirements are not missed. You may need to add subsections to a standard form to emphasize unique aspects of your product. In particular, the functional and performance portions of these outlines need more detail than any high-level standard format provides. One tailoring strategy is to expand the outline based on your operational concepts, which is especially helpful for products that have a sequence of operational phases. A spacecraft requirement document might have the performance subsections:

- Prelaunch
- Launch
- On-orbit
- Return
- Recovery

Another approach is to organize around the major functions that a system must perform. A performance-monitoring system might have these subsections:

♦ Optimization
♦ Historical data archiving
♦ Trend analysis
♦ Reporting

Note that having a large section of requirements for some aspect of your product does not necessarily mean that it is a separable chunk or subsystem of the product. The requirement document outline should not dictate product architecture.

You will most likely need to tailor the specification in the sections for reliability, maintainability, and availability. For example, if you can specify reliability and maintainability quantitatively, you will not need to specify availability. If you try to specify all three of these "-ilities," you risk introducing conflicting requirements. Adjust these sections to suit your product's criticalities.

In addition to content, you might want to tailor the section and subsection numbering. Our biggest complaint about the existing standards is their numbering systems. Many standards are based on old military standards that, for some reason, lumped all requirements into one section of a document and only used numbers 1 through 6 as major headers. This outline makes numbering the requirement sections very cumbersome. How do you feel when someone hands you a document that has a table of contents that runs for more than a few pages or has section numbers like 3.1.2.3.4.5.3.2? Even more difficult to use are documents that designate subsections with schemes like 1.A.1.a.1.A and indentation. This system makes it hard to tell from looking at any particular page where you are in the document. Readers are always flipping back to figure out a given requirement's context.

Many commercial organizations have abandoned these cumbersome subsection-numbering schemes, creating a more workable document out of the standards. One or another of these commercial standards may prove more suited to your organization than an existing international or military standard. Because the international and military standards are updated from time to time, their numbering problem may be resolved in the near future, so don't dismiss them entirely just on the basis of our numbering concerns.

Any subsection-numbering scheme will become a nightmare if your subsections are very small. It's tempting to use the subsection numbering as a means of tracking requirements. Keep in mind that the document numbering is intended to improve communication of the requirements, not track the requirements. Making each individual requirement its own subsection only appears to facilitate its tracking. You can number individual requirements to facilitate tracking and traceability, but use numbers that are not connected with an individual requirement's position in a document or sequence. Otherwise, moving a requirement will make your tracing useless.

Tailoring a standard is an ongoing process. Beyond your initial tailoring effort, we recommend implementing a fast, simple process to request a format waiver. A waiver policy can alleviate many concerns that your people have about the bureaucratic burden of a standard. This waiver process lets the writers know that they can make changes to the outline or format when needed. It also tells them exactly what is needed to justify a variation. Just knowing that they will not meet a concrete wall that cannot be moved is usually enough to get people to use the format instead of inventing a new format. Threats of "nothing can change" seem to drive the need to change. On the other hand, the option to change a standard can, in a disciplined environment, actually reduce people's desire to make changes.

What Is the Manager's Role in Formatting Requirements?

Except on very small projects, you probably won't be writing the specification. Your role will be choosing the format or specification outline, selling the format to your team and perhaps your seniors, tailoring it to your product's needs, and maintaining format discipline on your team.

Because you are ultimately responsible for producing the product, you want to make sure your team is working on the product, not on creating new outlines or new processes. You must make sure that they understand what must go into the requirement document and where it must go. You must also respond quickly to concerns that the format or outline is unduly burdensome. For example, you should implement a fast and simple waiver process.

Maintaining Perspective among the Piles of Paper

The point of using a standard format is not to be bureaucratic, or to impose structure for structure's sake. The format should help you. It should make defining requirements and then understanding them easier. If the format is making the job more difficult, you may be misusing the format, or perhaps you have the wrong format. It may be unsuitable for your product or just too complicated. If you are seeing "not applicable" in many, many parts of the outline or struggling to decide where to put each requirement, you have the wrong outline. Sanity check your outline choice with Table 11-3.

The final check for the specification is "Can you develop a product from it?" Until now, we have emphasized customer needs in writing requirements. Before deciding that the requirement document is complete, switch hats and read it from a developer's perspective. The requirement document is not an end in itself. It is a means to communicate (between customer and developers)

Table 11-3. Requirement Document Format Sanity Check

Can the format be used for all of your organization's products?

Is the format familiar to your customers and developers?

Is the format a comprehensive checklist to ensure completeness of requirements?

Does the format place all requirements in their proper context?

Is the format simple enough to prevent debate about where a requirement should be?

Can the format be tailored to your individual products or product lines?

Can a specification built on this format stand alone?

Can your customers understand a specification in this format?

Can your developers develop a product from a specification in this format?

what the product must do and to help focus the development team on solving the customer's real problem. It is also a means of communicating between levels (system and subsystems) in a complex development process. Regardless of complexity, the specification must completely define the needs for and verification of your product.

Chapter 12
Drawing a Line in the Sand
Preparing to Baseline Requirements

When are your requirements finished? A major concern for a manager is understanding when the requirements are solid enough to declare them a baseline and begin development.

Creating a baseline for requirements should be more than simply quitting requirement definition. Drawing the line between requirement definition and product design is a critical decision, one that should never be driven solely by a schedule milestone. Your requirements are never completely "done," but some point exists at which they are "done enough" to proceed with design. At this point, the cost of potential downstream changes will be less than the investment required to anticipate every possible requirement. We know of no simple indicator to tell you when your requirements are ready to baseline; however, you can do certain things to ensure that you have a good set of requirements and that you know the risk of proceeding with development. This chapter outlines these final steps to prepare requirements for baselining.

What's the Big Deal about a Baseline?

The baseline will control the product development pace and product evolution. To make your initial baseline as good as possible, your prebaseline effort should include review, clean up, and risk assessment. These actions will reduce postbaseline development rework, save change management resources, and reduce your vulnerability to risk.

Baseline preparation will reduce development rework. With design start, project staffing often increases dramatically. Your design team begins work on parallel tracks that must intersect downstream. If you are a customer contracting with others for product development, the contract must be completed and signed before the contractor's team can begin design. After the contract is signed, changes cost extra. Thus, whether you are managing an in-house effort or a contracted effort, design start is the point at which requirement changes become expensive. You must baseline your requirements and institute formal change control (Chapter 15) before design start or you will lose control of your budget and schedule. Some changes will be needed after the baseline, even if you do the best requirement definition job possible; however, a relatively small baseline preparation investment will prevent many late changes that increase cost, schedule, and risk.

Projects with poorly defined scope and requirements stemming from conflicting visions present the highest risk. Think about it: If you tell an army to march north, then two weeks later tell them "oops, I should have told you to march south," you must pay for the two weeks marching north, plus the time it takes them to turn around, march back to the starting point, and then march two weeks south. The turnaround time can be considerable with a large army, because it takes time for everyone to get word of the new orders, especially if they are scattered. You need to find the scope and requirement mistakes before you issue the orders to your product development army.

Documenting scope early (Chapter 4) and making sure that the requirements are in line with the scope can prevent expensive course-reversal problems. The prebaseline review confirms that the requirements are really in line with your vision and that everyone reading them will understand them within the same vision.

A rigorous prebaseline review and clean-up will save

change management resources. Using the formal postbaseline change process to fix grammatical errors, naming inconsistencies or other trivial errors is expensive. Finding and correcting the ambiguities and inconsistencies before baselining can save a great deal of trouble in the days ahead. As little as a week and a half of cleanup before baselining can keep these minor errors from clogging your change process. Otherwise, a flood of minor postbaseline changes can detract your team's attention from the really important changes, and you will have some really important changes.

Prebaseline risk assessment will reveal opportunities to decrease your risk exposure. As a good project manager, you begin development when you have reduced the development risks to an acceptable level. You cannot eliminate risks entirely, but you can assess them before taking them. If risk assessment shows that the requirement risks are unacceptably high, invest more before baselining. You may need more analysis, mockups, modeling, or prototypes to refine the requirements. These further investments will give you a better idea of what is needed and what is possible and reduce your risks.

Drawing the Line

Preparing the requirements for baselining takes time. Insert review and clean-up time into your schedule between requirement writing and baselining. Don't let your requirement writers think that the baseline date is their deadline; establish an earlier date that gives you and your reviewers the time needed to ensure a quality baseline. The bigger the project, the more time you will need for this prebaseline effort.

If you currently use a large team to simultaneously review requirements, a four-and-a-half step review will reduce the time to conduct the review and correct the document, reduce the amount of effort for individual reviewers, and give you the best results. The steps are (1) initial editorial, (2) goodness, (3) content, (4) risk assessment, and (4-1/2) final editorial.

Step 1: Initial Editorial

The first clean-up step is editorial. If you have access to professional editors, use them. If you are not so privileged—and many managers in small organizations are not—designate the most literate person on your staff as your editor for a few days. Have the editor find the format, grammar, spelling, and typographical errors in the requirements before you give them to your content reviewers. Make sure they know that this editorial cleanup is a valuable contribution to the project. You don't need ten or even just two people finding the same typo. Editorial cleanliness is not just a matter of preventing duplication of effort. Professional editors say that people think that they have finished "fixing" a sentence when they find the first error. People almost always stop looking for errors after that first find. Given an editorial error and a content error in the same requirement, what will your reviewers do? You guessed it: They will find the usually easy-to-spot editorial error and then move on, missing the more costly content error.

A document riddled with editorial problems will also make many reviewers feel overwhelmed. They may decide that it's a hopeless mess and limit their investment. It may seem more efficient to schedule only one editorial review after the content review, because changes will occur during the content review. This "efficiency" is an illusion! You need two editorial sweeps through your requirement document before baselining: one before your prebaseline review and another just before baselining to clean up after the reviewers. This process will maximize the benefit from the content review. A word of caution, however: Have the editor "redline" the requirement document, but reserve the right to accept or reject the changes during the next baseline step. Editors don't always understand a requirement's technical content and may accidentally introduce errors.

Table 12-1 provides a summary of the editorial sanity check.

Step 2: Goodness Review

The next step is a requirement "goodness" review by only a few people (including you) to look for obvious problems in the re-

Table 12-1. Editorial Sanity Check (Baseline Steps 1 and 4½)

Is each requirement
Grammatically correct?
In the form "product ABC shall XYZ?"
Using consistent terminology to refer to the product and its components?
Free of typographical errors and misspellings?

quirements that you have at this point: ambiguities, unverified assumptions, TBDs, implementation, lack of rationale or unintelligible rationale, and lack of traceability. Anything fixed now is one less item to deal with in the upcoming larger and more formal review. Of course, trained requirement engineers with domain expertise and experience are the ideal choice for this goodness review. We know of organizations that have such specialists to go from project to project helping with reviews. Their experience enables them to see the dangerous things that most people miss. Furthermore, if they haven't been involved in the project before this review, their fresh perspective helps them catch errors that you are too close to see.

Many of you will not be blessed with access to such a specialist. If this is your situation, identify the best requirement writer on your team and ask them to participate in the goodness review. Again, remember to reward this team member's good work.

A major objective of the goodness review is identifying requirements that don't meet the standards summarized in Chapter 7. Remember, a good requirement states a need clearly and is verifiable. The goodness reviewers must be especially alert to unclear or ambiguous requirements, which hide real issues and generate the most change traffic later. Recall, for example, that words like "support" (except in a structural requirement that reads something like "support 35 pounds") and "accommodate" are ambiguity flags (Table 7-2).

During the goodness review, identify all assumptions. Have you checked each assumption, converting it from "assumption" to "fact?" If you cannot validate a particular assumption by the time you must proceed into development, move it from the invalidated assumptions bucket to the risk bucket. You will not be able to validate all assumptions before you baseline. The possibility also exists that some now-valid assumptions may become invalid further downstream. Don't stop the baselining because you don't know everything; instead, identify the risks.

The key to identifying and validating assumptions is capturing rationale for each and every requirement. It is not enough to have the rationale—read it! If you don't understand it, your developers probably won't either. The percentage of your requirements supported with clear rationale is a more meaningful indicator of how close you are to a good baseline than the absolute requirement count.

Identify any "TBDs" during your goodness review. Prioritize them by impact on your product development. In general, we recommend that you don't baseline TBDs—a best guess is generally better than a TBD, as long as you keep track of it as a guess in the rationale. A guess will at least bind the technical problem. Consider: "The system shall update the display screen every TBD (time)." One developer might think of nanoseconds, another days. If your operational concepts suggest that the refresh interval should be on the order of seconds, rather than hours or days, replace the TBD with something like "10 seconds (estimated)" and include a note about how the estimate was derived in the rationale.

> One of my favorite methods for handling "TBD" appeared at the very beginning of a specification:
> "At this time several of the system requirement values are TBD, but are being used in various system analyses or pending confirmation. For purposes of this Specification these values are in brackets [ ] to indicate the working number, and likely final value unless trade studies indicate a better system can be achieved by changing the requirement."
> —Ivy Hooks

People will fight you on eliminating the TBDs. They don't want to commit to an estimated number. Why? If requirement authors put a TBD in a requirement, project managers will likely greet these authors with hugs and flowers when they finally do bring in the number. If these same authors include an estimate instead of a TBD, and then come in later with a different number, these same project managers will be more inclined to attack them. Remember that an early estimate helps you assess risk, technical feasibility, and cost. Take pains to encourage estimates. At the very least, don't punish people for refining their estimates!

Classify TBDs or estimates by the date when a change in the requirement will start costing money. The color of your product may not matter until you order paint late in manufacturing, but requirements that affect architecture must be made early to avoid major redesigns if the requirement is changed. Determine when you must refine the estimate and focus first on the critical ones. Perhaps a phased baseline is appropriate for your project. Maybe you can wait until the day the paint must be ordered to decide the color.

Use a complete tracing between requirements, scope, and operational concepts (for top-level requirements) or between requirements at different levels (for lower-level requirements) to reveal omissions and gold plating, as described in Chapter 9. Crosscheck your verification matrix (Chapter 10) to ensure that each requirement to be included in the baseline is verifiable. Finish your requirement goodness by checking requirement placement in the requirement document (Chapter 11). You don't want your content reviewers to waste their time looking for requirements.

Table 12-2 provides a summary of the "goodness" step checks.

Step 3: Content Review

Now you are ready to review for content. This review should involve a larger group of people. You want all of the stakeholders to take their best shot at the requirements before someone starts designing to them. Because you have corrected the editorial problems and have fixed the ambiguities and other obvious problems,

**Table 12-2. Requirement "Goodness" Sanity Check (Baseline
              Step 2)**

For each requirement, have you:
Eliminated descriptions of implementation?
Eliminated ambiguities?
Collected intelligible rationale?
Identified all assumptions?
Validated all assumptions?
Eliminated all TBDs?
Checked its lineage from scope and operational concepts?
Checked for correct document location and level?
Chosen a verification approach?

these reviewers will be able to find the really important content
errors, conflicts, or missing requirements.

When assembling your content review team, refer back to
your operational concepts. These concepts will remind you of
whom the product's stakeholders are. Once you have identified
all of your stakeholders, select reviewers from them. You need
representatives from developers, purchasers, maintainers, manufacturers, testers, installers, trainers, and (of course) users. Remember that requirement omissions and incorrect facts are often
the two biggest categories of requirement errors. Reviewers experienced in different life-cycle phases and aspects of use will be
best equipped to find the omissions and incorrect facts in those
phases and aspects. For example, a trainer will catch oversights
in your planned features for training new users, or an incorrect
assumption about how long a user will wait for a system response
before concluding that the system has a problem. An installer will
be able to tell you if the stated product size allows your product
to fit through a hatch between the decks of the ship that your
product is destined to serve on. The "outsiders"—people with
domain experience outside development—will also identify assumptions embedded in your requirements that you did not recognize as assumptions in your internal review.

If you have a choice within a stakeholder group (such as
users), pick reviewers open to change, if not enthusiastic about
it, to be on your review team. Look for articulate, imaginative

experts able to communicate their needs and expertise. The ideal expert on usage may not be the best operator in the pool. On the other hand, you need reviewers with enough experience to recognize potential problems. Always have at least one reviewer new to the product. This person can view the requirements without biases accumulated during the predesign effort. This person must be technically astute, perhaps another manager in your company responsible for different products.

Your reviewers must be committed to the review process as well as to your product. This review will take some of their time, and you want to do it well the first time. This commitment starts with their managers. You must convince each reviewer's manager that the review is a high priority.

Once you have chosen your reviewers, resist the temptation to fling your requirement document in their in-boxes and disappear for two weeks. Guide their effort! Start the review by having the reviewers read the operational concepts and scope. Include the rationale with the requirements. You don't want reviewers to have divergent visions of the project. If the reviewers have not had any requirement-writing training, they need to be taught what makes a good versus a bad requirement. Ask them to read Chapter 7 of this book. You don't want the reviewers undoing your goodness review, no matter how well intentioned they are. Clear instructions on what the reviewers should look for and how they should document their recommendations will make it easier to incorporate the review findings into the requirement document. At minimum, the reviewer must provide:

- Original requirement (if any)
- Recommended requirement or requirement change
- Rationale for change

You may also want to ask reviewers to classify their recommendations into categories, such as editorial, adding requirement, deleting requirement, or fixing incorrect requirement. Today's electronic tools enable a review team to make all of their input in electronic form. Some tools allow all members of a team to see each member's recommendation, which eliminates duplicate recommendations.

After the review, you will have to consolidate the recommendations into a single set of changes for the requirement document. Sort these recommendations into three groups: (1) definitely accept; (2) maybe accept; and (3) definitely not accept. Post all of these lists, along with the reasons for grouping them. For example, the "definitely not accept" list will include those recommendations that diverge from the scope. Explain the reasons for disapproval of any requested change; otherwise, you will see the same recommendation again and again until you do.

We suggest an open forum with your reviewers to sort the "maybes" into accept or not accept categories. If you don't know whether to accept a recommendation, perhaps not everyone is reading the requirement the same way. You may need to pull other experts into this discussion. Often, discussion will reveal that you have missing operational concepts or problems with your current operational concepts.

The main goal of the content review is identifying incorrect or missing requirements. Because you have involved representatives from all stakeholders, this review will find viewpoint issues, such as customer versus developer. At the same time, this review is a sanity check of the results of the previous two reviews that covered requirement readability and goodness. Table 12-3 summarizes step 3 of the baseline process.

Table 12-3. Requirement Content Sanity Check (Baseline Step 3)

Have you:

Before the content review:
Included representatives from all stakeholders on your review team?
Educated your review team on what constitutes a good requirement?
Provided instructions to the reviewers?
Reviewed project scope and operational concepts with your review team?
Provided a form for reviewer recommendations?
Provided rationale with the requirements?

After the content review:
Incorporated acceptable reviewer recommendations?
Circulated review recommendation summary to all review participants?
Explained why you are rejecting the recommendations not incorporated?

Step 4: Risk Assessment

To be a project manager, you have to be able to take risks. To be a good project manager, however, you must make a habit of driving the risk lower than the benefits. The first three baselining steps have eliminated risk from badly written, incorrect, and missing requirements. Now, you need to assess the true product development risk. Requirement volatility, technical feasibility, budget, and schedule risks may exist.

Volatile requirements

Volatile requirements are a major source of risk. They may be good, unambiguous requirements, but these requirements are likely to change during the product's life cycle. They may be volatile because a major customer won't commit to something, or because of other external events over which you have no control. External interfaces can be especially volatile.

Identifying the volatility now gives you an opportunity to reduce your long-term requirement change traffic. You may be able to convert volatile requirements into requirements that make your product tolerant of anticipated changes. For example, "ABC website shall contain a link to website www.notunderour-control.com" is a clear requirement, but the link will be useless if that website's proprietor changes the address. Perhaps you can add requirements for ABC website to have external link options easily reconfigured by a user, and to check its own external links. These additional requirements will prevent the ABC website from becoming obsolete when an external link changes. Your operational concepts will be helpful in identifying volatile requirements for nominal and off-nominal conditions and for all life-cycle phases. Review the operational concepts carefully in your risk assessment.

Requirement rationale also helps in volatility assessment. Are the requirements based on a solid, long-term perspective? Consider these examples:

- ◆ Will the outside vendor supplying a specific operating system or hardware item continue to make it available and support its purchasers?
- ◆ Is the Federal Communications Commission considering changes in radio frequency allocation?
- ◆ Will a demand exist for this product in countries where people do not speak English or do not use English units of measure?

Use rationale to check the lineage of any specific piece of data. If the source is unknown or poorly documented, assume the worst and add the requirement to your volatile list.

Once you identify a volatile requirement, assess your sensitivity to it. When might the requirement change? Will a change in the requirement make a significant difference to your development effort or product? Estimate the impact that a change in this requirement will have on your product at each stage of its life cycle. Schedule the date when you must have the volatility removed, and set an action to accomplish its removal. If the volatility cannot be removed before the critical date, try to write requirements that make your product less sensitive to possible changes.

Consider adding operational concepts involving potential changes to help you assess their impact. For example, if your software product will run on top of a particular third-party operating system, and the operating system supplier stops supporting it, will you have to redesign your product? Should you buy the rights to supply and start supporting the operating system yourself? Will your customers have to dedicate an otherwise obsolete system to run your product? Will you have to redesign major parts of your product to make it run on another operating system?

Use volatility operational concepts like these to rank volatile requirements by sensitivity. Then, you and your team should try to rewrite the sensitive requirements so that, if these anticipated changes occur, you won't have to change the requirement and you won't have to change the product. Consider these ideas on volatility-resistant requirements:

 ◆ Require that your product use only those operating system functions found in all major operating systems and
   that the operating system-specific parameters be isolated
   to data inputs in a single module.
 ◆ Require that all frequency-dependent functions be located
   on one field-replaceable component.
 ◆ Require that commands, displayed text, and measurement conversion factors be user-configurable and isolated to a single module.

   The last of these examples touches on human interface issues. Human interface requirements are generally volatile. People often do not know what they want until they see something
else. The exception might be a product whose human interface
must exactly emulate that of an existing product, or meet a precise standard. Should your requirements be straying from existing human interface conventions or no standard exists, we
recommend that your team do some user interface mockups or
prototypes to validate user interface requirements before baselining them.
   Sometimes a requirement may only appear volatile because
it depends on which design path your developers choose. If this
requirement is top level, this dependency may be a signal that
you have too much implementation in the requirements. If this is
the case, rewrite it to eliminate its dependence on design. Requirements that force your developers into a particular implementation limit flexibility in meeting the real requirements.
Recall from Chapter 9, however, that lower-level requirements
always depend somewhat on design. Before baselining, ensure
that the volatile requirements without global impact are in the
lower level documents, where the volatility impact is smaller.
   This prebaseline volatility identification, sensitivity analysis, and requirement rewrite take effort but will allow changing
needs to be incorporated without major requirements or design
changes. The investment will more than pay for itself. Some requirements will always exist that can't be rewritten to account
for every possible event, and these define your true requirement
volatility risk.

Before the Space Shuttle, NASA built one-of-a-kind items, flew them once, and dunked them in the ocean. They then plucked them out of the ocean, cleaned them up, and shipped them to the Smithsonian museum. The reusability requirement of the Shuttle presented NASA with new challenges. One reusability problem related to the software to make the vehicle fly. Each Shuttle has some unique hardware, and each launch is different. Thus, some portion of the software has to change for every flight. This problem was addressed very early, with a requirement to change the software related to these vehicle-to-vehicle or flight-to-flight items without recompiling the code. The solution was to imbed the flight- and vehicle-specific information in constants, called I-Loads, that could be inserted into the code without a recompilation and that could be quickly tested with a small subset of the total software tests.

This example is classic of "design for change," but first someone had to identify the problem and state the requirement to combat the problem.

—Ivy Hooks

Technical feasibility

The developer representatives on your content review team may have brought technical feasibility concerns to your attention. If they did not raise any feasibility concerns, however, you are not necessarily without technical risks. Technical risk is dependent on budget and schedule. Given unlimited time and money, you can solve almost any technical problem. You don't have that luxury, and your developer-reviewers may not have the budget and schedule visibility that you have. Add the facts that technical people (1) tend to be unrealistically optimistic about what they can accomplish (and American developers are ever so much more optimistic in general) and (2) enjoy a challenge, and it is easy to overlook or trivialize technical risks. Now is the time to rank these risks and map out alternatives if it turns out that you cannot solve these problems within the planned budget and schedule.

In the absence of alternatives, you may have to rewrite your requirements now to eliminate these technical risks. A compromise might be phasing in the technical risks: Adopt the most technically conservative requirements for the first version of the product, and then tackle a more ambitious feature in the second version. If you choose this approach, however, you must have requirements in the first version's baseline that drive the product design into something that can accept the ambitious feature add-on to the second version. You don't want to have to start all over again with the design to add these features later. The purpose of investing in requirement definition is to eliminate rework. Requiring "hooks" and "scars" (developer slang for future software and hardware additions, respectively) in the first version of the product will save you from rework later.

Schedule and budget

This risk assessment is an iterative process between requirement volatility, technical risk, schedule, and budget. Telling you how to cost or schedule your product development is beyond the scope of this book. If whatever costing and scheduling method that you use reveals that you do not have the resources to meet the requirements that you would like to baseline, we recommend reducing your project's scope to something more realistic. This process will entail revising operational concepts, interface definitions, and verification plans as well as the requirements and scope. A lot of work, but another requirement iteration is cheaper than a development effort abandoned before a useful product is delivered.

Table 12-4 provides a summary of the risk assessment sanity check.

Step 4-1/2: Final Editorial

Incorporating all of the recommendations from these reviews may have introduced some new spelling and grammar errors. We recommend that you return the requirement document to your

Table 12-4. Risk Assessment Sanity Check (Baseline Step 4)

Have you:

Requirement volatility
Identified volatile requirements?
Modified sensitive requirements to eliminate the need to change the
    requirement if the volatility becomes reality?
Modified sensitive requirements or added additional requirements to
    make the design robust to volatility?
Developed a plan to manage your development effort through
    requirement volatility when eliminating sensitivity is not possible?

Technical feasibility
Identified technical risks?
Modified requirements to reduce technical risk to match your budget and
    schedule?

Schedule and budget
Ensured that your schedule and budget are realistic for the requirements
    you want to include in the baseline?

editor for a final cleanup before baselining. As with the initial editorial review, check the editor's proposed changes to ensure that they clarify content rather than change it.

All at Once or Step-by-Step?

Some products are simple enough to have a single requirement specification document and an operational environment that is stable through their lifetime. If this is the case for your product, rejoice and plan a single requirement baseline.

Real life is often more complicated. In developing complex systems, you must baseline a top-level specification before you can do system-level design that will spawn the next level of specifications. You must then baseline the subsystem specifications before designing subsystems, and so on. The baselining process is repeated for each level.

Phased product capability may also dictate phased baselining. Long-lived products or those used in a dynamic environment need to evolve. This situation may require an evolving baseline. Because developing to a moving target is difficult, if not impossible, you will probably define new baselines at intervals. You might collect new requirements until a certain date or until you have a number that agrees with your product support budget. Then, you will baseline them, assign a new version or release number, and begin development of a new release. During that version's development, all change requests are held for the next version.

Note that phased baselining—baselining some of a product's requirements before others—is not the same thing as phased requirement definition. You can baseline all of a product's requirements at one time, but plan to implement some requirements before others. Chapter 13 covers prioritizing requirements for implementation.

What Is the Manager's Role in Baselining?

You will make the decision to baseline the requirements. If you keep an eye on requirements throughout their definition, involve all of the stakeholders, emphasize your commitment to quality requirements, and back this commitment by recognizing people doing a good job on requirements, you should have good quality requirements at your projected baseline date. Still, it is up to you, not the calendar, to determine when the requirements are ready for design.

You will have to orchestrate editorial and content reviews. Many poor reviews are due to poor reviewer choices. You must request and insist on the right people for the review, many of whom may work in other areas. Your counterparts in other areas will be tempted to send their least experienced or least productive employees. Even if the inexperienced reviewers are sincere and motivated, you will get an editorial review but not much help with real issues.

You will also coordinate and participate in risk assessment and mitigation. If you have a good set of requirements, a good review, and few risks identified in the specification, go ahead, baseline, and pat yourself on the back. If the requirement quality is poor, it will take considerable courage to refuse to baseline. You will feel great pressure to meet a milestone! Remember that if you allow poor requirements into your baseline document, you will pay dearly later. The other milestones are much more important, and now is the time to ensure meeting those later milestones.

If most of your specification is in good shape, but problems still exist, you can assess the risk of baselining now versus resolving the problems and baseline later. As a manager, you are responsible for the assessing the risk, and it is your decision to accept the risk and baseline or to delay the baselining until the risk is reduced to an acceptable level.

The Bottom Line on Drawing the Line

A tendency exists to set the baselining date for a product's requirements by backing up on the calendar from a desired product delivery date. People allocate a reasonable amount to testing, manufacturing, and design, perhaps based on historical data. Then, they assign whatever is left (if anything) to requirement definition. Whatever requirements are available on the date that the schedule calls "design start" become the baseline. Unfortunately, their design, manufacture, and test time allocations are "reasonable" only for a good set of requirements, which don't exist. They spend much more time and money in each of the nonrequirement phases fixing the problems that poor requirements cause than they would if they had ensured good requirements before beginning the design.

We have seen projects in which people baselined a set of poor requirements, and then spent an amazing amount of effort in the formal change process to fix the requirements. Although they ended up with good requirements, most of the changes could have been made before the baseline at a fraction of the formal change control cost. Applying the change process' rigorous standards for requirements before the baseline would have also saved a significant portion of the development resources wasted in re-work.

Your best defense against change is: Don't baseline bad or sloppy requirements! Put as much rigor into the baseline as in changes that follow the baseline. Your downstream savings will more than pay for the prebaseline investment.

Chapter 13
Not All Requirements Are Created Equal
The Case for Prioritizing Requirements

In my classes, I ask my students, "Have any of you prioritized requirements on any programs?" In a class for managers, one of the participants replied, "We all prioritize requirements on every program, it's just a matter of when."

—Ivy Hooks

You now have a good initial requirement baseline and are poised to dive into design. Before you start design, however, we recommend that you prioritize the requirements—that is, group them by relative importance. If you are a development manager, not the customer, you will have to enlist the customer or marketing in prioritizing the requirements. Do so now! If you prioritize the requirements early in the project, before you spend resources on them, you have greater flexibility in tradeoffs, design, and implementation. If you wait until the product is partially implemented, you lose this flexibility.

If you postpone requirement prioritization, and you face a resource shortfall, your team may have to throw away work already done on the lower priority requirements in a panic effort to focus on and finish the truly important ones. By the time the crisis looms, it may too late to fix it with prioritization. The portion of the product implementing the low-priority requirements may be too tightly intertwined with the portion implementing the high-priority requirements. Dropping some requirements late in development may require major, expensive surgery on the product.

The Case for Early Prioritization

Knowing requirement priorities early can help avoid the late-stage implementation train wreck. Prioritizing your requirements before design start provides options to manage requirement additions and risk, enables delivery of a useful product in spite of changes in schedule and resource allocations, and guides architecting and design tradeoffs.

Prioritizing provides options to manage requirement additions and risks. Even when you have a high-quality set of requirements and use them to derive the initial development cost and schedule, the product design process will reveal new requirements. Perhaps the marketing department gets wind of features in your competitor's next product that you must add in your product to stay competitive. You must add development time and money, or drop other requirements to add the new requirement. If you prioritize the requirements, you know where to find the resources to use for the important latecomers. You know which requirements can be postponed for later implementation to make room for the new ones.

Sometimes all of your risk calculations on a project go against you, and you find yourself running low on time and resources to implement all of your requirements. Early prioritization will position you to postpone the less important product features until the big ones have been implemented, thus ensuring that you have a useful product to deliver on time and on budget. In short, requirement priorities can provide options to manage development risk.

Prioritizing enables delivery of a useful product in spite of changes in schedule and resource allocations. Marketing may decide that you have to deliver this new product sooner than originally planned, or your budget gets cut. With requirement prioritization, you can react to these squeezes by developing a product with the most important features now, and put the lower priority requirements in a second- or third-generation product.

Prioritizing guides architecting and design tradeoffs. Prioritizing requirements before a schedule or budget crunch can guide you to a product architecture that allows postponing less important requirements without forcing redesign. Prioritization can drive the architecture so that adding the lower priority features later won't require rework of the rest of the product. If you expect to add more to a product at a later time, you can put the "more" into the requirements in a manner that allows the developers to architect for the total future product. The product can be developed incrementally with the high-priority requirements in the earliest version and lower priority requirements in later versions of the product.

Prioritization can help resolve requirement conflicts. The development team may discover in the design phase that they cannot simultaneously meet all of the performance, maintainability, portability, and reliability requirements while containing the cost and schedule; they must make tradeoffs between the requirements. If the conflicting requirements have been prioritized, the developers know how to conduct trade studies to get the most customer-pleasing compromise between performance and these "-ilities."

Selling the Concept of Prioritizing Requirements

Defining requirements is all about communication between customers and developers. Requirement priorities improve communication between these parties. The payoff is not obvious to everyone, however, and you will probably have to sell the concept of prioritization to your stakeholders.

A common product development scenario is a commercial company developing a consumer product. In this case, your stakeholders will include your marketing department (surrogate for your customers) as well as developers, manufacturers, users (in some cases, different from your customers), and maintainers.

Some of the product development managers among you might be thinking:

> This prioritization stuff is all well and good, if you are your own customer or your marketing department defines your customer, but my customer is outside my company. They are the ones who have to do the prioritization, and they won't do it! They want all of the requirements. Why else would they be asking for them? They believe all of their requirements are equally important. If we ask them to prioritize requirements, they will know we are going to cut out some and that's not acceptable to them. They think that our development problems are our problems, not theirs.

An external customer is probably the hardest stakeholder of all to sell on the concept of prioritization. Customers have difficulty with the concept. Once, we found a requirement in a specification that read, "All requirements in this document shall be equal." We thought it might be a mistaken use of "shall" until we found this requirement in the verification matrix—to be verified "by analysis." Unless a customer has spelled out such a requirement in writing, however, try marketing the concept of prioritization to them.

Requirement prioritization may appear to the customer to benefit the developer over the customer, so if you are the development manager you may have a tough selling job. Many customers initially view a request to prioritize requirements as a backdoor way to reduce the number of requirements. A prioritization effort involving both customer and developer perspectives will separate essential from desirable, needs from wants, in a way not possible from only one side's perspective. The customer may decide to drop the low-priority "desirables" after such a review. The customer must reach this conclusion, not those of you on the development side. You signed up to do them all!

Sell requirement prioritization in a positive light. It is not just about preventing development disasters. If the customer will prioritize requirements early, you will find opportunities to phase the product's development in a way that improves your customer's satisfaction. For example, you might be able to offer a preliminary product incorporating the most important requirements earlier than the customer expects. Because most customers buy a product to improve their productivity and effectiveness, early delivery of functionality translates into more money on their bottom line. It is also a great opportunity for the customers to exercise the product on their own terms and turf before completion.

Customers want to preserve some flexibility in requirements. Emphasize how priorities help them select which of the original requirements can be deferred in favor of implementing important latecomers without delaying the scheduled delivery or overrunning the budget. Point out to the customer insisting that all requirements are Priority 1 that this can only be the case if requirements are missing. Some requirements always exist that are merely useful or desirable, not critical, which you can defer to a later phase.

Another point to make with your customer is how important their priorities are in driving trade studies during design and ultimately in their own satisfaction with the final product. For example, most of your developers have never been out in the field in freezing temperatures trying to fix broken equipment. It's hard to imagine what that's like from the security of an air-conditioned office. In the absence of priority information, your developers will tend to resolve tradeoffs between ease of development and maintainability in favor of, you guessed it, ease of development. As a result, what will your customer be doing next winter? Alternately cursing the weather, their frozen fingers, and your product.

Don't be surprised if you encounter resistance to prioritization from your developers, because the priorities may make the implementation job harder. They will no longer be able to schedule work simply to minimize development effort. Customer priorities often conflict with the most expeditious implementation scheme. Include the developers in the priority discussions to avoid adding to their problems unnecessarily and to gain their support.

If you are the manager responsible for acquiring a product and you are defining requirements, you have to convince your own people of the need to prioritize. Remind them of recent problems, such as how late requirements drove the product acquisition into cost and schedule overruns, how you cut some testing to get the delivery back on schedule and then had trouble with the product in operations, or the war over what part of the product must be discarded to make room for a really important new requirement. Why would you ever want to be in that position again?

How Do You Prioritize Requirements?

Whether you are on the customer side managing requirements or on the other side managing product development, you need a simple method for realizing the benefits of prioritizing requirements. Formal prioritization methods exist, such as quality function deployment (QFD), a Japanese technique developed at the Kobe Shipyard.[1] In addition to helping the customer to prioritize needs, QFD provides a structure for the development team to evaluate all of their candidate designs against the customer's priorities.

Most projects, however, do not need a QFD-scale investment in prioritization. The benefits of prioritization have to exceed the cost of doing it. We recommend QFD only for large, complex projects in which diverse stakeholders have very different viewpoints and are having trouble agreeing. Most projects can reap the benefits of requirement prioritization with the following simple five-step program:

1. Define priority classes.
2. Classify the requirements.
3. Resolve the differences.
4. Create priority-based development schedules.
5. Maintain the priorities.

Let's expand on each of these steps.

Define Priority Classes

Keep them simple. A numbering system of 1-2-3 works well. Number the essential, nonnegotiable, and urgent requirements with priority 1. Assign priority 2 to the useful, negotiable, or slightly deferrable requirements. Save priority 3 for merely desirable, flexible, or "someday" requirements. Educate all stakeholders—internal and external, customers and developers—on the prioritization scheme.

Classify the Requirements

Next, ask all stakeholders to classify the requirements by priority, which should be an informal sorting process. Don't give people time to agonize over the exactness of the classification. The priority of the prioritization process is getting a relative sense of each requirement's priority. A review of the product's operational scenarios (Chapter 5) helps stakeholders classify requirements. Often, it's easiest to identify 1's and 3's first and allow everything else to default to 2.

Resolve the Differences

Once everyone has had a chance to do their prioritization, resolve the differences. Start by throwing all of the requirements that everyone has ranked the same into the appropriate bucket. That is, if everyone prioritizes requirement A as 1, it's definitely a 1. Then, move to building a consensus on the requirements that different people prioritized differently. Get the stakeholders together, and show them the requirements that they agreed on and then the ones that they ranked differently. Often, people will find agreement after some informal discussion. If not, note who is disagreeing. When you are managing development of a product for a particular customer, that customer's prioritization obviously carries the most weight.

When you are managing development of a commercial product for many customers, your marketing department has a large say-so, but your development organization must balance marketing's input because they understand the requirement's implementation cost and complexity. Ask the development expert about disputed requirements: Some can be done early regardless of priority because the developer can save total development effort by implementing them along with related high-priority requirements. If so, or if implementing the requirement represents a very small effort for other reasons, put it in the higher priority class. Solicit the developer priority viewpoint very carefully to ensure that you get the most in the least amount of time.

If a strong disagreement continues over a particular requirement's priority, put the requirement in the higher class to stop the debate. If you have a single holdout insisting that requirement D is a 1 while everyone else thinks it's a 2, go ahead and put it in class 1, with a note to put it behind the other priority 1's in the schedule. Keep the process simple and speedy. At this stage of your product, you don't know enough to find a perfectly optimized solution anyway.

Create Priority-Based Development Schedules

After you have a set of priorities, use them to create priority-based development schedules. Show everyone where work begins and ends on each requirement. This information helps you define intermediate products or "releases" containing the high-priority requirement implementations. These schedules will also help your developers synchronize work on particular requirements.

Maintain the Priorities

Throughout the development effort, you must maintain the priorities. You don't finish with prioritization until you finish the last version of the product. Revisit them as the team analyzes design trades to make sure that the priorities are still driving the effort on realistic schedules. When the customer brings new requirements that require deferring some old requirements, reassess priorities to make certain that the least important priorities are the ones being deferred.

What Is the Manager's Role in Prioritizing Requirements?

Your first priority in requirement prioritization may be selling the stakeholders on the concept of prioritizing requirements before design start. Once they agree to it, you will guide the stakeholders through the prioritization process. Then, you will incorporate the results into product development schedules and budgets. You must enforce the priorities throughout the development process.

As development progresses, you will identify situations that trigger use of the priorities: impending resource shortages, changes in external constraints or expectations, and conflicts. You must ensure that the priorities rule the outcome.

The Bottom Line on Prioritizing Requirements

Requirement prioritization early in development helps a manager control project risk and change. Knowing requirement priorities focuses a product development team and guides intelligent choices for phasing in product features over time. It prevents the "bailing" that so often occurs just before delivery, in which partially implemented requirements are thrown overboard in a frantic effort to save dwindling resources for finishing the critical components. Above all, it's one more communication channel between customers and developers. Table 13-1 provides a check to see if you are taking full advantage of this communication opportunity.

Table 13-1. Prioritizing Requirements Sanity Check

Have you :
Sold stakeholders on the benefits of requirement prioritization?
Defined priority classes?
Classified all requirements by priority?
Resolved the priority differences between stakeholders?
Created priority-based development schedules?
Maintained the priorities throughout development?

While developing a requirement class for Honeywell, Ivy and I suggested prioritizing requirements to a group of managers and senior engineers. They were adamant that customers would never allow it. After reworking the material to sell the idea, the first class was eager to try it, seeing the benefit. In the second class, one project group said they were [already] applying the technique. After three years of customer frustration and massive overtime for the development team, the customer recommended prioritizing the requirements. The additional understanding the development team obtained enabled them to do a much better job of planning. The developers were able to show the customer more realistic schedule estimates and plan the delivery phases better. While prioritizing requirements, the customer dropped some low priority requirements. The customer is much happier now, as they are getting what they need in a timely manner. The developers are able to cruise through acceptance testing with little overtime and none of the panic rework that marked their effort prior to the change in planning and prioritization philosophy. Customer expectations match product delivery, and there is a lot less stress all around. Though not quantitatively measured, the improvements are tangible. These gains came from increased requirement definition and analysis as well as prioritization, of course. It's nice to know that doing these things to improve product quality can also make life easier for the people who do the actual work of satisfying the customer.[2]

—Larry Fellows
Staff Consultant
Honeywell Software Initiative
Phoenix, AZ

Chapter 14
Keeping Sane
Automating Requirement Management

Scope, constraints, operational concepts, interface details, verification assessments, requirement, and review notes, you may feel like you are smothered in lists before your team finishes the first iteration of requirement definition. It can get worse before it gets better. The process must be repeated for every requirement level in the product's development.

Throughout a product's development and use, your team must refer back to these requirement documents. You must measure your team's progress against these requirement documents. If requirement changes are justified, you must change these documents.

Is this process a management nightmare? Possibly. In a complex project, requirements can drop through the cracks between disciplines, contractors, and customers. Out-of-date requirement documents can lead developers astray and are often undiscovered until integration of subsystems or, worse, until customer acceptance testing. Staying on top of the product's requirements is a major project management responsibility.

Automated tools may be the answer to keeping on top of your requirements throughout product development. Tools are not magic, however. Tools enable you to automate a process. If no process exists to begin with, however, imposing a tool will only make matters worse.

> In the early days of the international space station development effort, NASA struggled to integrate inputs from thousands of stakeholders into one coherent requirement set. As one of the "phase B" or feasibility study contractors, we were deluged with these inputs and proposed responses to them. As people experimented with various ideas, backing up to a previous baseline was common enough to make us reluctant to part with old versions of documents. It didn't help that our feasibility study results were often tied to a particular version.
>
> The growing mountain of paper stimulated some dark but innovative proposals to cope with less-than-hoped-for development budgets. "We don't need rockets to get Station to orbit," read one e-mail. "We can just build a stairway to heaven out of all this paper, and carry Station up there piece by piece."
>
> —Kristin Farry

Why Automate?

Judicious use of automated requirement management tools will improve your team's communication, improve product quality, help enforce discipline, and reduce development and life-cycle costs.

Automation can improve your team's communication. Even common electronic office tools can enhance requirement definition, documentation, and dissemination. Some tools, such as web-based document managers, enable unduplicated and orderly input from all stakeholders without loss of control by the responsible party. Other document manager capabilities can help capture and show various views of clarifying rationale and verification methods along with the requirement in an easy-to-access form. Making it easier for team members to access the latest version of all documents (perhaps on an internal company Website) may prevent some team members from missing a change.

Automation improves product quality. Automating some parts of the requirement management process can aid and even enable follow-through critical for quality. For example, consider just one of the many uses for a requirement management tool: tracing. A good tool can trace the requirements back to scope, operational concepts, and constraints and trace them forward from parent (system) to child (subsystem or component) requirements and verification plans.

ISO 9000 says that you shall trace requirement lineage. The U.S. Department of Defense has required traceability for years. Now, the FDA and other government customers are following its lead. More and more commercial customers are demanding traceability.

Typically, product developers have done the tracing only one time during the program. Even a single trace can help you identify holes and gold plating in a requirement document, but the job doesn't end there. Although this single trace meets the customer requirement for tracing, it is not useful as a management tool.

When people do tracing without automation, they laboriously build matrices—high-level requirements to lower-level requirements or requirements to verification method—manually. We have hardly ever seen a manual matrix that was correct one minute past its completion. Someone makes a single change to the requirements or verification and the matrix is wrong. It's hard to tell if the trace was ever completely right—few people have the time to check the traceability matrices. A thorough review involves opening all of the product documents and jumping back and forth—a difficult and tedious process at best, impossible at worst. The effort required to update these matrices is so great that they are usually abandoned after the one iteration required by the customer. If this database is not maintained throughout the product's development and test, it is worthless as a project management tool. You cannot use an outdated traceability matrix to assess the impact of a proposed change.

Tracking bits of information is something that computers do well. Computerizing this data tracking can save personnel time, help detect requirement problems early, assess impact of proposed changes, and prepare for verification. A requirement management tool can make it easy to assess the correctness and completeness of a linkage without opening any documents.

Automation enforces discipline. You may have a requirement-tracing process in place, but how do you know if it is being rigorously implemented? In a manual system, it is often easy to rationalize away an apparent gap in, say, traceability between parent and child requirements as your imagination. The computer won't lie to you. It requires good inputs to give you good outputs, but it won't tell you that links exist where there are none.

Automation reduces development and life-cycle costs. Note that this process does not necessarily mean a reduction in requirement management costs! In fact, you will see some increases in the costs of requirement management beyond that of introducing the tool, because the discipline required will shift costs toward the front end of your product development. Capability increases, such as being able to track requirements throughout the product's life, may lead you to expand your management processes. The automation payoff will be in lowering overall costs rather than lowering requirement process costs, because you will reduce development rework and postdevelopment change headaches. Product quality will improve.

> We used a requirement management tool to document our system level requirements and associated data. Ultimately we placed master control of the management tool with the developer of our system. The development contractor was the heaviest user at that time so it was in the interest of both parties that the contractor have control and the configuration management task. We amended our contract and required the contractor to add their lower level documents into the common database with the tool and to perform linkages between requirements while maintaining this as the configuration management database for our program. We could therefore watch, virtually real-time, as lower level requirements were written into the database as updates took place.
>
> The utilization of this approach greatly reduced the work associated with managing requirements as the system developed and it greatly reduced the cost and efforts associated with change management throughout the development phases. This management and engineering tool enabled us to

perform better as an Integrated Process Team (IPT) vice as separate groups with intermittent alliances to accomplish integration.

This process was a great time saver in many ways. In the past, we would not have seen the lower level documents until very late. Mistakes that we identified would already have been incorporated into the design and correcting the problems required redesign and large efforts, time, and with higher costs. We liked our new integrated team RM&RE [Requirement Management and Requirement Engineering] approach because utilizing the tools enabled us to identify most problems before design had occurred; this saved us cost and time. The contractor liked it, because it reduced redesign and rework, and increased his profit margin while greatly reducing risk.

Formal reviews took much less time because we assigned cognizant individuals on both the contractor team and on our team to regularly review individual requirements, spending a very short time period each day, instead of spending many days reviewing many requirements in a large group effort. All issues were addressed only by the two parties responsible at an early stage thus preventing or at least greatly reducing the number of issues to be presented as problems at the larger formal program review sessions. We prevented our IPT from getting lost in a multitude of problems and enabling them to concentrate on a few more worthy issues at the formal reviews.[1]

—Harry Botsford
Senior Software Technologist
Patuxent River Naval Air Station, MD

How Do You Automate?

Table 14-1 summarizes some automation opportunities in requirement management. Consider them carefully before you begin. Remember that automating should help you do something better. It should enable you to finish a product faster, save product development resources, improve the product's quality, or all three. How can you accomplish this? How will you know that the path you have chosen is accomplishing this? You must know your

Table 14-1. Requirement Management Automation Opportunities

Opportunity	Implementation Options
Publishing and maintaining documents	• Word processor with autonumbering and change bar features • Requirement management tool
Capturing requirement rationale	• Word processor with hidden text capability • Requirement management tool
Searching rationale	• Word processor with search capability • Requirement management tool
Locating requirements containing ambiguous or unverifiable words	• Word processor with search capability • Requirement management tool
Locating TBDs	• Word processor with search capability • Requirement management tool
Summarizing requirements containing ambiguous or unverifiable words or TBDs	• Requirement management tool
Capturing input from stakeholders	• Web publishing and network document manager with user-traceable "notes" features • Requirement management tool
Capturing input from reviewers	• Web publishing and network document manager with user-traceable "notes" features • Requirement management tool
Parsing existing requirement document into database	• Requirements management tool
Identifying requirements missing rationale or other data	• Requirement management tool

Table 14-1. Requirement Management Automation Opportunities
(continued)

Opportunity	Implementation Options
Ensuring that requirements cover full scope, constraints, and operational concepts	• Requirement management tool
Identifying unnecessary requirements (orphans)	• Requirement management tool
Assessing verification coverage	• Requirement management tool
Assessing change impact	• Requirement management tool
Allocating requirements	• Requirement management tool
Tracking source of requirements	• Requirement management tool
Maintaining history of changes	• Requirement management tool

current costs to justify the "delta" cost of automation, the investment required to realize these gains.

Your first thought should be: What can we do with the tools that we already have? No doubt you are already automating some of your requirement document maintenance by using a word processor, which is a good starting point. Are you using all of the capabilities of a word processor that can streamline your requirement management? For example, you can use the "hidden text" function of the word processor to store a requirement's rationale right next to the requirement. Print all text (requirements and rationale) for reviews, and print requirements only for formal signature. A word processor's automated number features can save the headaches associated with moving a requirement from one section to another, or adding a late-coming requirement in with related requirements. You might use different fonts to draw attention to TBDs or requirements from different sources. Web-publishing capability in word processors can make posting the evolving document on a project website with password access.

In reviews involving a number of people (such as your baseline reviews), reviewers can make their comments on a central site using the "notes" feature of some word processors. These notes are automatically tagged with the author's name and time entered. Several reviewers may have the same or similar comment, and seeing the requirement already tagged with an appropriate comment will save others the effort of documenting the comment again. This process will reduce the time required to integrate everyone's comments after the review.

A major headache in requirement management is traceability. Requirement traceability requires database functions, and word processors do not contain these functions. Word processors are great for capturing the requirement and its rationale, but trying to use a word processor for any more than that is going to cost more than it's worth.

Databases are better than word processors for capturing rationale, because the database can allow you to maintain one rationale for many requirements. Although you can duplicate the same rationale for each of those requirements in a word processor, a change in the rationale means many changes in the document. You will often have to change the rationale in only one place if you are using a database. Also, databases and requirement management tools offer more options for searching of rationale. For example, it is difficult to identify requirements that are missing rationale or source data in a word processor, but requirement management tools can do this well.

Realizing that database functionality is needed for tracing, many people decide to whip up their own traceability tool using a handy database manager. This process can become a quagmire, tying up product development resources without yielding a useful product. These in-house traceability tool efforts typically fail. The prime reason for these failures is a lack of understanding of the requirements for the tracing tool. Tool builders are often developing the process to be automated at the same time they are building the automation. They solve one problem at a time, and end up reworking the solution on the way to solving the next problem. Rework may involve reentering requirement data, which is expensive! In addition, this requirement tool building is not your team's real job. Ultimately, the tool project gets neglected or becomes a hobby shop, a major distraction from developing the real product.

> "If I had all the money that companies have spent on building their own requirement traceability tools in-house, I'd be richer than Bill Gates."
>
> —Ivy Hooks

> On one big project, our systems engineering department decided to build a tool to manage the product's requirements. They spent man-years on it. The white papers they circulated throughout the project extolling its capability and benefits made it sound wonderful. I requested an output of the requirements allocated to my area—at that time, software—and got nothing. Only a few high-level requirements were entered into the tool's database. When I asked why, the systems engineering lead said that they were waiting for the other departments to come in with requirements and allocate them to various disciplines and subsystems.
>
> The systems engineering department had become a tool development department. They had totally forgotten that "systems engineering" usually collects requirements, architects the system, and allocates requirements downward to initiate implementation.
>
> —Kristin Farry

Requirement management tools are commercially available for purchase, and their cost will be lower than anything that you can build in-house for most product development efforts. Remember, however, that the decision to buy a commercial, off-the-shelf requirement tool doesn't save you from thinking through your own requirements for good requirement management. You must define your requirements for the tool before you buy. Then, you must ensure that the tool purchased meets those requirements. Develop and consider the operational concepts for tool usage carefully.

Buying a requirement management tool requires investment

beyond the initial purchase. Your team must train to use the tool, enter the requirements and supporting data, back up the data, generate the reports, and maintain their tool usage skills. You may need a tool administrator to keep the tool up and running. Table 14-2 is an automation tool sanity check and cost worksheet for your project. You must weigh the cost of this process against the cost of the requirement errors that the tool will prevent. If you don't have a good case for the benefits, you will find yourself stuck with the accounting department's idea of a bargain.

A tendency exists in large companies to want to buy one tool for everything and everyone: "We're going to have a standard, by golly!" Elsewhere in this book, we have recommended adopting a standard requirement document outline for every project in an organization, so it may seem strange that we hesitate to recommend that every organization adopt a standard requirement management tool. A standard tool can give you benefits, such as reduced training costs and ease of use for those overseeing many projects. We caution that it is easier to get caught in a "one size fits none" trap on requirement management tools than it is on specification outlines, because outlines can be tailored by anyone, but tools cannot.

Big projects may need a tool with extensive capability. They can afford the overhead associated with that capability's inevitable complexity, because the tool's use may be the difference be-

Table 14-2. Automation Cost-Benefit Sanity Check

Have you considered:
Purchase price of tool?
Cost of hosting tool (computer time, hardware upgrades required)?
Tailoring of tool to your process?
Purchase price of companion tools (such as word processors) to streamline integration?
Training of personnel (training course cost, time lost from real job)?
Entry of data (clerical for basic entry, skilled labor for linking tasks and verifying data entry)?
Maintenance of entered data?
Purchase price of tool upgrades? (cost of tool upgrades, annual maintenance, retraining, reentering, or reconfiguring data)

tween success and failure. Little projects in the same company can't afford the overhead associated with that complex tool. Therefore, they don't use it and aren't allowed to use anything else, even though using a simpler tool would save project resources. Some companies with projects varying in size or complexity have saved by standardizing on several requirement management tools that span the spectrum of complexity.

Your accounting department may also want to buy many copies of a requirement management tool at one time to get bulk-buy savings. Bulk buys often clutter shelves unused, making the real unit cost far higher than it might have been with a smaller purchase. Even if analysis shows that an automated requirement management tool will pay off on all projects in your organization, it does not make sense for all of the projects to start using the tool at once. A trial project led by an outstanding, disciplined manager should work out the problems in integrating organization processes with the tool. This trial can determine what needs to be done to make the tool and the team effective. This trial project's team will pay a price for going where no one else in the organization has gone before—the trial team needs extra resources and support required to successfully integrate the tool into the organization's process. The "lessons learned" by this team will smooth the application of the requirement management tool to other projects, especially if you can use trained personnel from the trial project to help implement the tool on the next project.

If your trial project is critical to the success of your organization, the learning curve may prove to be an albatross. Choose a trial project that is representative of typical projects but is not critical to the year's financials or your organization's survival. If a critical project requires automation, chose a trial project that leads the critical project, so the trial project lessons learned can be applied to the critical project.

A company I know recognized the need to automate the requirement process. Despite warnings of the dangers and potential problems, the Systems Engineering Manager made the decision to use the tool for the first time on the largest, most

> complex project the company had ever done. The project was in trouble from the start, as engineers struggled to learn the tool, develop the product, and maintain an aggressive schedule. As the schedule continued to slip, the customer became increasingly dissatisfied with the company's performance. The customer soon lost confidence in the company and canceled the contract. The company had lost the work that was to be its lifeblood for five to ten years. As a result of this disaster, many managers were replaced, but the company never recovered. It ceased to be a major player in the market. Although not the only cause, the ill-fated introduction of requirement automation without proper planning was a major contributor to the demise.[2]
>
> —Larry Fellows
> Staff Consultant
> Honeywell Software Initiative
> Phoenix, AZ

During the trial project, you will learn that everyone needs the reports output by the tool but not everyone needs to use the tool. Tool training takes time and money. Unless you are a frequent user of a tool, you will quickly lose proficiency. Inefficient tool users can cost your project much more than efficient tool use could ever save. Errors introduced into your requirement database can waste the time of many people.

We have seen highly successful requirement management in which a single person is the only automated tool user for one or many projects. Having a tool specialist reduces tool purchase and training investment and lowers the frustration level of most of the team. This single specialist takes input from the entire team (either in writing or electronically), enters the requirements and other data into the tool, generates reports and documents, and keeps everything up-to-date. Having only one tool specialist does put your development effort at risk if something happens to that person. We recommend spreading the tool-oriented work between two people to reduce your project's vulnerability to turnover and absences. Note that the tool specialist needs a good understanding of requirements and the product—this is not a clerical job!

Some tools offer an option between "everyone has the tool" and "everyone has to go to a single tool specialist." They have a "view" mode that many users can use to see data. These users can use the view mode without understanding everything about the tool, and the viewers cost less than the full-capability tool.

In short, you don't have to equip everyone on the project with the requirement management tool and the training to use all of its features. All members of the project team do need to know what the tool can and cannot do for them. Then, everyone can provide and ask for the right information.

The fact that everyone doesn't need to use the tool for it to have a big impact on your product is good news. You have no doubt noticed that not everyone in your organization lines up eagerly for the latest software purchase. Some people don't like computers and don't want to use software tools. Other people feel that they are too busy to learn how to use yet another tool.

What Is the Manager's Role in Automating Requirement Management?

As manager, you are the one with the visibility to assess the costs and benefits of your requirement management automation options. You have the big process picture and can tell where the weaknesses exist. You must determine which weaknesses are process weaknesses (which automation can't help) and which are throughput bottlenecks (which automation can help).

You can make the decision to automate some or all of your requirement management functions. You have control of the budget and can allocate resources for tools and their use. Finally, you will motive your team to use the tools.

No Magic Here

Tools will not create process for you. They only automate process. You have to have the process before you can automate it.

You must identify your requirement problems and determine what process you can use to avoid the problems. Then, and only then, should you look at tools to automate your requirement management. Automation begins with choosing the tools. You must still train people and integrate the use of the tools into the project's routine. You must then see that your team keeps the data current throughout the project.

No magic exists in automation. A spreadsheet program will not make you an accountant. A word processor won't make you a writer. A requirement management tool won't miraculously make you a requirement genius. It certainly won't write or manage requirements for you.

Chapter 15
Death, Taxes, and Requirement Change
Managing Change

> Some years ago, I called an old acquaintance who had just assumed management of a troubled program. I told him that I would like to help him manage his requirements. He told me that he did not need any help. He was using the advice of a friend: "Just say 'no' to all proposed changes."
>
> This advice was not necessarily bad, but it was inappropriate for his specific project. The program had baselined poor requirements that could not be satisfied within budget or schedule, if at all. I have no idea what this program manager actually did, but the program has since been canceled.
>
> —Ivy Hooks

If we waited until we knew everything we needed to know to build something, we would never get started. Increasing investment in requirement definition greatly reduces change requests. A prebaseline effort to write requirements to drive the design to be tolerant of probable changes (Chapter 12) is crucial to preventing change requests. Even with a thorough requirement definition effort, however, something will always be missed or something external will change during development, such as the customer's needs or a regulation, requiring a corresponding modification in your product. Your requirement management process must allow but control postbaseline requirement change. We recommend a rigorous process.

Why Formal Change Control?

A rigorous, formal change approval process will enable you to maintain control of your resources and integrate approved changes into the product development flow. Many large development organizations already have a formal change proposal review and approval process. If you manage projects in such an organization, bear with us while we review the reasons for its existence.

A change approval process maintains your resource control. Postbaseline changes are trouble—the purpose of the baseline was to drive a stake in the ground that signaled the beginning of development and a large increase in the rate of spending. Before you "just say no" to a proposed change, however, you must understand the change and its impact. Some proposed changes are necessary for the product to succeed, whereas others are only nice to have. Among the necessary changes are those that "fix" a bad requirement; those that remove unnecessary requirements; those that add forgotten, but needed requirements; and those that alter existing good requirements to meet a new customer or market goal or objective. Almost all change proposals, if approved, will require some development rework, taxing limited resources. Your team cannot build a product to a moving target. You must limit the changes to those that are absolutely necessary.

A rigorous change proposal review process gives proposed changes visibility before implementation. It ensures that you will know about all change proposals, their justification, and their cost. It also enables you to veto the proposals that are unnecessary or impossible within existing resource allocation. It protects individuals on the development team from external change pressure.

A formal change approval process helps integrate changes into the development flow. Once a change is approved, you must quickly and fully integrate it into the product development flow. You must do this change implementation without derailing the entire development effort. A rigorous change proposal review process gives you and your team the data required for thorough project replanning and change implementation. These data include a complete assessment of the change impact and its cost.

How Do You Control Change?

Controlling postbaseline requirement change is a four-step process:

1. Documenting and evaluating the change justification.
2. Performing a thorough change impact assessment.
3. Making the decision to approve or disapprove the change.
4. Implementing the change if approved.

These steps must be repeated for each change proposed.

The first step in evaluating a prospective change is documenting and evaluating the reasons for the proposed change. The person proposing the change should provide this rationale, just as your original requirement writers provided their rationale (Chapter 8). Weigh the change rationale against the original requirement rationale.

The change process highlights the importance of capturing rationale along with requirements. If you don't clearly understand how a requirement came into being, it is very difficult to determine if a proposed change is suitable. This problem has two sides. On the one hand, you may make a change without considering some very important point. This "ignorance is bliss" change may be very expensive and potentially catastrophic.

On the other hand, great battles may be fought over a very minor change. The lack of information feeds natural fears of making a mistake, which could also be costly. At best, days spent finding the reasons for the original requirement are days your product development army is marching in the wrong direction.

> The Space Station requirements were written to interface with a Space Shuttle that had its remote manipulator arm on the starboard side. The actual Space Shuttle has the arm on its port side. Perhaps someone saw an early "artist's concept" with the arm on the starboard, or someone got a viewgraph reversed, or forgot which was the Shuttle's right side when they were looking out the back window—who knows? It took years to have the error corrected in the requirement specification.
>
> —Ivy Hooks

If the change survives the first test—good rationale exists for making the change and you understand what you are changing—you can proceed to the second step, a change impact assessment. If it is a necessary change, you need the assessment to effect the change. If it is a nice-to-have change, you need the impact assessment to perform a cost-benefit analysis of the change. A thorough and accurate change impact assessment is also a powerful weapon against political pressure.

> Historically, between full-scale development start and launch, spacecraft grow in mass 30–50 percent. Lunar Prospector had only 5 percent mass growth, due primarily to the unforeseen requirement to include a self-destruct system that range safety officers would use to destroy the spacecraft if the launch vehicle went out of control. "We didn't try to build a broad consensus. . . . We defined our objectives up front and we stuck to them!" said Dr. Alan Binder, the Lunar Prospector principal investigator. "Don't try to do everything! Don't bite off so much that you choke on it.
>
> "Give engineers time and money, and they will increase the mass of the spacecraft. Every time I'd come back from a trip out of town, I'd find that the spacecraft had grown 10 kilograms. I had to beat it back down.

"We had to buy the propellant tanks early—they were a long lead time item. And I sized them at 1400 meters/seconds delta-V. So any spacecraft mass growth would shorten the mission, reducing the amount of data. The profit—up to $4 million—was tied to the data quantity. That was a pretty good stick to beat the mass down with. To be fair to the engineers, the scientists cause problems, too. They are always trying to add an instrument."

One scientist wanted to add an instrument after spacecraft testing was done. He claimed that it would have zero impact on anything else and would merely replace ballast in a spacecraft boom. "There is no such thing as a zero-impact change," Dr. Binder stated with the conviction of experience.[1]

—Dr. Alan Binder,
Director, Lunar Research Institute
Tucson, AZ

Assessing requirement change impact begins with identifying related requirements, those that could also be affected or invalidated by the proposed change. The effort invested in traceability pays off here. Check all parent requirements to ensure that the requirement, as modified by the change proposal, will still comply with its parent requirements. If not, you cannot make the proposed change without a higher-level change being approved.

Next, look at all child requirements to assess the ripple from the proposed change. Automating requirement traceability (Chapter 14) makes this change assessment go quickly. It can also prevent errors from being introduced with changes, by identifying all affected requirements. Without traceability and rationale to guide your team in evaluating change, everyone must review every proposed change for potential impact in their area. This effort eats up precious development time. It also gets old fast, and people may start ignoring requests to review proposed changes or give them only superficial review. With so many pieces of paper crying "wolf," it becomes easy to miss the one with real teeth. Everyone's job generally becomes no one's job.

Change impact assessment will vary considerably, depending on where you are in the development cycle. If change is early or small, it may have little schedule and budget impact. If change is late or large, there will be considerable schedule and budget impact. If you are well into design, you must assess design impact as well as test and manufacturing plans and procedures. The change may also affect test equipment and manufacturing tooling on parallel development tracks. If your product is already in test, the change may invalidate the test results that you already have as well as requiring changes in test procedures and test equipment. Late in development, the change may affect parts on order as well as manufacturing tooling. All of these impacts must be incorporated into a revised schedule and budget, which in turn must be factored into the change decision.

The third step in the change process is deciding whether to make the change. You may determine early in the impact assessment that the change is not affordable or that its benefit cannot outweigh the impact. If so, you do not need a thorough assessment to disapprove the change. Similarly, if the change is essential, you must approve it, but you will still need a thorough change impact assessment to incorporate it and to ensure that nothing is missed. If the change decision is not obvious, you will need a thorough change assessment just to make the decision.

The final step in change management is implementing the change. You must ensure that the approved change is documented and disseminated to everyone that your change assessment shows should be involved, as soon as possible. Every day's delay in implementation adds to its cost. Back the change approval with the resources necessary to implement the change. Your change impact assessment is now your roadmap for implementation action. Implentation includes making changes throughout all affected documents, for all related requirements that must be changed. If the assessment is thorough, your change implementation should go smoothly. Even with thorough preparation, however, you and your team must be vigilant for unanticipated ripples from the change.

What Is the Manager's Role in Change Management?

You must have a rigorous change management process in place. Checks and balances must be implemented to ensure that necessary changes are made and that unnecessary changes are not. You must have information that covers all impacts of a change to prevent creating worse problems than the one the change is fixing. You must also allocate resources and see that your team has the data and tools necessary to assess the impact of proposed changes. Finally, you must ensure that team members affected by an approved requirement change know about the change immediately and have the resources to implement it.

The Apollo spacecraft had 28-volt electrical systems. When North American (prime contractor) awarded the contract for the oxygen tanks to Beech Aircraft, they specified that the tank's heaters, fans, and sensors—required to keep the oxygen at an optimum 340 degrees Fahrenheit below zero—run at this voltage. The Beech engineers selected components that would handle the maximum current the spacecraft electrical system could deliver at 28 volts. Unfortunately, that requirement was only valid while the spacecraft was flying. Prior to launch, it would spend weeks in tests on the launch pad, connected to external generators—which ran at 65 volts.

North American noticed this oversight during design and redirected Beech to redesign the tank electrical system for 65 volts. Beech engineers did the redesign to comply with the change request, but overlooked the thermostat switches on the heaters. These switches were supposed to open, turning off the heaters, when the temperature reached 80 degrees, to protect the tank from pressurizing to the point of exploding. No one foresaw a situation where the tanks would ever get or need to get hotter than 80 degrees, so these little safety thermostat switches didn't get much attention. North American and NASA reviewers also missed the error.

The change error did not cause a problem on the flights prior to Apollo 13 because the tank temperatures never got close to 80 degrees. It might never have caused a problem if it hadn't been for other changes in the tank design made after Apollo 13's tanks were completed. The tanks had been installed in the Apollo 10 spacecraft, but engineers decided to remove the service module containing these tanks from Apollo 10 and replace it with one containing upgraded tanks. Unfortunately, workers dropped the module 2 inches during its removal.

Inspectors found no damage to the tanks, so they were upgraded and installed in Apollo 13's service module. After the Apollo 13 final countdown rehearsal, however, oxygen tank 2 failed to empty. Engineers concluded that a tube in its drain system had been loosened when it was dropped. This was a frustrating and seemingly trivial problem—it was the last time the tanks would ever have to be drained. Since the drain wasn't needed during the flight, why risk removing the otherwise healthy and completely tested service module?

Someone cooked up a work-around that seemed quite ingenious: open the tank vent and use the tank's own internal heaters to warm up the liquid oxygen to a gaseous state and let it escape through the vent. The thermostat switches would cut the heaters off if the temperature got above 80 degrees. A technician would monitor the tank temperature to make sure that it stayed below 80 degrees.

The heaters were on for eight hours. During that time, the 65-volt overload on the 28-volt thermostat switch welded it shut when it tried to turn the heaters off at 80 degrees. Since the designers had never had a requirement to measure a temperature above the 80-degree safety threshold, they had designed the temperature sensor to measure up to 80 degrees, but no higher. So the technician monitoring the procedure saw a steady 80 degrees on the gauge while the temperature inside the tank actually climbed to 1000 degrees. This temperature severely degraded the Teflon insulation on the fan motor wires inside the tank.

Seventeen days later, in space, Apollo 13 crew member Jack Swigert switched on a fan inside the tank. A short circuit in the damaged wiring ignited the remains of the Teflon and caused the tank to explode, converting Apollo 13 from a mission to the moon to a desperate race to rescue Swigert, Lovell, and Haise.[2]

—Kristin Farry

A Balancing Act

Table 15-1 provides a sanity check on your requirement change management process. As project manager, it is up to you to find a balance between being too rigid—automatically rejecting all change just to make the development job easier—and trying to develop to a moving target. Capturing rationale and doing thorough, accurate change impact assessments is critical to making the right change decision and making the change happen. Time is not on your side: As soon as you know that something needs changing, get the change started. Remember that the cost of fixing an error goes up astronomically as development progresses (Figure 1-3).

Table 15-1. Change Management Sanity Check

Have you:
Established a change control process?
Developed standard forms for collecting requirement changes that include justification?
Created a set of procedures that ensure thorough impact assessments?
Implemented a method to communicate potential changes to all who are impacted?
Implemented a method to communicate approved changes quickly to the people who need to know?
Implemented a procedure to ensure all documents are updated when changes are approved?

Chapter 16
Cap'n, Are We There Yet?
Measuring Requirement Quality

My father started farming late—it was his third career—and he figured that he had a lot to do to catch up with his new neighbors, all of whom had farmed all their lives. He read books on farming, visited other farms, took soil samples, wrote letters to university experts, and read more books. He began to notice that the other farmers around weren't doing things like the books and experts suggested. He worried that there might be factors that the experts were missing. He decided to test some of his ideas on our veterinarian instead, who knew everyone and their farming practices.

"If I throw the dirt uphill like so," Dad motioned with his hands, "in that hilly area above the creek, I think it'll hold the water better and reduce the run-off, don't you?" he asked one day when Doctor Matt came out to doctor calves.

"Uh-huh," Doctor Matt grunted as he grabbed the next calf's tail.

"But do you think I should try it?" Dad pressed him for an opinion.

"Why not?" Doctor Matt grunted again.

"Well, no one else around here plows that way," Dad informed him.

"What difference does that make?"

"Some of these fellows have forty years' experience farming!" Dad protested.

> The vet straightened up and looked at him. "Some of these fellows have forty years' experience farming," he said, punctuating in the air with the syringe. "And some of them have one year's experience, forty times."
>
> —Kristin Farry

Measurement is the foundation of improvement. It's unfortunate that many managers believe that measuring requirement quality is complex and costly. They assume that they do not have room in their project budgets for it. Other managers assume that they can't assess requirement quality until the project is finished. We believe that a manager can and should assess requirement quality throughout a project. Our approach to achieving "better, cheaper, faster" is to invest a little more up front, in requirement definition, to prevent rework. Quality measurement can show you where to put scarce project budget dollars to get the most from them.

The first step in requirement quality measurement occurs during the baselining process (Chapter 12). You measure the quality of the requirements before baselining to determine if your team should proceed to product development. Beyond baselining, we recommend requirement quality measurement both within a given project and across projects. In this chapter, we offer quick and simple ways to measure requirement quality.

Why Measure Requirement Quality?

Measuring requirement quality reveals opportunities for long-term improvements in requirement definition, shows you where to invest for improvements, and helps you develop your team.

Quality measurement reveals opportunities for improvement. If requirement quality isn't measured, there will be no improvement in requirements. Every project will be a rerun of the last. Did your last project have rework, crisis in testing, customer complaints? A review of that project's requirements may now show you how to avoid some of those same headaches on your current project.

Quality measurement shows you where to invest to realize improvements. If you don't know where the problems are, you can't fix them. The consequences of requirement errors usually don't become apparent until late in the development process. It's easy to confuse them with design errors or testing problems. Given our cultural predisposition toward firefighting, developers will focus on the design or test phase fires caused by these errors rather than the errors themselves. Because the spending rate is higher in these latter phases, managers will also focus on putting out fires, as opposed to preventing them. The latest CAD tools or the best test engineers, however, can at most trim the cost of requirement errors, not fix them. You need to know if your problems stem from bad requirements or from something else. It is not enough to simply allocate 10 percent of the project's resources to requirement definition to realize a 50 percent savings in implementation and test. You must invest the 10 percent where it will have the greatest impact.

Requirement quality measurement helps you develop your team. As you learn more about where your errors are, you can invest wisely in training for your people. For example, numerous ambiguous requirements suggest that they need training in writing requirements. Lots of omitted requirements signal a need for training in the domain where the omissions occurred. Alternatively, instead of domain training for people you already have, perhaps you should recruit someone with field experience on similar products.

Using Common Data for Quality Measurement

Two levels or perspectives of quality measurement should be considered: within a particular project and across projects. On a given project, certain requirement statistics can tell you whether you are converging on a good set of requirements. Baseline review redlines can show which team members are doing the best requirement work, so you can recognize their contribution. Within and across ongoing projects, discrepancy reports (DRs) and change requests (CRs) can be pointers to requirement definition process problems.

Requirement Statistics

One simple check is a requirement count. If you are building a system out of primarily commercial off-the-shelf components, and you have more than a thousand requirements at the system level, something is wrong! Perhaps your development effort is not focused enough, or you may be going too deep in your specification process. You may have gone beyond requirements and into design. Over a thousand requirements at any one level on any project should be cause for concern. Having only three or four requirements may also be a problem, unless the product is very simple—even a common bolt is built to more than four requirements! Don't try to read anything into, say, the difference between 500 and 550 requirements, however. Outside of the extremes, absolute numbers are seldom meaningful—no one has done enough research. If you build many similar products, absolute numbers, such as the total number of requirements, may become meaningful over time. In general, a better measure of your requirement process is the number of requirements for a given product at the end of each development stage. If you see significant increases in the requirement count after baselining, for example, you need to pay more attention to operational concepts and communication between stakeholders, especially those in support functions, such as test and maintenance.

Wherever possible, we recommend that you look at requirement statistics primarily as percentages of a total rather than absolute numbers. It is particularly useful to look at these percentages as a function of the development stage in which the discrepancies are discovered. This view (Figure 16-1) will enable you to check for convergence. For example, the percentage of your requirements supported by good rationale is a better indicator of requirement quality than absolute requirement count.

It's easy for people to fall into a "bean counter mindset" and begin playing games to increase numbers. If people figure out that they are scored on traceability between requirements, for example, they will link everything to everything, even if the link is meaningless. The result will be just as useless as no traceability at all.

Figure 16-1. Discrepancy Analysis

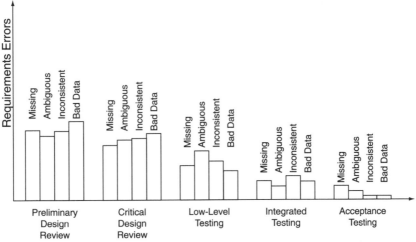

Baseline Review Redlines

Your requirement writers have submitted requirements as "ready for baselining." Thus, redlines from each stage of the pre-baseline reviews (Chapter 12) are a measure of their understanding of what is a good requirement. Review redlines will always exist, but should you find that 50 percent or more of the requirements submitted have to be changed before baselining, you have a serious problem. The nature of the problem depends on where (in the baselining reviews) redlines occur. Large numbers of editorial step-format redlines suggest that your team members need a format review or work on their writing skills. Excessive goodness review corrections may suggest that your writers are having trouble understanding what is a true requirement, or it may show that your customer is unwilling to commit. Content review problems may point toward weak operational concepts or perhaps inadequate verification assessment.

Review redlines can give you an idea of who are your best requirement writers, although an assessment of individual performance has its pitfalls. As you try to evaluate individual requirement writers, keep in mind that only the initial editorial review grades the original writers alone. Redlines coming out of the goodness review are against both the original writers and the editor, whereas content review redlines grade writers, editors, and goodness reviewers. Look at percentages, not absolute counts, when evaluating an individual's contributions. A large number of redlines against a person's contribution may indicate that she wrote the most requirements, not necessarily that she is a poor requirement writer. She may have valuable insight into requirements that are often missed by others, and you don't want to punish that when a little help on writing skills might make her your best requirement definition person.

Discrepancy Analysis

DRs are reports of problems—generally mismatches in expectations (requirements) and performance. Most people associate them with testing, but they can come from anyone noticing a problem at any time, including design reviews and analysis. Analyzing a DR can give you important information about requirements. Were requirements (wrong or misunderstood) the reason for the problem? Was it a bad assumption? What could have been done to identify the problem earlier? You can track DRs throughout the product life cycle. Simply counting them can be misleading, however, because all DRs are not created equal. You may have many DRs addressing one particular problem, generated by different parts of your development organization. If the cause of a DR is not addressed and fixed right away, several DRs, spread over time, may be traced to the first DR's cause. Not all organizations consolidate related DRs into one final DR, so you might have to do this before your analysis.

After you consolidate the DRs, group them by category. Simple categories that we find useful for analysis include:

1. Did not comply with requirement
2. Requirement problem
   a. Incorrect data
   b. Misunderstood requirement

      c. Ambiguous requirement
      d. Missed requirement
  3. Did not follow standards

The key to meaningful DR analysis is to separate problems in meeting a requirement from requirement problems. Pay attention to the timing of the DRs. *When* the discrepancy is revealed can tell you a lot about the nature of your requirement errors. Plot DRs versus milestones or project phases (Figure 16-1). Early DRs from developers and design reviews are often caused by ambiguity in the requirements or misunderstanding of the problem that the product is to solve. Designers often flag conflicting, duplicate, or inconsistent requirements. A test engineer will write a DR when the product fails to meet a requirement. If the requirement is a good requirement, the DR indicates a design problem rather than a requirement problem. A test engineer's DR may also reveal ambiguity where the test engineer read the requirement differently from the design engineer. Why are your people getting confused? Is it terminology or format? Could a change in the presentation, say, using a visual aid instead of text alone, have resolved the ambiguity?

In integrated testing of systems, DRs in testing are often rooted in interface requirement problems. DRs generated in acceptance testing may reveal problems communicating with your customers, because people often use DRs to say they don't like the product, not just to report discrepancies between the product's performance and the requirements. If you see these "fails to meet expectations" DRs, you didn't capture the customer's expectations in the beginning or didn't keep the customer "on board" with you throughout development.

The goal of DR analysis is to understand how to fix anything in the requirement process that is causing rework. Fixing everything can be overwhelming. Look for patterns. First fix the ones that cause the most problems, cost the most, and occur the most often. Implement changes in your requirement definition process to eliminate repeating mistakes. For example, if you don't see a decrease in the number of DRs flagging ambiguous requirements as the product development progresses, you might have a problem with follow-up on DRs.

Discrepancy analysis should be linked to the change process. In a disciplined organization, DR's due to requirement problems lead to a CR to fix the requirements. When a DR in design reveals an ambiguous requirement, don't just say, "Oh, now we know what that requirement means," and go on building. Change the requirement! Otherwise, the confusion will be repeated in testing. DRs should be accompanied by a commitment to follow through and change the requirements so they will be correct or cannot be misinterpreted. Without follow-through, your people will lose faith in the DR process and spend less effort on writing DRs.

Change Analysis

You can learn a lot from reading CRs. In a qualitative analysis, ask, "Was an incorrect, ambiguous, or missing requirement the change driver? What could have been done to identify the problem earlier?"

Certain statistics derived from CRs can tell you how good your requirement baseline was. These statistics include the percentages of requirements changed, added, or deleted after the baseline. Normally, the baseline marks the beginning of formal change control, so every requirement change after the baseline should be documented with a CR. Be careful in counting CRs: As with DRs, not all CRs should be counted equally. The value of these numbers depends on your organization's definition of a change. Some organizations use CRs for everything from a requirement change to a minor procedural or schedule change. Before you start counting CRs, sort them into at least three groups:

1. CRs that affect design, requiring rework (usually involving a significant requirement change, addition, or deletion)
2. Other CRs that involve other requirement changes (usually involving clarifying a requirement's wording, but not changing it, or a requirement deletion)
3. All other CRs

The first group is your expensive requirement errors. Study these changes the most. If you can quantify the cost of the development rework due to these requirement problems, you will be well on your way to understanding how much more you have to invest in requirement definition on the next product.

Follow-through on change analysis is also important. Like DR analysis, CR analysis should be accompanied by a commitment to change the requirement definition process. People will get tired of giving you data if they don't see action resulting. They will invest less and less time in producing that data. Eventually, the data will be meaningless.

In summary, you need to:

• Determine where improvement would give the biggest payoff
• Determine if problems in different areas have a common or unique source
• Show how much improvement is occurring over time

Pick a past program, and plot your DRs by category over time or product development cycle. If your analysis indicates that adding rationale could have prevented the problems you encountered, add capturing requirement rationale (Chapter 8) to your process. Plot the DRs from the next project (in which you implement rationale capture), and compare the trends in DRs. Compare projects in the context of "big picture" customer satisfaction as well as "little picture" DR statistics. Although it is wonderful to reduce the number of DRs and this may help you deliver your product on time and within budget, you have only succeeded if your customer is happy with the product. A good project manager takes responsibility for the requirements' content as well as for meeting them. Simply declaring victory short of your objectives does not make it a victory. Meeting cost without meeting objectives is just as bad as blowing cost in meeting objectives!

The Fifth Amendment Syndrome

Many managers want to measure quality and progress, but they find their people won't cooperate by providing the necessary data. The data are evidence of mistakes, and they don't want to be punished for these mistakes, particularly if they feel that their mistakes are because of a faulty process that traps them into making the mistakes. You must create an environment where people can bring forward data documenting mistakes without fear of punishment. Use that data to find recurring problems with the process, implement fixes, and look for improvement. If the first fix doesn't work, try another. Reserve your wrath for reluctance to cooperate on the fixes. Shooting the messenger will leave you without any messages of opportunities for improvement. Protect your messengers from the wrath of outsiders by protecting the data and their privacy.

Your people may also resist your data collection efforts because they are already overloaded with doing their product development job. They may not be able to see how the data collection is going to help them. In fact, they may see evidence that it will hurt them—taking time away from their product development assignments to collect data about the process may put them behind their peers in job performance evaluations. You, as manager, must make it clear that the data collection and analysis will help your team, and you must make allowances for the time spent on it in their schedules. Implement change based on the results of the measurement effort, and reward its participants.

What Is the Manager's Role in Measuring Requirement Quality?

Only managers can change the process to provide the data needed to track requirement quality. Managers must commit the resources to evaluate the data. Managers are responsible for implementing reward systems to encourage improved quality. A project manager has quality assessment responsibility during the baselining decision, which is oriented toward an individual project's success. A line manager or people manager must also assess quality with an eye toward improving requirement definition on all of the organization's products.

You must look at the data already available and ask for

more or different data, if necessary. You must motivate your people to give you useful and accurate data by ensuring that people are rewarded, never punished, for bringing forward data showing a problem. You must spot trends and pointers toward the highest payoff process improvements. Finally, only a manager, you, can make the decision to change the process and enforce its implementation.

Measurement Is the Foundation of Improvement

Start measuring requirement quality today (Table 16-1). Otherwise, you will never know if you are converging on the quality requirements that will lead you to better products built faster and cheaper. You don't need a fancy system. You are better off choosing a simple measure and following through to improvements than a complex, resource-hogging measure that you can't convert into process improvements with the resources you have available.

Table 16-1. Measuring Requirement Quality Sanity Check

Do you have a requirement quality measurement procedure:
    For individual projects?
    Across projects?
Do you have a discrepancy (or problem) reporting (DR) procedure for all phases?
Do you have a method for assessing the relationship between DRs and requirements?
Do you have a change request (CR) tracking procedure?
Do you have a method for assessing the relationship between CRs and requirements? Can you measure improvements?

Chapter 17

It Can Happen on Your Watch

Making Changes in an Organization's Requirement Definition Process

> My 10-year old granddaughter asked what I did when I worked. I tried to give her a less-than-3-minute statement of the problem that I try to help people solve:
>
> "When someone wants a new product, they try to define what they want so that they can buy it or have someone make it for them. If they don't describe what they want in terms that the other person understands, or if they omit something that they need, they don't get what they want. Often, they have to start all over after having spent a lot of money and time," I explained.
>
> "Oh, I've got it. It's like playing video games," Jackie responded. "You get to the last level and then get killed and have to go back to the first level."
>
> —Ivy Hooks

Quality products begin long before manufacture. They begin before design—with quality requirements.

Nothing can change without a management commitment.

Change starts from the top. You can send your people to classes to learn to write good requirements, but people feel powerless to implement this new way of doing business without visible management commitments and understanding. A manager's attitude about requirement definition is echoed all the way to the bottom of the project pyramid. You face a host of technical and cultural challenges in shifting the product development investment toward requirement definition.

Is it just your imagination, or is product development getting harder?

We believe that it is harder than it used to be to get a quality product out the door, and the problems begin with increasing difficulties in getting a quality set of requirements together. Much of the new difficulty stems from the technology that was supposed to save us.

Consider, for example, the word processor. Before this amazing "labor-saver," someone had to type the entire document. You couldn't cut and paste almost effortlessly from other documents or old versions of the same document. Because retyping was so hard, you invested more thought in each version. In fact, you may have just done it right the first time! Verbosity was also a problem—if your document was too big, no one would type it. The electronic thesaurus hasn't helped communications in general and requirement clarity in particular, because it's so easy for people to find fancy alternatives to plain-Jane but well-understood words.

The option of putting a computer into nearly every product hasn't helped. In fact, the computer industry has ratcheted people's expectations up to impossible levels. A printed piece of paper doesn't impress anyone now. You have to have cute, animated graphics on a Web page. A product has to have more flexibility. In products where hardware has traditionally been the order of the day, designers see opportunities to lift traditional constraints imposed by embedding a computer. The precomputer design placed a premium on ease of control or inherent simplicity of operation, but now designers assume that the "black box" can fix anything, compensating for all sorts of hardware flaws. We now have airplanes, for example, that human beings cannot fly without the aid of a computer.

The possibilities of computers have broken the molds in many fields. For a long time, people have refined or modified existing products to make new products. Now, we demand major leaps and assume that the computer makes these leaps feasible. A gap is growing between what we want and our understanding of its real cost. The high ratio of personnel turn-over to development cycle length—now common in our development staffs—makes a lack of recorded rationale a problem when a product is ready for testing or a refinement is needed.

—Kristin Farry and Ivy Hooks

The Process

In this book, we have presented nine steps to good requirements. Together, these nine steps address all five groups of requirement errors noted in Chapter 1 (Figure 1-1). Some steps are particularly effective at reducing certain types of errors (Table 17-1). For example, properly written requirements have no ambiguities. Detailed operational concepts for all portions of the life cycle, early verification assessment, and a rigorous baseline involving all stakeholders will prevent requirement omissions. Capturing rationale for each requirement and early interface evaluation are your best defenses against incorrect facts. Formatting your requirements in a form well-understood by your team will prevent them from losing a requirement during implementation. If you have an especially high count of one type of requirement error in your projects, phase-in the appropriate process steps immediately.

We emphasize once again that these steps do not always form a tidy little waterfall in which the output of each step flows neatly to the next; rather, this is often an iterative process. You may get to verification assessment and realize that your scope is too big, or some requirement rationale may reveal a bad assumption that ripples back to scope. Furthermore, you will repeat these steps for each level of a complex system (i.e., system level, subsystem level, and major component level).

Table 17-1. Nine Steps to Eliminating Requirement Errors

Requirement Definition Step		Chapter	Incorrect Facts	Omissions	Inconsistencies	Ambiguities	Misplacement
				Requirement Errors Prevented			
1	Scope product	4	X	X	X		
2	Develop operational concepts	5	X	X	X		
3	Identify interfaces	6	X	X	X		
4	Write requirements	7				X	
5	Capture rationale	8	X			X	
6	Level requirements	9	X	X	X		X
7	Assess verification	10		X		X	
8	Format requirements	11		X			X
9	Baseline requirements	12	X	X	X	X	X

The common thread throughout this process is effective communications. Indeed, requirements are communication of a need to the developers—no more, no less. Although we have admonished you to "put it in writing" throughout this book, and written requirements are the standard, everything in this process lends itself to other means of communication, such as video, multimedia presentations, mockups, simulations, and rapid prototypes. We encourage you to consider using these other media, both to enliven your requirement definition process for your team and to bridge language gaps. Remember that a language gap exists between domain experts and lay people as well as between people of different nationalities.

Beyond the requirement definition stage of your project, you must manage your product's requirements throughout the development cycle. Hence, we have also covered prioritizing requirements to give yourself options in case of schedule or budget problems (Chapter 13), automating requirement management to ensure currency and complete coverage (Chapter 14), and controlling changes to control your budget and schedule (Chapter 15).

Requirement management is key to controlling your product development risk. The major risk areas in product development are often cited as requirements, schedule, budget, personnel, and technical. The prime requirement risk is the risk of building an inadequate or dangerous product. The secondary risk is requirement errors that will wreck your schedule and budget, or lead you to attempt a solution with inappropriate technical tools. The added pressure to meet schedules that are mismatched with requirements increases personnel risks. Thus, poor requirements can add risk in all areas. Of course, a chance always exists that you can underestimate the resources or the technology required to meet a well-defined set of requirements, or that you can lose key people. Starting with a great set of requirements, complete with rationale, however, leaves you margin and memory to handle the risks unrelated to requirements.

The Culture

Now you have a proven, well-documented requirement definition process. Educating your team on it and making it your policy will address the five corporate myths we described in Chapter 2. This is a good start, but it will take more than passing around a summary of the process to realize "faster, better, cheaper" product development. Training for you and your team must go beyond discussion of the process itself. Your team needs education in the nuts and bolts of requirement writing. As you schedule your people for requirement training, consider it an opportunity to show your commitment to improved requirements by attending the courses with them. Yes, you are busy, but how much of your busyness is crises brought on by bad requirements? Make it an investment in future sanity.

Some of your team will also need training in basic communications skills. You know who they are. Sign them up for remedial writing courses. No matter how good they are technically, their future and their immediate usefulness to you in requirement definition hinges on communications skills.

You have to tackle broader cultural issues head-on to implement this process and reap the rewards. Recall from Chapter 2 that the four American cultural factors most problematic during requirement definition are impatience (to start design), easy acceptance of mistakes, a high regard for improvisation, and a tendency to make assumptions. The American cultural bias toward action and low regard for planning makes us respond to a request for "faster" with less upfront planning and less requirement definition. We assume that we have to dive into development faster, when in fact a compressed schedule might require more upfront planning than a longer, more relaxed schedule would. Being positive and committed to good requirements is important, but will not, alone, overcome the impatience to start designing and building the product.

You must deal with this impatience in American culture by making requirement definition more fun and substantive. Engage your team in developing and playing out operational concepts. Your developers probably define "fun" as problem solving. Promote verification assessment as a major challenge deserving of their best problem-solving effort. Mockups, simulations, or rapid prototypes can be cost-effective communications or risk-reduction tools. Have your team build them wherever appropriate in your requirement effort. This process will make requirement definition feel more like product development, and your product developers would rather be doing product development than anything else!

The usual American practice is to push through all the "oopses" stemming from our lack of good requirement definition with frantic effort. We believe that the mistakes and the burnout-inducing workload are inevitable. Question this assumption! Question it with your team, as a group. Schedule postmortem time, even after success. Too often, if a product was ultimately successful, we don't revisit the mistakes that, but for some team member's ingenuity and sacrifice, might have killed it prematurely. For example, if you have a DR during testing, and it can be traced to a requirement error, discuss the requirement error in addition to rewarding the "fixer" who salvaged the project with a clever eleventh-hour workaround. Remember the American cultural fascination with "fixers." Address the imbalance proactively: Every time you pass out kudos to a firefighter, cite a fire-preventor for avoiding a problem. During the requirement definition, keep notes on who thought up the not-so-obvious requirements. Glance back at the requirement rationale to remind yourself of the problem that these obscure requirements were preventing, and reward their author in front of others on your team. If you have the opportunity, mention these authors to higher level managers: These people should become tomorrow's project managers. Until we start rewarding people for doing it right the first time, people will be fixers. You, the manager, can break this cycle. Give people enough time and other resources to do it right the first time, and then begin rewarding quality requirement work.

You must also create an environment where people will ask the question that they assume is "dumb." Simply put, there are no dumb questions with respect to requirements. Strive to replace assumptions with questions. Start by asking these questions yourself. Work also on making people comfortable and committed to telling you about a looming problem. One survey[1] showed that 30 percent of all employees don't speak up when something is wrong and needs fixing. The main reason most people cite for not speaking up about a problem is a perception that no one cares or nothing will be done about it. Other people just don't want to risk embarrassment or causing trouble for somebody else. Still other people believe that it's not their job. You must convey an attitude of willingness to listen and develop a reputation for acting on requirement problems immediately. Don't dwell on who caused the problem publicly—this will discourage people from bringing up future problems. Focus on understanding and fixing the problem, before it causes a schedule train wreck. This focus will flow naturally from simply taking ownership of the requirements. When your team sees that you have made quality requirements your job, they will make quality requirements their job.

Your subordinates notice what you notice. They listen to their managers for clues on what will get them promoted! The minute a manager says, "This is a bad requirement. It can be read four different ways," people will begin to pay attention to requirements.

You must turn the cultural tide toward good requirement definition. You must make your team gain (both personally and as a group) from investing in requirement definition. Does a category called requirement definition performance appear on your personnel evaluations? Put it in! Are you promoting your requirement writers before you know whether they have done a good job on requirement writing? On many projects, the requirement writers aren't around to see their mistakes show up in test or operations. Seeing even a single project from beginning to end can alert a requirement writer to communications pitfalls or omissions.

We've summarized the cultural issues and actions for you in Table 17-2 (see page 255).

The walls at NASA's Johnson Space Center are plastered with safety posters admonishing passers-by with slogans such as "If it's not safe, say so!" Yet deadlines can shout louder. The top manager at a company holding a contract to assist with Space Shuttle launches lost his perspective and his temper one day when a junior engineer was attempting to explain his safety concerns.

"I don't have time to listen to this crap," he said angrily, dismissing the engineer. Some minutes after the engineer left, however, he realized the potential impact of his mistake. In hours, the grapevine would have everyone in the company talking about his lack of concern for the safety of the people aboard the Space Shuttle. He had made himself into a monster with nine lousy words. There was only one thing that he could do to have a chance to turn it around. Fortunately, he had the commitment and courage to do it. He called an "all-hands" meeting and apologized to the engineer in front of everyone in the company.

—Kristin Farry

The Pitfalls

Most product developers (especially those in the United States, because of American cultural biases) don't spend enough time on requirement definition. Occasions occur, however, when the opposite is true. Don't confuse how much you spend before that final requirement review with good requirements. Yes, it is possible to spend too much time and effort on requirement definition, or, at least, on things that are hard for the casual observer to distinguish from requirement definition, which is why we advocate measuring requirement quality.

What can bog your project down during requirement definition? Systems engineering people tend to be process oriented. They may focus so much on the process that they forget the product. Other people are reluctant to commit to building something because it's easier to judge a prototype than a document. They lack the confidence to move forward into development. As more and more of our product developers start their careers well-grounded in theory but without "hands on" practical education, more and more projects get bogged down in "viewgraph engineering."

People can simply lose their way on large or lengthy projects. Organizations that are floundering are doing so because they have lost sight of their objectives. Even people not ordinarily fascinated by processes at the expense of producing a product

Table 17-2. Countering Cultural Problems in Requirement Definition

Cultural Factor	Counter Action
U.S. Culture	
Impatience with time	• Involve your team in operational concepts development • Have them develop simulations, mock-ups, and rapid prototypes to validate high-risk requirements
Acceptance of mistakes	• Document and analyze mistakes to determine if requirements errors contributed • Discuss mistakes with your team constructively, emphasizing prevention • Reward those not making requirement mistakes
The urge to improvise	• Reward fire-preventors instead of firefighters • Turn planning into an improvisation exercise by asking your team to anticipate problems and solutions in operational concepts
Bias toward assumptions	• Question assumptions • Insist on quality requirement rationale • Reward those pushing all the way to the facts

can get bogged down in short-term action items. You must write the objectives and post them everywhere to remind you and your team that you are ultimately building a product, not a pile of paper. These objectives, like the requirements, must be specific. "Do good!" is simply not enough guidance.

Finally, politics always exist. Our requirement process can help you prevent the "oops, I'm sorry" kind of requirement problems. We can't guarantee that this process will keep you from

Table 17-2. Countering Cultural Problems in Requirement Definition (*continued*)

Cultural Factor	Counter Action
Corporate Culture	
Lack of knowledge of the project's big picture	• Document and circulate project scope and objectives
Lack of knowledge about writing requirements	• Arrange training classes for your team • Attend these training classes yourself to underscore their importance
Poor or nonexistent requirement management process	• Implement a proven, standard requirement management process • Use the process yourself • Enforce the process discipline
Lack of understanding the requirement management process	• Document the process and circulate the documentation • Educate your team on the process
Belief that nothing can be done about bad requirements	• Reject bad requirements • Make requirement definition performance part of your personnel evaluations • Reward good requirement writers • Assist your customer in defining good requirements

falling victim to maliciousness or dishonesty. People can delay a project's development start by refusing to agree to a set of requirements or running you in circles with their inputs during reviews. We have seen this happen when other managers believed that an automation project's success would result in staffing and budget cuts in their organizations. Sometimes, people are reluctant to reveal everything about their work to a requirement analyst for fear of losing their own jobs to the product. In other cases, people perceive that approval of a project or product will in-

Table 17-2. Countering Cultural Problems in Requirement Definition (*continued*)

Cultural Factor	Counter Action
Individual Factors	
Johnny doesn't know what to do	• Give training in requirement definition • Give remedial writing and other communications skills training • Document, circulate, and discuss intermediate requirement definition products (needs, scope, operational concepts, etc.) as a team
Johnny doesn't understand why	• Keep requirement writers involved with the entire life cycle of at least one product to see the impact of their work • Give requirement writers the help and information that they request promptly
Johnny would rather be doing something else	• Emphasize the importance of requirements in design of a quality product • Make requirement definition feel "real" with operational concepts development, customer interaction, mockups, and prototypes • Give requirement writers adequate time for the job • Emphasize that the review process can't fix everything
Johnny sees no reward	• Measure requirement quality • Reward good requirement definition effort • Ensure that reviewers understand the difference between good and bad requirements

crease another department's budgets at the expense of their own department, or prevent approval of a pet project of their own.

Some organizations or people might profit from a lot of change traffic on your project. If you are a customer writing requirements for a contractor to develop and deliver a product to you, be especially alert to the fact that an unscrupulous contractor might view post-award change traffic as profitable. Unambiguous requirements will reduce change traffic in development; if you find someone resisting you in reducing ambiguity, consider whether they would benefit from change traffic.

We can only caution you to be alert for these conflicts of interest when you encounter difficulties in converging on a stable set of requirements. There are really no technical problems, only people problems. Get enough people committed to solving a particular technical problem, and it is only a matter of time before it will be solved. Getting the people to commit is the hard part!

Your best protection from these problems is a commitment to quality requirements, which is not the same thing as a commitment to expend effort on the requirement definition process.

> The Ford Motor Company invested more in market and customer research for the Edsel than they had for any other car they had produced up to that time. But, it was a legendary flop.
>
> What went wrong? They spent a long time developing the car after their marketing research, and apparently didn't stay in touch with their customer base while they were developing it. Customer preferences changed during the development time. The biggest problem was a change in the economy, accompanied by a big rise in gasoline prices. The Edsel was a huge, expensive gas-guzzler. People were asking for smaller, more economical cars by the time the Edsel entered the marketplace.[2]
>
> —Bob Collings, D.B.A.
> Chairman of the Board of Trustees
> Daniel Webster College
> Nashua, NH

The Price

Good requirements can make development go faster and cheaper by preventing rework and make the customer think the product is better simply by making it a closer match to what they need. Unfortunately, the payoff for the effort in requirement definition is not obvious and few organizations have quantified it. You will have to educate people above you as well as below you to make these changes and find the right level of requirement investment. Throughout this book, we've built our summaries and figures to provide you with material for this purpose. We've constructed the "sanity checks" to help you stay on course in a hectic project management environment.

There is no magic in good requirement engineering. No be-all–end-all requirement engineering tools or analysis models exist. Nor is there any substitute for hard work and discipline. You, the manager, must set the pace by taking personal responsibility for the requirements. No one can review or analyze "good" into a requirement. You must read your requirements and understand them every step of the way, throughout the entire product life cycle.

Your attitude will become your team's attitude.

Endnotes

Introduction

1. T. H. Davenport, *Information Ecology* (New York: Oxford University Press, 1997), p. 6.

2. S. Branch, "P&G system is causing flawed data," *The Wall Street Journal*, 11/22/99. N. E. Boudette, "Europe's SAP scrambles to stem big glitches—Software giant to tighten its watch after snafus at Whirlpool, Hershey," *The Wall Street Journal*, 11/04/99.

Chapter 1

1. R. Dion, "Process improvement and the corporate balance sheet," *IEEE Transactions on Software Engineering*, vol. 10, July 1993, pp. 283–285.

2. D. Leffingwell, "Calculating the return on investment from more effective requirements management," *American Programmer*, Cutter Information Corp., Arlington, MA, April 1997, pp. 19–24.

3. R. Spinrad, "Systems Architecture," speech at University of Southern California, November 21, 1988.

4. M. Sue White, "Requirements: A quick and inexpensive way to improve testing," *Test Techniques Newsletter*, Software Research, Inc., San Francisco, CA, December 1994, pp. 5–6.

5. B. W. Boehm, et al., "Some experience with automated aids to the design of large-scale reliable software," *IEEE Transactions on Software Engineering*, vol. 1, issue 1, March 1975, pp. 125–133. P. Tavolato and K. Vincena, "A prototyping methodology and its tool," in *Approaches to Prototyping*, R. Budde, et al., editors. Berlin: Springer-Verlag, 1984, pp. 434–445.

6. V. Basili and D. Weiss, "Evaluation of a software requirements document by analysis of change data," Presented at Fifth International Conference on Software Engineering, Washington, D.C.: IEEE Computer Society Press, 1981, pp. 314–323.

7. G.L. Dillingham, "Perspectives on FAA's Effort to Develop New

Technology," United States General Accounting Office, GAO/T-RCED-95-193, May 16, 1995.

8. T. S. Perry, "In search of the future of air traffic control," *IEEE Spectrum*, vol. 34, no. 8, August 1997, pp.18–35. Appendix II, "FAA budget: Issues related to the fiscal year 1996 request," Testimony before the Subcommittee on Transportation and Related Agencies, Committee on Appropriations, House of Representatives, United States General Accounting Office.

9. G. L. Dillingham, *op. cit.*

10. "Advanced automation system: Implications of problems and recent changes," Testimony before the Subcommittee on Public Works and Transportation, House of Representatives, April 13, 1994.

11. A. Hall, "Using formal methods to develop an ATC information system," *IEEE Transactions on Software Engineering*, vol. 13, March 1996, pp 66–76.

12. B. W. Boehm, *Software Engineering Economics* (Englewood Cliffs, NJ: Prentice-Hall), 1981.

13. A. Hall, *op. cit.*

14. A. Davis, *Software Requirements: Analysis and Specification* (Englewood Cliffs, NJ: Prentice-Hall, 1990), p. 20.

15. D. Leffingwell, *op. cit.*

16. W. Gruehl, NASA Comptroller's Office, 1990.

17. *Fast Track Study*, NASA APM-23, Strategic Resources, Inc., Falls Church, VA, November 1996, p. iii.

18. A. Davis, *op. cit.*

19. Interview of Dr. Alan Binder by author Farry, July 7, 1998. Some participants in this effort place its pre-NASA level as high as 10 engineer-years. "Missions to the Moon, Sun, Venus, and a comet picked for discovery," NASA Press Release 95-19, February 28, 1995.

20. Robert and Jean McMath, http://www.showlearn.com.

21. B. Laurence, "Requirements Happens," *American Programmer,* Cutter Information Corporation, Arlington, Massachusetts, April 1997, pp. 6–7.

22. M. A. Dornheim, "'Service ready' goal demands more tests," *Aviation Week and Space Technology*, April 11, 1994, pp. 43–44.

23. K. Sabbagh, *21st-Century Jet: The Making and Marketing of the Boeing 777* (New York: Scribner, 1996), p. 90.

24. R. G. O'Lone, "Service readiness is key objective in Boeing 767-X development," *Aviation Week and Space Technology*, August 20, 1990, pp. 95–97.

25. K. Sabbagh, *21st-Century Jet: The Making and Marketing of the Boeing 777* (New York: Scribner, 1996), pp. 47–48.

26. "Working together: Celebrating the Boeing 777's first flight," *Aviation Week and Space Technology*, June 27, 1994, p. S3.

27. K. Sabbagh, *op. cit.*

28. "Boeing airplanes cost less to operate," http://www.boe ing.com.

Chapter 2

1. J. Hammond and J. Morrison, *The Stuff Americans Are Made Of* (New York: Macmillan, 1996), p. 5–6.

2. *Ibid.*, p. 184, 202–203.

3. S. Traweek, *Beamtimes and Lifetimes: The World of High Energy Physicists* (Cambridge, MA: Harvard University Press, 1988), p. 86.

4. J. Hammond and J. Morrison, *The Stuff Americans Are Made Of* (New York: Macmillan, 1996), p. 207.

5. B. S. Blanchard and W. J. Fabrycky, *Systems Engineering and Analysis*, 3rd ed. (Englewood Cliffs, N J: Prentice-Hall, 1998), p. 57–61. L. Cohen, *Quality Function Deployment: How to Make QFD Work for You* (Reading, MA: Addison-Wesley, 1995).

Chapter 3

1. "Understand customer needs and expectations," System Engineering CMM (SE-CMM), Process Area (PA) 06.

2. M. C. Paulk, B. Curtis, M. B. Chrissis, and C. V. Weber, "Capability maturity model for software, version 1.1," CMU/SEI-93-TR-24, Software Engineering Institute, Carnegie-Mellon University, Pittsburgh, PA, February 1993.

3. "Quality systems—Model for quality assurance in design/development, production, installation, and servicing," International Standards Organization (ISO) 9001, 1987(E), Section 4.2.

4. *Ibid,* Section 4.4.3

5. Paulk, *op. cit.,* CMU/SEI-93-TR-25.

6. *Ibid.*

7. An excellent text is Karl E. Wiegers, *Software Requirements* (Redmond, WA: Microsoft Press), 1999.

8. S. and J. Robertson, *Mastering the Requirements Process* (Addison-Wesley, 1999).

9. B. S. Blanchard and W. J. Fabrycky, *Systems Engineering and Analysis*, 3rd ed. (Englewood Cliffs, NJ: Prentice-Hall, 1998), pp. 30-31.

10. A. Davis, *Software Requirements: Analysis and Specification* (Englewood Cliffs, NJ: Prentice-Hall, 1990). J. Grady, *Systems Requirements Analysis* (McGraw-Hill, 1993).

11. A. Davis, *op. cit.*

12. J. Hammond and J. Morrison, *The Stuff Americans Are Made Of* (New York: Macmillan, 1996), p. 82–83.

Chapter 4

1. J. Hammond and J. Morrison, *The Stuff That Americans Are Made Of* (New York: MacMillan), 1996, pp. 82–83.

Chapter 5

1. B. S. Kelsey, *The Dragons Teeth? The Creation of U.S. Air Power for World War II* (Washington D.C.: Smithsonian Institution Press, 1982).

2. M. Schwartz and R. Maguglin, *The Howard Hughes Flying Boat* (Oakland, CA: Scenic Art, Inc., 1983).

3. R. Ebbets, Excel Homes, Inc., Liverpool, PA, January 1999 interview with K. Farry.

4. J. Lienhard, "The Engines of Our Ingenuity," Episode No. 1122 KUHF, Houston, TX.

5. A. Farry, Sr., Madison, VA, May 1991 interview with K. Farry.

6. Kelsey, *op. cit.*

7. D. Freedman, "Intensive Care," *Inc.,* February 1999, p. 78, permission granted by Copyright Clearance Center.

Chapter 6

1. Bernard Kuchta, as quoted in E. Rechtin, *Systems Architecting: Creating and Building Complex Systems* (Englewood Cliffs, NJ: Prentice-Hall), 1991, p. 89.

2. J. Grady, *Systems Requirements Analysis* (McGraw-Hill, 1983).

Chapter 8

1. C. Gliens, *Grand Old Lady* (Cleveland: Pennington Press, 1949).
2. B. Roberts, Futron Corporation, Houston, TX, October 1999 interview with I. Hooks.

Chapter 9

1. H. Jordan, "Computer SNAFU may cost state millions," San Jose Mercury News, May 2, 1997. T. Walsh, "California, Lockheed Martin part ways over disputed SACSS deal," Government Computer News, February 1998.
2. W. Rice, Adsystech, Inc., Silver Spring, MD, December 1999 interview with I. Hooks.
3. B. Webb, California, November 1999 interview with I. Hooks.
4. E. Rechtin, *Systems Architecting: Creating and Building Complex Systems* (Englewood Cliffs, NJ: Prentice-Hall, 1991). Grady, *Systems Requirements Analysis* (McGraw-Hill, 1993) B. S. Blanchard and W. J. Fabrycky, *Systems Engineering and Analysis*, 3rd ed. (Englewood Cliffs, NJ: Prentice-Hall, 1998).

Chapter 10

1. H. Mark, "Conversations with Hans Mark," *Aerospace America,* November 1999, p. 12.

Chapter 11

1. W. Perry, Quality Assurance Institute, Orlando, FL.

Chapter 13

1. B. S. Blanchard and W. J. Fabrycky, *Systems Engineering and Analysis*, 3rd ed. (Englewood Cliffs, N J: Prentice-Hall, 1998),

p. 57–61. L. Cohen, *Quality Function Deployment: How to Make QFD Work for You* (Reading, MA: Addison-Wesley, 1995).

2. L. Fellows, Honeywell, Phoenix, AZ, August 1999 interview by I. Hooks.

Chapter 14

1. H. Botsford, NAVAIR Software Technology and Environments, Patuxent River NAS, MD, October 1999 interview by I. Hooks.

2. L. Fellows, Honeywell, Phoenix, AZ, August 1999 interview by I. Hooks.

Chapter 15

1. A. Binder, Lunar Prospector Principal Investigator, Lunar Research Institute, Tuscon, AZ, July 7, 1998 interview by K. Farry.

2. E.M. Cortright, "Report of Apollo 13 Review Board," National Aeronautics and Space Administration, Washington, D.C., Chapters 4–5. J. Lovell and J. Kluger, *Apollo 13* (New York: Pocket Books, Simon and Schuster, Inc., 1994), pp. 372–378.

Chapter 17

1. A national survey conducted by the Wirthlin Group for the American Quality Foundation, cited by J. Hammond and J. Morrison, *The Stuff Americans Are Made Of* (New York: MacMillan, 1996), p. 207.

2. R. Collings, Danielle Webster College, Nashua, NH, August 1999 interview by K. Farry.

About the Authors

Ivy F. Hooks is a nationally renowned expert in requirements development and management who educates and consults organizations on the importance of writing good requirements. She received a B. S. degree and a M. S. degree, both in mathematics, from University of Houston.

Ms. Hooks is currently president and CEO of Compliance Automation, Inc. She has managed a small business for the past 15 years. She has provided training and consulting in requirements for companies, including Rockwell-Collins, Lockheed-Martin, Hughes, Raytheon, Kodak, and Allied Signal, and government organizations, including NASA, NOAA, FAA, and the Navy. Her seminars have been presented across the United States, in Canada, and in Great Britain.

Before her private sector career, Ms. Hooks had a 20-year career with NASA, where she was manager of Flight Software Development for the Space Shuttle, verification manager of Flight Software for the Space Shuttle, and integration manager for the Shuttle Separation Systems. She also was a manager in the Shuttle Program Office, executive assistant to the director of engineering, and executive assistant to the director of the Johnson Space Center.

Ms. Hooks is the recipient of the Washington, D.C. Jaycee's Arthur S. Flemming Award for outstanding young civil servant, NASA's Exceptional Service Medal, NASA's Outstanding Speaker Award, as well as many other awards.

She is a charter member of INCOSE (International Council on Systems Engineering), a Fellow of the Society of Women Engineers, an Associate Fellow of the AIAA, and a member of IEEE.

She currently resides in the Texas Hill Country.

Kristin A. Farry, Ph.D., is a versatile engineer with over two decades of experience in aerospace, robotics, and biomedical engineering. She received her B.S. degree in aerospace engineering from the University of Virginia in 1980. She then earned an M.S.E. degree from Princeton University, also in aerospace engineering, in 1988. In 1995, she earned her Ph.D. degree in electrical engineering, robotics, and bioengineering from Rice University. She served in the U.S. Air Force (USAF) (Captain, Regular) for four years (1982–1986), working on flight control systems (including that of the X-29) and robotics. She worked for Rockwell International (1986–1988) on the Space Station and National Aerospace Plane. At Rockwell Space Operations, she served as a Space Shuttle flight controller and mission planner (1988–1990). Since 1990, she has worked on control of artificial hands, industry robotics, and spacecraft development.

In parallel with her technical work, Dr. Farry has also acquired business management experience. She is founder and president of One DGE, Inc., a technical consulting company. She is cofounder and president of Intelligenta, Inc., a company specializing in bionics. She founded Win-Com Publications, a computer-oriented publications company with international sales, and operated it for two years in the early 1980s. In addition, she gained contract management experience in the USAF and at Rockwell International.

Among the awards she has received are the USAF Systems Command Aeronautical Systems Division's (ASD) 1985 Business Woman of the Year, USAF ASD Flight Dynamics Laboratory 1985 Engineer of the Year, and a 1988 Rockwell International Space Systems Division Engineer of the Year award.

Outside of professional pursuits, Dr. Farry is a pilot and mechanic, activities that give her additional insight into operability and maintainability requirements. She is active with the Collings Foundation, a museum of actively flying historic aircraft; she serves as crew chief and pilot on a B-25 Mitchell.

She currently resides near Houston, Texas.

Index

accountability, 50
administrative gridlock, 138–139
Allied Waste Industries, Inc., xxix
allocation, requirement, 140–141, 151
ambiguities, 5, 111–114
American culture, 16–20, 251–252, 255
Americans with Disabilities Act, 165
analysis techniques, 39–40
API, *see* application programmer's interface
Apollo spacecraft, 232–233
application programmer's interface (API), 87, 96
assumptions, 19–20, 50, 107–108, 122–123, 128, 255
attainability, 104
automation of requirement management, 212–225
  benefits of, 213–216
  manager's role in, 224
  tools for, 216–224

bad assumptions, 107–108, 122–123
bad grammar, avoiding, 114
bad requirements, 24–25
baselining, 40–41, 183–201
  benefits of, 183–185
  and changes, 227
  manager's role in, 199–200
  phased, 198–199
  steps in, 185–198
  time needed for, 185, 200
big picture, 136–137
Binder, Alan, 11, 229–230
Boehm, Barry, on rework costs, 3
Boeing, 13–14
Botsford, Harry, on Integrated Process Teams, 215–216
budgeting, 197
bugs, 4
business case, 48–49

Capability Maturity Model (CMM), 34, 36
CD-ROMs, 137
change analysis, 242–243
change management, 226–234

benefits of, 227–228
  manager's role in, 231–233
  steps for, 228–231
change requests (CRs), 242–243
clarity, 105–107
CMM, *see* Capability Maturity Model
Collings, Bob, on Edsel, 258
comebacks, 17–18
commitment, management, 246–247
communication, 22
  and automation of requirement management, 213
  with operational concepts, 61–62
  of project scope, 54–55
  and rationale, 124
conciseness, 129
consistency, 5, 63
constraints, 50
content review, 189–192
cost(s)
  of good requirements, 259
  overruns in, 9
  project, xxvii
  of verification, 159, 160
CRs, *see* change requests
culture, 250–254
  American, 16–20, 251–252, 255
  German, 20
  Japanese, 21
  Russian, 20–21
customer needs, 4
  describing, 103–104
  and prioritizing requirements, 211
  and project scope, 46–47

data tracking, 214
defects, product, 3
definition, requirement, 15–31
  achieving success in, 29–31
  cultural obstacles to, 16–21
  individual obstacles to, 25–29
  management myths about, 21–25
  practical process for, 32–41
  and verification, 158–168
  see also written requirements
Department of Defense, 36, 214